Semiparametric Regression for the Applied Econometrician

This book provides an accessible collection of techniques for analyzing nonparametric and semiparametric regression models. Worked examples include estimation of Engel curves and equivalence scales; scale economies; semiparametric Cobb–Douglas, translog, and CES cost functions; household gasoline consumption; hedonic housing prices; and, option prices and state price density estimation. The book should be of interest to a broad range of economists, including those working in industrial organization, labor, development, urban, energy, and financial economics.

A variety of testing procedures are covered such as simple goodness-of-fit tests and residual regression tests. These procedures can be used to test hypotheses such as parametric and semiparametric specifications, significance, monotonicity, and additive separability. Other topics include endogeneity of parametric and nonparametric effects as well as heteroskedasticity and autocorrelation in the residuals. Bootstrap procedures are provided.

Adonis Yatchew teaches economics at the University of Toronto. His principal areas of research are theoretical and applied econometrics. In addition, he has a strong interest in regulatory and energy economics and is Joint Editor of the *Energy Journal*. He has received the social science undergraduate teaching award at the University of Toronto and has taught at the University of Chicago.

Further Praise for *Semiparametric Regression for the Applied Econometrician*

"This fluent book is an excellent source for learning, or updating one's knowledge of semi- and nonparametric methods and their applications. It is a valuable addition to the existent books on these topics."

– Rosa Matzkin, *Northwestern University*

"Yatchew's book is an excellent account of semiparametric regression. The material is nicely integrated by using a simple set of ideas which exploit the impact of differencing and weighting operations on the data. The empirical applications are attractive and will be extremely helpful for those encountering this material for the first time."

– Adrian Pagan, *Australian National University*

"At the University of Toronto Adonis Yatchew is known for excellence in teaching. The key to this excellence is the succinct transparency of his exposition. At its best such exposition transcends the medium of presentation (either lecture or text). This monograph reflects the clarity of the author's thinking on the rapidly expanding fields of semiparametric and nonparametric analysis. Both students and researchers will appreciate the mix of theory and empirical application."

– Dale Poirier, *University of California, Irvine*

Themes in Modern Econometrics

Managing editor
PETER C.B. PHILLIPS, *Yale University*

Series editors
RICHARD J. SMITH, *University of Warwick*
ERIC GHYSELS, *University of North Carolina, Chapel Hill*

Themes in Modern Econometrics is designed to service the large and growing need for explicit teaching tools in econometrics. It will provide an organized sequence of textbooks in econometrics aimed squarely at the student population and will be the first series in the discipline to have this as its express aim. Written at a level accessible to students with an introductory course in econometrics behind them, each book will address topics or themes that students and researchers encounter daily. Although each book will be designed to stand alone as an authoritative survey in its own right, the distinct emphasis throughout will be on pedagogic excellence.

Titles in the series

Statistics and Econometric Models: Volumes 1 and 2
CHRISTIAN GOURIEROUX and ALAIN MONFORT
Translated by QUANG VUONG

Time Series and Dynamic Models
CHRISTIAN GOURIEROUX and ALAIN MONFORT
Translated and edited by GIAMPIERO GALLO

Unit Roots, Cointegration, and Structural Change
G.S. MADDALA and IN-MOO KIM

Generalized Method of Moments Estimation
Edited by LÁSZLÓ MÁTYÁS

Nonparametric Econometrics
ADRIAN PAGAN and AMAN ULLAH

Econometrics of Qualitative Dependent Variables
CHRISTIAN GOURIEROUX
Translated by PAUL B. KLASSEN

The Econometric Analysis of Seasonal Time Series
ERIC GHYSELS and DENISE R. OSBORN

SEMIPARAMETRIC REGRESSION FOR THE APPLIED ECONOMETRICIAN

ADONIS YATCHEW

University of Toronto

CAMBRIDGE
UNIVERSITY PRESS

CAMBRIDGE UNIVERSITY PRESS
Cambridge, New York, Melbourne, Madrid, Cape Town, Singapore, São Paulo

Cambridge University Press
The Edinburgh Building, Cambridge CB2 2RU, UK

Published in the United States of America by Cambridge University Press, New York

www.cambridge.org
Information on this title: www.cambridge.org/9780521812832

First published 2003

A catalogue record for this publication is available from the British Library

Library of Congress Cataloguing in Publication data

Yatchew, Adonis.
Semiparametric regression for the applied econometrician / Adonis Yatchew.
p. cm. – (Themes in modern econometrics)
Includes bibliographical references and index.
ISBN 0-521-81283-6 – ISBN 0-521-01226-0 (pbk.)
1. Econometrics. 2. Regression analysis. I. Title. II. Series.
HB139 .Y38 2003
330′.01′519536 – dc21 2002041002

ISBN-13 978-0-521-81283-2 hardback
ISBN-10 0-521-81283-6 hardback

ISBN-13 978-0-521-01226-3 paperback
ISBN-10 0-521-01226-0 paperback

Transferred to digital printing 2006

To Marta, Tamara and Mark.
Your smiles are sunlight,
your laughter, the twinkling of stars.

Contents

List of Figures and Tables

Preface

This book has been largely motivated by pedagogical interests. Nonparametric and semiparametric regression models are widely studied by theoretical econometricians but are much underused by applied economists. In comparison with the linear regression model $y = z\beta + \varepsilon$, semiparametric techniques are theoretically sophisticated and often require substantial programming experience.

Two natural extensions to the linear model that allow greater flexibility are the partial linear model $y = z\beta + f(x) + \varepsilon$, which adds a nonparametric function, and the index model $y = f(z\beta) + \varepsilon$, which applies a nonparametric function to the linear index $z\beta$. Together, these models and their variants comprise the most commonly used semiparametric specifications in the applied econometrics literature. A particularly appealing feature for economists is that these models permit the inclusion of multiple explanatory variables without succumbing to the "curse of dimensionality."

We begin by describing the idea of differencing, which provides a simple way to analyze the partial linear model because it allows one to remove the nonparametric effect $f(x)$ and to analyze the parametric portion of the model $z\beta$ as if the nonparametric portion were not there to begin with. Thus, one can draw not only on the reservoir of parametric human capital but one can also make use of existing software. By the end of the first chapter, the reader will be able to estimate the partial linear model and apply it to a real data set (the empirical example analyzes scale economies in electricity distribution using a semiparametric Cobb–Douglas specification).

Chapter 2 describes the broad contours of nonparametric and semiparametric regression modeling, the categorization of models, the "curse of dimensionality," and basic theoretical results.

Chapters 3 and 4 are devoted to smoothing and differencing, respectively. The techniques are reinforced by empirical examples on Engel curves, gasoline demand, the effect of weather on electricity demand, and semiparametric translog and CES cost function models. Methods that incorporate heteroskedasticity, autocorrelation, and endogeneity of right-hand-side variables are included.

Chapter 5 focuses on nonparametric functions of several variables. The example on hedonic pricing of housing attributes illustrates the benefits of nonparametric modeling of location effects.

Economic theory rarely prescribes a specific functional form. Typically, the implications of theory involve constraints such as monotonicity, concavity, homotheticity, separability, and so on. Chapter 6 begins by outlining two broad classes of tests of these and other properties: goodness-of-fit tests that compare restricted and unrestricted estimates of the residual variance, and residual regression tests that regress residuals from a restricted regression on all the explanatory variables to see whether there is anything left to be explained. Both of these tests have close relatives in the parametric world. The chapter then proceeds to constrained estimation, which is illustrated by an option pricing example.

Chapter 7 addresses the index model with an application to equivalence scale estimation using South African household survey data. Chapter 8 describes bootstrap techniques for various procedures described in earlier chapters.

A cornerstone of the pedagogical philosophy underlying this book is that the second best way to learn econometric techniques is to actually apply them. (The best way is to teach them.[1]) To this purpose, data and sample programs are available for the various examples and exercises at www.chass.utoronto.ca/~yatchew/. With the exception of constrained estimation of option prices, all code is in *S-Plus*.[2] The reader should be able to translate the code into other programs such as *Stata* easily enough.

By working through the examples and exercises,[3] the reader should be able to

- estimate nonparametric regression, partial linear, and index models;
- test various properties using large sample results and bootstrap techniques;
- estimate nonparametric models subject to constraints such as monotonicity and concavity.

Well-known references in the nonparametrics and semiparametrics literature include Härdle (1990), Stoker (1991), Bickel et al. (1993), Horowitz (1998),

1 Each year I tell my students the apocryphal story of a junior faculty member complaining to a senior colleague of his inability to get through to his students. After repeating the same lecture to his class on three different occasions, he exclaims in exasperation "I am so disappointed. Today I thought I had finally gotten through to them. This time even *I* understood the material, and they still did not understand."

2 Krause and Olson (1997) have provided a particularly pleasant introduction to *S-Plus*. See also Venables and Ripley (1994).

3 Many of the examples and portions of the text draw upon previously published work, in particular, Yatchew (1997, 1998, 1999, 2000), Yatchew and Bos (1997), Yatchew and No (2001), and Yatchew, Sun, and Deri (2001). The permission for use of these materials is gratefully acknowledged.

and Pagan and Ullah (1999).[4] It is hoped that this book is worthy of being squeezed onto a nearby bookshelf by providing an applied approach with numerical examples and adaptable code. It is intended for the applied economist and econometrician working with cross-sectional or possibly panel data.[5] It is expected that the reader has had a good basic course in econometrics and is thoroughly familiar with estimation and testing of the linear model and associated ideas such as heteroskedasticity and endogeneity. Some knowledge of nonlinear regression modeling and inference is desirable but not essential. Given the presence of empirical examples, the book could be used as a text in an advanced undergraduate course and certainly at the graduate level.

I owe a great intellectual debt to too many to name them individually, and regrettably not all of them appear in the references. Several anonymous reviewers provided extensive and valuable comments for which I am grateful. Thanks are also due to Scott Parris at Cambridge University Press for his unflagging efforts in this endeavor. My sister Oenone kindly contributed countless hours of proofreading time. Finally, it is indeed a special privilege to thank Peter Phillips, whose intellectual guidance shaped several aspects of this book. It was Peter who from the start insisted on reproducible empirical exercises. Those who are acquainted with both of us surely know to whom the errors belong.

[4] There are also several surveys: Delgado and Robinson (1992), Härdle and Linton (1994), Powell (1994), Linton (1995a), and Yatchew (1998). See also DiNardo and Tobias (2001).

[5] With the exception of correlation in the residuals, time-dependent data issues have not been covered here.

1 Introduction to Differencing

1.1 A Simple Idea

Consider the nonparametric regression model

$$y = f(x) + \varepsilon \tag{1.1.1}$$

for which little is assumed about the function f except that it is smooth. In its simplest incarnation, the residuals are independently and identically distributed with mean zero and constant variance σ_ε^2, and the x's are generated by a process that ensures they will eventually be dense in the domain. Closeness of the x's combined with smoothness of f provides a basis for estimation of the regression function. By averaging or smoothing observations on y for which the corresponding x's are close to a given point, say x_o, one obtains a reasonable estimate of the regression effect $f(x_o)$.

This premise – that x's that are close will have corresponding values of the regression function that are close – may also be used to remove the regression effect. It is this removal or *differencing* that provides a simple exploratory tool. To illustrate the idea we present four applications:

1. Estimation of the residual variance σ_ε^2,
2. Estimation and inference in the partial linear model $y = z\beta + f(x) + \varepsilon$,
3. A specification test on the regression function f, and
4. A test of equality of nonparametric regression functions.[1]

[1] The first-order differencing estimator of the residual variance in a nonparametric setting appears in Rice (1984). Although unaware of his result at the time, I presented the identical estimator at a conference held at the IC2 Institute at the University of Texas at Austin in May 1984. Differencing subsequently appeared in a series of nonparametric and semiparametric settings, including Powell (1987), Yatchew (1988), Hall, Kay, and Titterington (1990), Yatchew (1997, 1998, 1999, 2000), Lewbel (2000), Fan and Huang (2001), and Horowitz and Spokoiny (2001).

1.2 Estimation of the Residual Variance

Suppose one has data $(y_1, x_1), \ldots, (y_n, x_n)$ on the pure nonparametric regression model (1.1.1), where x is a bounded scalar lying, say, in the unit interval, ε is i.i.d. with $E(\varepsilon \mid x) = 0$, $Var(\varepsilon \mid x) = \sigma_\varepsilon^2$, and all that is known about f is that its first derivative is bounded. Most important, the data have been rearranged so that $x_1 \leq \cdots \leq x_n$. Consider the following estimator of σ_ε^2:

$$s_{diff}^2 = \frac{1}{2n} \sum_{i=2}^{n} (y_i - y_{i-1})^2. \tag{1.2.1}$$

The estimator is consistent because, as the x's become close, differencing tends to remove the nonparametric effect $y_i - y_{i-1} = f(x_i) - f(x_{i-1}) + \varepsilon_i - \varepsilon_{i-1} \cong \varepsilon_i - \varepsilon_{i-1}$, so that[2]

$$s_{diff}^2 \cong \frac{1}{2n} \sum_{i=2}^{n} (\varepsilon_i - \varepsilon_{i-1})^2 \cong \frac{1}{n} \sum_{i=1}^{n} \varepsilon_i^2 - \frac{1}{n} \sum_{i=2}^{n} \varepsilon_i \varepsilon_{i-1}. \tag{1.2.2}$$

An obvious advantage of s_{diff}^2 is that no initial estimate of the regression function f needs to be calculated. Indeed, no consistent estimate of f is implicit in (1.2.1). Nevertheless, the terms in s_{diff}^2 that involve f converge to zero sufficiently quickly so that the asymptotic distribution of the estimator can be derived directly from the approximation in (1.2.2). In particular,

$$n^{1/2}\left(s_{diff}^2 - \sigma_\varepsilon^2\right) \xrightarrow{D} N(0, E(\varepsilon^4)). \tag{1.2.3}$$

Moreover, derivation of this result is facilitated by the assumption that the ε_i are independent so that reordering of the data does not affect the distribution of the right-hand side in (1.2.2).

1.3 The Partial Linear Model

Consider now the partial linear model $y = z\beta + f(x) + \varepsilon$, where for simplicity all variables are assumed to be scalars. We assume that $E(\varepsilon \mid z, x) = 0$ and that $Var(\varepsilon \mid z, x) = \sigma_\varepsilon^2$.[3] As before, the x's have bounded support, say the unit interval, and have been rearranged so that $x_1 \leq \cdots \leq x_n$. Suppose that the conditional mean of z is a smooth function of x, say $E(z \mid x) = g(x)$ where g' is

[2] To see why this approximation works, suppose that the x_i are equally spaced on the unit interval and that $f' \leq L$. By the mean value theorem, for some $x_i^* \in [x_{i-1}, x_i]$ we have $f(x_i) - f(x_{i-1}) = f'(x_i^*)(x_i - x_{i-1}) \leq L/n$. Thus, $y_i - y_{i-1} = \varepsilon_i - \varepsilon_{i-1} + O(1/n)$. For detailed development of the argument, see Exercise 1. If the x_i have a density function bounded away from zero on the support, then $x_i - x_{i-1} \cong O_P(1/n)$ and $y_i - y_{i-1} \cong \varepsilon_i - \varepsilon_{i-1} + O_P(1/n)$. See Appendix B, Lemma B.2, for a related result.

[3] For extensions to the heteroskedastic and autocorrelated cases, see Sections 3.6 and 4.5.

bounded and $Var(z \mid x) = \sigma_u^2$. Then we may rewrite $z = g(x) + u$. Differencing yields

$$\begin{aligned} y_i - y_{i-1} &= (z_i - z_{i-1})\beta + (f(x_i) - f(x_{i-1})) + \varepsilon_i - \varepsilon_{i-1} \\ &= (g(x_i) - g(x_{i-1}))\beta + (u_i - u_{i-1})\beta \\ &\quad + (f(x_i) - f(x_{i-1})) + \varepsilon_i - \varepsilon_{i-1} \\ &\cong (u_i - u_{i-1})\beta + \varepsilon_i - \varepsilon_{i-1}. \end{aligned} \tag{1.3.1}$$

Thus, the direct effect $f(x)$ of the nonparametric variable x and the indirect effect $g(x)$ that occurs through z are removed. Suppose we apply the OLS estimator of β to the differenced data, that is,

$$\hat{\beta}_{diff} = \frac{\sum(y_i - y_{i-1})(z_i - z_{i-1})}{\sum(z_i - z_{i-1})^2}. \tag{1.3.2}$$

Then, substituting the approximations $z_i - z_{i-1} \cong u_i - u_{i-1}$ and $y_i - y_{i-1} \cong (u_i - u_{i-1})\beta + \varepsilon_i - \varepsilon_{i-1}$ into (1.3.2) and rearranging, we have

$$n^{1/2}(\hat{\beta}_{diff} - \beta) \cong \frac{n^{1/2}\frac{1}{n}\sum(\varepsilon_i - \varepsilon_{i-1})(u_i - u_{i-1})}{\frac{1}{n}\sum(u_i - u_{i-1})^2}. \tag{1.3.3}$$

The denominator converges to $2\sigma_u^2$, and the numerator has mean zero and variance $6\sigma_\varepsilon^2\sigma_u^2$. Thus, the ratio has mean zero and variance $6\sigma_\varepsilon^2\sigma_u^2/(2\sigma_u^2)^2 = 1.5\sigma_\varepsilon^2/\sigma_u^2$. Furthermore, the ratio may be shown to be approximately normal (using a finitely dependent central limit theorem). Thus, we have

$$n^{1/2}(\hat{\beta}_{diff} - \beta) \xrightarrow{D} N\left(0, \frac{1.5\,\sigma_\varepsilon^2}{\sigma_u^2}\right). \tag{1.3.4}$$

For the most efficient estimator, the corresponding variance in (1.3.4) would be $\sigma_\varepsilon^2/\sigma_u^2$ so the proposed estimator based on first differences has relative efficiency $2/3 = 1/1.5$. In Chapters 3 and 4 we will produce efficient estimators.

Now, in order to use (1.3.4) to perform inference, we will need consistent estimators of σ_ε^2 and σ_u^2. These may be obtained using

$$\begin{aligned} s_\varepsilon^2 &= \frac{1}{2n}\sum_{i=2}^{n}((y_i - y_{i-1}) - (z_i - z_{i-1})\hat{\beta}_{diff})^2 \\ &\cong \frac{1}{2n}\sum_{i=2}^{n}(\varepsilon_i - \varepsilon_{i-1})^2 \xrightarrow{P} \sigma_\varepsilon^2 \end{aligned} \tag{1.3.5}$$

and

$$s_u^2 = \frac{1}{2n}\sum_{i=2}^{n}(z_i - z_{i-1})^2 \cong \frac{1}{2n}\sum_{i=2}^{n}(u_i - u_{i-1})^2 \xrightarrow{P} \sigma_u^2. \tag{1.3.6}$$

The preceding procedure generalizes straightforwardly to models with multiple parametric explanatory variables.

1.4 Specification Test

Suppose, for example, one wants to test the null hypothesis that f is a linear function. Let s^2_{res} be the usual estimate of the residual variance obtained from a linear regression of y on x. If the linear model is correct, then s^2_{res} will be approximately equal to the average of the true squared residuals:

$$s^2_{res} = \frac{1}{n}\sum_{i=1}^{n}(y_i - \hat{\gamma}_1 - \hat{\gamma}_2 x_i)^2 \cong \frac{1}{n}\sum_{i=1}^{n}\varepsilon_i^2. \tag{1.4.1}$$

If the linear specification is incorrect, then s^2_{res} will overestimate the residual variance while s^2_{diff} in (1.2.1) will remain a consistent estimator, thus forming the basis of a test. Consider the test statistic

$$V = \frac{n^{1/2}\left(s^2_{res} - s^2_{diff}\right)}{s^2_{diff}}. \tag{1.4.2}$$

Equations (1.2.2) and (1.4.1) imply that the numerator of V is approximately equal to

$$n^{1/2}\frac{1}{n}\sum \varepsilon_i\,\varepsilon_{i-1} \xrightarrow{D} N\left(0, \sigma_\varepsilon^4\right). \tag{1.4.3}$$

Since s^2_{diff}, the denominator of V, is a consistent estimator of σ^2_ε, V is asymptotically $N(0,1)$ under H_0. (Note that this is a one-sided test, and one rejects for large values of the statistic.)

As we will see later, this test procedure may be used to test a variety of null hypotheses such as general parametric and semiparametric specifications, monotonicity, concavity, additive separability, and other constraints. One simply inserts the restricted estimator of the variance in (1.4.2). We refer to test statistics that compare restricted and unrestricted estimates of the residual variance as "goodness-of-fit" tests.

1.5 Test of Equality of Regression Functions

Suppose we are given data $(y_{A1}, x_{A1}), \ldots, (y_{An}, x_{An})$ and $(y_{B1}, x_{B1}), \ldots, (y_{Bn}, x_{Bn})$ from two possibly different regression models A and B. Assume x is a scalar and that each data set has been reordered so that the x's are in increasing order. The basic models are

$$\begin{aligned} y_{Ai} &= f_A(x_{Ai}) + \varepsilon_{Ai} \\ y_{Bi} &= f_B(x_{Bi}) + \varepsilon_{Bi} \end{aligned} \tag{1.5.1}$$

where given the x's, the ε's have mean 0, variance σ_ε^2, and are independent within and between populations; f_A and f_B have first derivatives bounded. Using (1.2.1), define consistent "within" differencing estimators of the variance

$$s_A^2 = \frac{1}{2n}\sum_i^n (y_{Ai} - y_{Ai-1})^2$$
$$s_B^2 = \frac{1}{2n}\sum_i^n (y_{Bi} - y_{Bi-1})^2. \qquad (1.5.2)$$

As we will do frequently, we have dropped the subscript "*diff*". Now pool *all* the data and reorder so that the pooled x's are in increasing order: $(y_1^*, x_1^*), \ldots\ldots, (y_{2n}^*, x_{2n}^*)$. (Note that the pooled data have only one subscript.) Applying the differencing estimator once again, we have

$$s_p^2 = \frac{1}{4n}\sum_j^{2n} \left(y_j^* - y_{j-1}^*\right)^2. \qquad (1.5.3)$$

The basic idea behind the test procedure is to compare the pooled estimator with the average of the within estimators. If $f_A = f_B$, then the within and pooled estimators are consistent and should yield similar estimates. If $f_A \neq f_B$, then the within estimators remain consistent, whereas the pooled estimator overestimates the residual variance, as may be seen in Figure 1.1.

To formalize this idea, define the test statistic

$$\Upsilon \equiv (2n)^{1/2}\left(s_p^2 - 1/2\left(s_A^2 + s_B^2\right)\right). \qquad (1.5.4)$$

If $f_A = f_B$, then differencing removes the regression effect sufficiently quickly in both the within and the pooled estimators so that

$$\Upsilon \equiv (2n)^{1/2}\left(s_p^2 - 1/2\left(s_A^2 + s_B^2\right)\right)$$
$$\cong \frac{(2n)^{1/2}}{4n}\left(\sum_j^{2n}\left(\varepsilon_j^* - \varepsilon_{j-1}^*\right)^2 - \sum_i^n (\varepsilon_{Ai} - \varepsilon_{Ai-1})^2 - \sum_i^n (\varepsilon_{Bi} - \varepsilon_{Bi-1})^2\right)$$
$$\cong \frac{(2n)^{1/2}}{2n}\left(\sum_j^{2n}\varepsilon_j^{*2} - \varepsilon_j^*\varepsilon_{j-1}^* - \sum_i^n \varepsilon_{Ai}^2 - \varepsilon_{Ai}\varepsilon_{Ai-1} - \sum_i^n \varepsilon_{Bi}^2 - \varepsilon_{Bi}\varepsilon_{Bi-1}\right)$$
$$\cong \frac{1}{(2n)^{1/2}}\left(\sum_i^n \varepsilon_{Ai}\varepsilon_{Ai-1} + \sum_i^n \varepsilon_{Bi}\varepsilon_{Bi-1}\right) - \frac{1}{(2n)^{1/2}}\left(\sum_j^{2n}\varepsilon_j^*\varepsilon_{j-1}^*\right). \qquad (1.5.5)$$

Consider the two terms in the last line. In large samples, each is approximately $N(0, \sigma_\varepsilon^4)$. If observations that are consecutive in the individual data

Within estimators of residual variance

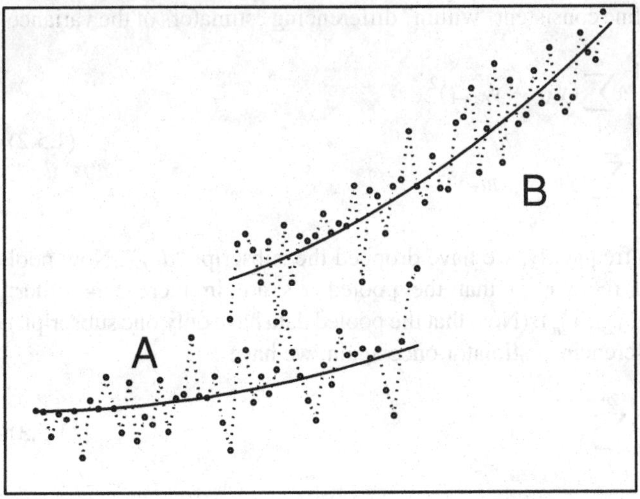

Pooled estimator of residual variance

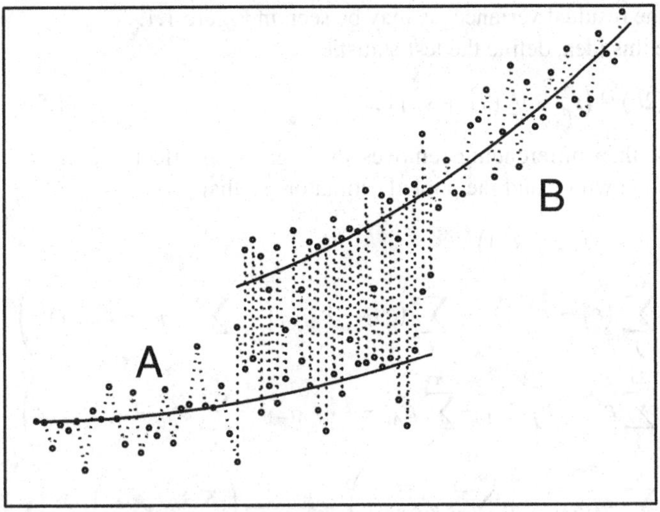

Figure 1.1. Testing equality of regression functions.

sets tend to be consecutive after pooling and reordering, then the *covariance* between the two terms will be large. In particular, the covariance is approximately $\sigma_\varepsilon^4(1-\pi)$, where π equals the probability that consecutive observations in the pooled reordered data set come from *different* populations.

It follows that under $H_o : f_A = f_B$,

$$\Upsilon \xrightarrow{D} N\left(0, 2\pi\sigma_\varepsilon^4\right). \tag{1.5.6}$$

For example, if reordering the pooled data is equivalent to stacking data sets A and B – because the two sets of x's, x_A and x_B, do not intersect – then $\pi \cong 0$ and indeed the statistic Υ becomes degenerate. This is not surprising, since observing nonparametric functions over different domains cannot provide a basis for testing whether they are the same. If the pooled data involve a simple interleaving of data sets A and B, then $\pi \cong 1$ and $\Upsilon \rightarrow N(0, 2\sigma_\varepsilon^4)$. If x_A and x_B are independent of each other but have the same distribution, then for the pooled reordered data the probability that consecutive observations come from different populations is ½ and $\Upsilon \rightarrow N(0, \sigma_\varepsilon^4)$.[4] To implement the test, one may obtain a consistent estimate $\hat{\pi}$ by taking the proportion of observations in the pooled reordered data that are preceded by an observation from a different population.

1.6 Empirical Application: Scale Economies in Electricity Distribution[5]

To illustrate these ideas, consider a simple variant of the Cobb–Douglas model for the costs of distributing electricity

$$\begin{aligned} tc = {} & f(cust) + \beta_1 wage + \beta_2 pcap \\ & + \beta_3 PUC + \beta_4 kwh + \beta_5 life + \beta_6 lf + \beta_7\, kmwire + \varepsilon \end{aligned} \tag{1.6.1}$$

where *tc* is the log of total cost per customer, *cust* is the log of the number of customers, *wage* is the log wage rate, *pcap* is the log price of capital, *PUC* is a dummy variable for public utility commissions that deliver additional services and therefore may benefit from economies of scope, *life* is the log of the remaining life of distribution assets, *lf* is the log of the load factor (this measures capacity utilization relative to peak usage), and *kmwire* is the log of kilometers of distribution wire per customer. The data consist of 81 municipal distributors in Ontario, Canada, during 1993. (For more details, see Yatchew, 2000.)

[4] For example, distribute n men and n women randomly along a stretch of beach facing the sunset. Then, for any individual, the probability that the person to the left is of the opposite sex is ½. More generally, if x_A and x_B are independent of each other and have different distributions, then π depends on the relative density of observations from each of the two populations.

[5] Variable definitions for empirical examples are contained in Appendix E.

Because the data have been reordered so that the nonparametric variable *cust* is in increasing order, first differencing (1.6.1) tends to remove the nonparametric effect f. We also divide by $\sqrt{2}$ so that the residuals in the differenced Equation (1.6.2) have the same variance as those in (1.6.1). Thus, we have

$$\begin{aligned}
&[tc_i - tc_{i-1}]/\sqrt{2} \\
&\quad \cong \beta_1[wage_i - wage_{i-1}]/\sqrt{2} + \beta_2[pcap_i - pcap_{i-1}]/\sqrt{2} \\
&\qquad + \beta_3[PUC_i - PUC_{i-1}]/\sqrt{2} + \beta_4[kwh_i - kwh_{i-1}]/\sqrt{2} \\
&\qquad + \beta_5[life_i - life_{i-1}]/\sqrt{2} + \beta_6[lf_i - lf_{i-1}]/\sqrt{2} \\
&\qquad + \beta_7[kmwire_i - kmwire_{i-1}]/\sqrt{2} + [\varepsilon_i - \varepsilon_{i-1}]/\sqrt{2}. \qquad (1.6.2)
\end{aligned}$$

Figure 1.2 summarizes our estimates of the parametric effects β using the differenced equation. It also contains estimates of a pure parametric specification in which the scale effect f is modeled with a quadratic. Applying the specification test (1.4.2), where s^2_{diff} is replaced with (1.3.5), yields a value of 1.50, indicating that the quadratic model may be adequate.

Thus far our results suggest that by differencing we can perform inference on β as if there were no nonparametric component f in the model to begin with. But, having estimated β, we can then proceed to apply a variety of nonparametric techniques to analyze f as if β were known. Such a modular approach simplifies implementation because it permits the use of existing software designed for pure nonparametric models.

More precisely, suppose we assemble the ordered pairs $(y_i - z_i\hat{\beta}_{diff}, x_i)$; then, we have

$$y_i - z_i\hat{\beta}_{diff} = z_i(\beta - \hat{\beta}_{diff}) + f(x_i) + \varepsilon_i \cong f(x_i) + \varepsilon_i. \qquad (1.6.3)$$

If we apply conventional smoothing methods to these ordered pairs such as kernel estimation (see Section 3.2), then consistency, optimal rate of convergence results, and the construction of confidence intervals for f remain valid because $\hat{\beta}_{diff}$ converges sufficiently quickly to β that the approximation in the last part of (1.6.3) leaves asymptotic arguments unaffected. (This is indeed why we could apply the specification test after removing the *estimated* parametric effect.) Thus, in Figure 1.2 we have also plotted a nonparametric (kernel) estimate of f that can be compared with the quadratic estimate. In subsequent sections, we will elaborate this example further and provide additional ones.

1.7 Why Differencing?

An important advantage of differencing procedures is their simplicity. Consider once again the partial linear model $y = z\beta + f(x) + \varepsilon$. Conventional

Variable	Quadratic model		Partial linear model[a]	
	Coef	SE	Coef	SE
cust	−0.833	0.175	–	–
$cust^2$	0.040	0.009	–	–
wage	0.833	0.325	0.448	0.367
pcap	0.562	0.075	0.459	0.076
PUC	−0.071	0.039	−0.086	0.043
kwh	−0.017	0.089	−0.011	0.087
life	−0.603	0.119	−0.506	0.131
lf	1.244	0.434	1.252	0.457
kmwire	0.445	0.086	0.352	0.094
s_ε^2	.021		.018	
R^2	.618		.675	

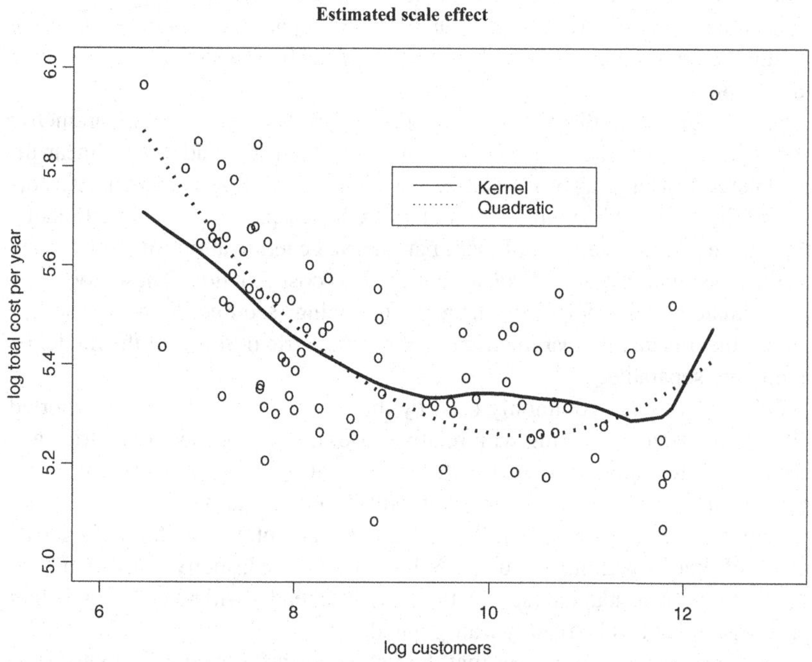

[a] Test of quadratic versus nonparametric specification of scale effect: $V = n^{1/2}(s_{res}^2 - s_{diff}^2)/s_{diff}^2 = 81^{1/2}(.021 - .018)/.018 = 1.5$, where V is $N(0,1)$, Section 1.4.

Figure 1.2. Partial linear model – Log-linear cost function: Scale economies in electricity distribution.

estimators, such as the one proposed by Robinson (1988) (see Section 3.6), require one to estimate $E(y \mid x)$ and $E(z \mid x)$ using nonparametric regressions. The estimated residuals from each of these regressions (hence the term "double residual method") are then used to estimate the *parametric* regression

$$y - E(y \mid x) = (z - E(z \mid x))\beta + \varepsilon. \tag{1.7.1}$$

If z is a vector, then a separate nonparametric regression is run for each component of z, where the independent variable is the nonparametric variable x. In contrast, differencing eliminates these first-stage regressions so that estimation of β can be performed – regardless of its dimension – even if nonparametric regression procedures are not available within the software being used. Similarly, tests of parametric specifications against nonparametric alternatives and tests of equality of regression functions across two or more (sub-) samples can be carried out without performing a nonparametric regression.

As should be evident from the empirical example of the last section, differencing may easily be combined with other procedures. In that example, we used differencing to estimate the parametric component of a partial linear model. We then removed the estimated parametric effect and applied conventional nonparametric procedures to analyze the nonparametric component. Such modular analysis does require theoretical justification, which we will provide in Section 4.12.

As we have seen, the partial linear model permits a simple semiparametric generalization of the Cobb–Douglas model. Translog and other linear-in-parameters models may be generalized similarly. If we allow the parametric portion of the model to be nonlinear – so that we have a partial parametric model – then we may also obtain simple semiparametric generalizations of models such as the constant elasticity of substitution (CES) cost function. These, too, may be estimated straightforwardly using differencing (see Section 4.7). The key requirement is that the parametric and nonparametric portions of the model be additively separable.

Other procedures commonly used by the econometrician may be imported into the differencing setting with relative ease. If some of the parametric variables are potentially correlated with the residuals, instrumental variable techniques can be applied, with suitable modification, as can the Hausman endogeneity test (see Section 4.8). If the residuals are potentially not homoskedastic, then well-known techniques such as White's heteroskedasticity-consistent standard errors can be adapted (see Section 4.5). The reader will no doubt find other procedures that can be readily transplanted.

Earlier we have pointed out that the first-order differencing estimator of β in the partial linear model is inefficient when compared with the most efficient estimator (see Section 1.3). The same is true for the first-order differencing estimator of the residual variance (see Section 1.2). This problem can be corrected using higher-order differencing, as demonstrated in Chapter 4.

Most important, however, the simplicity of differencing provides a useful pedagogical device. Applied econometricians can begin using nonparametric techniques quickly and with conventional econometric software. Indeed, all the procedures in the example of Section 1.6 can be executed within packages such as *E-Views, SAS, Shazam, Stata*, or *TSP*. Furthermore, because the partial linear model can easily accommodate multiple parametric variables, one can immediately apply these techniques to data that are of practical interest.

Simplicity and versatility, however, have a price. One of the criticisms of differencing is that it can result in greater bias in moderately sized samples than other estimators.[6] A second criticism is that differencing, as proposed here, works only if the dimension of the model's nonparametric component does not exceed 3 (see Section 5.3). Indeed, in most of what follows we will apply differencing to models in which the nonparametric variable is a scalar. More general techniques based on smoothing will usually be prescribed when the nonparametric variable is a vector. However, we would argue that, even if differencing techniques were limited to one (nonparametric) dimension, they have the potential of significant "market share." The reason is that high-dimensional nonparametric regression models, unless they rely on additional structure (such as additive separability), suffer from the "curse of dimensionality" which severely limits one's ability to estimate the regression relationship with any degree of precision. It is not surprising, therefore, that the majority of applied papers using nonparametric regression limit the nonparametric component to one or two dimensions.

1.8 Empirical Applications

The target audience for this book consists of applied econometricians and economists. Thus, the following empirical applications will be introduced and carried through various chapters:

- Engel curve estimation (South African data)
- Scale economies in electricity distribution (data from Ontario, Canada)
- Household gasoline consumption (Canadian data)
- Housing prices (data from Ottawa, Canada)
- Option prices and state price densities (simulated data)
- Weather and electricity demand (data from Ontario, Canada)
- Equivalence scale estimation (South African data).

Empirical results presented in tables and in figures are worked through in exercises at the end of each chapter along with additional empirical and theoretical problems. The reader is especially urged to do the applied exercises for

[6] Seifert, Gasser, and Wolf (1993) have studied this issue for differencing estimators of the residual variance.

this is by the far the best way to gain a proper understanding of the techniques, their range, and limitations.

For convenience, variable definitions are collected in Appendix E. Other data sets may be obtained easily. For example, household survey data for various developing countries are available at the World Bank Web site www.worldbank.org/lsms. These are the Living Standard Measurement Study household surveys from which our South African data were extracted.

1.9 Notational Conventions

With mild abuse of notation, symbols such as y and x will be used to denote both the variable in question and the corresponding column vector of observations on the variable. The context should make it clear which applies. If x is a vector, then $f(x)$ will denote the vector consisting of f evaluated at the components of x. If X is a matrix and δ is a conformable parameter vector, then $f(X\delta)$ is also a vector.

We will frequently use subscripts to denote components of vectors or matrices, for example, β_i, A_{ij} or $[AB]_{ij}$. For any two matrices A, B of identical dimension, we will on a few occasions use the notation $[A \odot B]_{ij} = A_{ij} B_{ij}$.

When differencing procedures are applied, the first few observations may be treated differently or lost. For example, to calculate the differencing estimator of the residual variance $s^2_{diff} = \sum_i^n (y_i - y_{i-1})^2/2n$, we begin the summation at $i = 2$. For the mathematical arguments that follow, such effects are negligible. Thus, we will use the symbol $\doteq$ to denote "equal except for end effects." As must be evident by now, we will also use the symbol $\cong$ to denote approximate equality, $\xrightarrow{P}$ for convergence in probability, and $\xrightarrow{D}$ for convergence in distribution. The abbreviation "i.i.d." will denote "independently and identically distributed."

Because differencing will be one of the themes in what follows, several estimators will merit the subscript "*diff*", as in the preceding paragraph or in (1.3.2). For simplicity, we will regularly suppress this annotation.

To denote low-order derivatives we will the use the conventional notation f', f'', f'''. Occasionally we will need higher-order derivatives which we will denote by bracketed superscripts; for example, $f^{(m)}$.

1.10 Exercises[7]

1. Suppose $y = f(x) + \varepsilon$, $|f'| \leq L$ for which we have data (y_i, x_i) $i = 1, \ldots, n$, where the x_i are equally spaced on the unit interval. We will derive the distribution

[7] Data and sample programs for empirical exercises are available on the Web. See the Preface for details.

of $s_{diff}^2 = \sum_i^n (y_i - y_{i-1})^2/2n$, which we may rewrite as

$$s_{diff}^2 = \frac{1}{2n}\sum_{i=2}^{n}(\varepsilon_i - \varepsilon_{i-1})^2 + \frac{1}{2n}\sum_{i=2}^{n}(f(x_i) - f(x_{i-1}))^2$$
$$+ \frac{1}{n}\sum_{i=2}^{n}(f(x_i) - f(x_{i-1}))(\varepsilon_i - \varepsilon_{i-1}).$$

(a) Show that the first term on the right-hand side satisfies

$$n^{1/2}\left(\frac{1}{2n}\sum_{i=2}^{n}(\varepsilon_i - \varepsilon_{i-1})^2 - \sigma_\varepsilon^2\right) \xrightarrow{D} N(0, E(\varepsilon^4)).$$

(b) Show that the second term is $O(\frac{1}{n^2})$.
(c) Show that the variance of the third term is $O(\frac{1}{n^3})$ so that the third term is $O_P(\frac{1}{n^{3/2}})$. Thus,

$$n^{1/2}\left(s_{diff}^2 - \sigma_\varepsilon^2\right) = \left(\frac{1}{2n}\sum_{i=2}^{n}(\varepsilon_i - \varepsilon_{i-1})^2 - \sigma_\varepsilon^2\right) + O\left(\frac{1}{n^{3/2}}\right) + O_P\left(\frac{1}{n}\right).$$

2. Consider the restricted estimator of the residual variance (1.4.1) used in the differencing specification test. Show that

$$s_{res}^2 = \frac{1}{n}\sum_{i=1}^{n}(y_i - \hat{\gamma}_1 - \hat{\gamma}_2 x_i)^2 = \frac{1}{n}\sum_{i=1}^{n}(\varepsilon_i + (\gamma_1 - \hat{\gamma}_1) - (\gamma_2 - \hat{\gamma}_2 x_i))^2$$
$$= \frac{1}{n}\sum_{i=1}^{n}\varepsilon_i^2 + O_P\left(\frac{1}{n}\right).$$

Combine this with (1.2.2) and the results of the previous exercise to derive the distribution of V in Section 1.4.

3. Derive the covariance between the two terms in the last line of (1.5.5). Use this to obtain the approximate distribution of the differencing test of equality of regression functions (1.5.6). How would the test statistic change if the two subpopulations were of unequal size?

4. *Scale Economies in Electricity Distribution*

(a) Verify that the data have been reordered so that the nonparametric variable *cust*, which is the log of the number of customers, is in increasing order.
(b) Fit the quadratic model in Figure 1.2, where all variables are parametric. Estimate the residual variance, the variance of the dependent variable *tc*, and calculate $R^2 = 1 - s_\varepsilon^2/s_{tc}^2$.
(c) Transform the data by first differencing as in (1.6.2) and apply ordinary least-squares to obtain estimates of the parametric effects in the partial linear model. To obtain the standard errors, rescale the standard errors provided by the OLS procedure by $\sqrt{1.5}$, as indicated in (1.3.4).

(d) Remove the estimated parametric effects using (1.6.3) and produce a scatterplot of the ordered pairs $(y_i - z_i\hat{\beta}_{diff}, x_i)$, where the x variable is the *log* of the number of customers.
(e) Apply a smoothing or nonparametric regression procedure (such as *ksmooth* in *S-Plus)* to the ordered pairs in (d) to produce a nonparametric estimate of the scale effect.
(f) Apply the specification test in (1.4.2) to the ordered pairs in (d) to test the quadratic specification against the nonparametric alternative.

2 Background and Overview

2.1 Categorization of Models

We now turn to a description of the range of models addressed in this book. Consider first the pure nonparametric model $y = f(x) + \varepsilon$, where ε is i.i.d. with mean 0 and constant variance σ_ε^2. If f is only known to lie in a family of smooth functions $\Im$, then the model is nonparametric and incorporates weak constraints on its structure. We will soon see that such models are actually difficult to estimate with precision if x is a vector of dimension exceeding two or three. If f satisfies some additional properties (such as monotonicity, concavity, homogeneity, or symmetry) and hence lies in $\bar{\Im} \subset \Im$, we will say that the model is constrained nonparametric. Figure 2.1 depicts a parametric and a pure nonparametric model at opposite corners.

Given the difficulty in estimating pure nonparametric models with multiple explanatory variables, researchers have sought parsimonious hybrids. One such example is the partial linear model introduced in Chapter 1. One can see in Figure 2.1 that for any fixed value of x, the function is linear in z. Partial parametric models are an obvious generalization, where $y = g(z; \beta) + f(x) + \varepsilon$ and g is a known function. For the partial parametric surface in Figure 2.1, g is quadratic in z – a shape that is replicated for any fixed value of x.

Index models constitute another hybrid. In this case $y = f(x\beta) + \varepsilon$. For any fixed value of the index $x\beta$, the function $f(x\beta)$ is constant. The index model depicted in Figure 2.1 is given by $f(x\beta) = \cos(x_1 + x_2)$; thus, the function is flat along lines where $x_1 + x_2 = \mathit{constant}$. Partial linear index models are yet another generalization, where $y = f(x\beta) + z\delta + \varepsilon$.

Finally, if we can partition x into two subsets x_a and x_b such that f is of the form $f_a(x_a) + f_b(x_b)$, where f_a and f_b are both nonparametric, then the model is called additively separable. (Of course, partial linear and partial parametric models are also additively separable, but in these cases one component is parametric and the other nonparametric.)

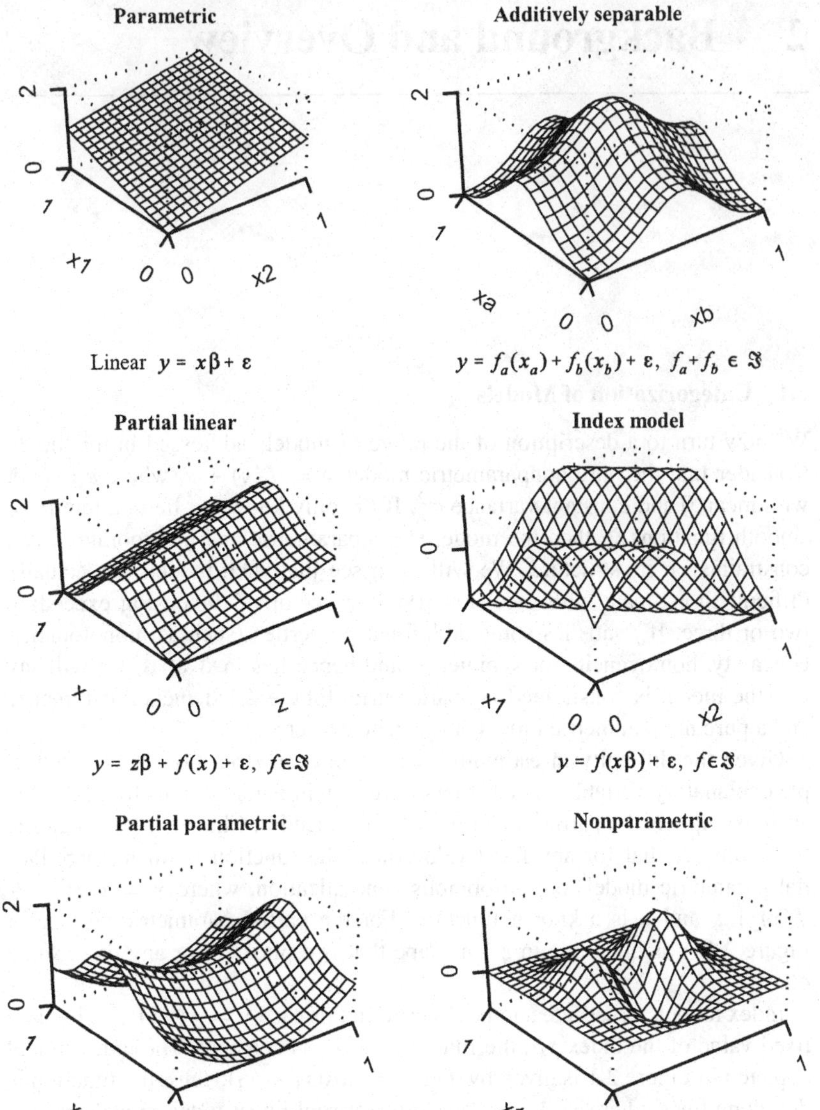

$\Im$ is a family of smooth functions. $\bar{\Im}$ is a smooth family with additional constraints such as monotonicity, concavity, symmetry, or other constraints.

Figure 2.1. Categorization of regression functions.

2.2 The Curse of Dimensionality and the Need for Large Data Sets

2.2.1 Dimension Matters

In comparison with parametric estimation, nonparametric procedures can impose enormous data requirements. To gain an appreciation of the problem as well as remedies for it, we begin with a deterministic framework. Suppose the objective is to approximate a function f. If it is known to be linear in one variable, two observations are sufficient to determine the entire function precisely; three are sufficient if f is linear in two variables. If f is of the form $g(x; \beta)$, where g is known and β is an unknown k-dimensional vector, then k judiciously selected points are usually sufficient to solve for β. No further observations on the function are necessary.

Let us turn to the pure nonparametric case. Suppose f, defined on the unit interval, is known only to have a first derivative bounded by L (i.e., $\sup_{x\in[0,1]} |f'| \leq L$). If we sample f at n equidistant points and approximate f at any point by the closest point at which we have an evaluation, then our approximation error cannot exceed $\frac{1}{2} L/n$. Increasing the density of points reduces approximation error at a rate $O(1/n)$.

Now suppose f is a function on the unit square and that it has derivatives bounded in all directions by L. To approximate the function, we need to sample throughout its domain. If we distribute n points uniformly on the unit square, each will "occupy" an area $1/n$, and the typical distance between points will be $1/n^{1/2}$ so that the approximation error is now $O(1/n^{1/2})$. If we repeat this argument for functions of k variables, the typical distance between points becomes $1/n^{1/k}$ and the approximation error is $O(1/n^{1/k})$. In general, this method of approximation yields errors proportional to the distance to the nearest observation.

Thus, for $n = 100$, the potential approximation error is 10 times larger in 2 dimensions than in 1 and 40 times larger in 5 dimensions. One begins to see the virtues of parametric modeling to avoid this curse of dimensionality.[1]

2.2.2 Restrictions That Mitigate the Curse

We will consider four types of restrictions that substantially reduce approximation error: a partial linear structure, the index model specification, additive separability, and smoothness assumptions.

Suppose a regression function defined on the unit square has the partial linear form $z\beta + f(x)$ (the function f is unknown except for a derivative bound). In this case, we need two evaluations along the z-axis to completely determine β (see the partial linear surface in Figure 2.1). Furthermore, n equidistant evaluations

[1] For an exposition of the curse of dimensionality in the case of density estimation, see Silverman (1986) and Scott (1992).

along the x-axis will ensure that f can be approximated with error $O(1/n)$ so that the approximation error for the regression function as a whole is also $O(1/n)$, the same as if it were a nonparametric function of one variable.

Now consider the index model. If β were known, then we would have a nonparametric function of one variable; thus, to obtain a good approximation of f, we need to take n distinct and say equidistant values of the index $x\beta$. How do we obtain β? Suppose for simplicity that the model is $f(x_1 + x_2\beta)$. (The coefficient of the first variable has been normalized to 1.) Beginning at a point (x_{1a}, x_{2a}), travel in a direction along which f is constant to a nearby point (x_{1b}, x_{2b}). Because $f(x_{1a} + x_{2a}\beta) = f(x_{1b} + x_{2b}\beta)$ and hence $x_{1a} + x_{2a}\beta = x_{1b} + x_{2b}\beta$, we may solve for β. Thus, just as for the partial linear model, the approximation error for the regression function as a whole is $O(1/n)$, the same as if it were a nonparametric function of one variable.

Next, consider an additively separable function on the unit square: $f(x_a, x_b) = f_a(x_a) + f_b(x_b)$, where the functions f_a and f_b satisfy a derivative bound ($f_b(0) = 0$ is imposed as an identification condition). If we take $2n$ observations, n along each axis, then f_a and f_b can be approximated with error $O(1/n)$, so approximation error for f is also $O(1/n)$, once again the same as if f were a nonparametric function of one variable.

The following proposition should now be plausible: For partially linear, index, or additively separable models, the approximation error depends on the maximum dimension of the nonparametric components of the model.

Smoothness can also reduce approximation error. Suppose f is twice differentiable on the unit interval with f' and f'' bounded by L and we evaluate f at n equidistant values of x. Consider approximation of f at $x_o \in [x_i, x_{i+1}]$. Using a Taylor expansion, we have

$$\begin{aligned} f(x_o) &= f(x_i) + f'(x_i)(x_o - x_i) \\ &\quad + {}^1\!/\!_2\, f''(x^*)(x_o - x_i)^2 \qquad x^* \in [x_i, x_o]. \end{aligned} \tag{2.2.1}$$

If we approximate $f(x_o)$ using $f(x_i) + f'(x_i)(x_o - x_i)$, the error is $O(x_o - x_i)^2 = O(1/n^2)$. Of course we do not observe $f'(x_i)$. However, the bound on the second derivative implies that $f'(x_i) - [f(x_{i+1}) - f(x_i)]/[x_{i+1} - x_i]$ is $O(1/n)$ and thus

$$f(x_o) = f(x_i) + \frac{[f(x_{i+1}) - f(x_i)]}{[x_{i+1} - x_i]}(x_o - x_i) + O\left(\frac{1}{n^2}\right). \tag{2.2.2}$$

This local linear approximation involves nothing more than joining the observed points with straight lines. If third-order (kth order) derivatives are bounded, then local quadratic ($k - 1$ order polynomial) approximations will reduce the error further.

In this section, we have used the elementary idea that if a function is smooth, its value at a given point can be approximated reasonably well by using evaluations of the function at neighboring points. This idea is fundamental to nonparametric estimation where, of course, f is combined with noise to yield the observed data. All results illustrated in this section have analogues in the nonparametric setting. Data requirements grow very rapidly as the dimension of the nonparametric component increases. The rate of convergence (i.e., the rate at which we learn about the unknown regression function) can be improved using semiparametric structure, additive separability, and smoothness assumptions. Finally, the curse of dimensionality underscores the paramount importance of procedures that validate models with faster rates of convergence. Among these are specification tests of a parametric null against a nonparametric alternative and significance tests that can reduce the number of explanatory variables in the model.

2.3 Local Averaging Versus Optimization

2.3.1 Local Averaging

In Chapter 1 we introduced the idea of differencing, a device that allowed us to remove the nonparametric effect. Suppose the object of interest is now the nonparametric function itself. A convenient way of estimating the function at a given point is by averaging or smoothing neighboring observations. Suppose we are given data $(y_1, x_1) \ldots (y_n, x_n)$ on the model $y = f(x) + \varepsilon$, where x is a scalar. Local averaging estimators are extensions of conventional estimators of location to a nonparametric regression setting. If one divides the scatterplot into neighborhoods, then one can compute local means as approximations to the regression function. A more appealing alternative is to have the "neighborhood" move along the x-axis and to compute a moving average along the way. The wider the neighborhood, the smoother the estimate, as may be seen in Figure 2.2. (If one were in a vessel, the "sea" represented by the solid line in the bottom panel would be the most placid.)

2.3.2 Bias-Variance Trade-Off

Suppose then we define the estimator to be

$$\begin{aligned}\hat{f}(x_o) &= \frac{1}{n_o}\sum_{N(x_o)} y_i \\ &= f(x_o) + \frac{1}{n_o}\sum_{N(x_o)}(f(x_i) - f(x_o)) + \frac{1}{n_o}\sum_{N(x_o)}\varepsilon_i \qquad (2.3.1)\end{aligned}$$

where summations are taken over observations in the neighborhood $N(x_o)$ around x_o, and n_o is the number of elements in $N(x_o)$. Conditional on the x's, the bias of the estimator consists of the second term, and the variance is determined by the third term.

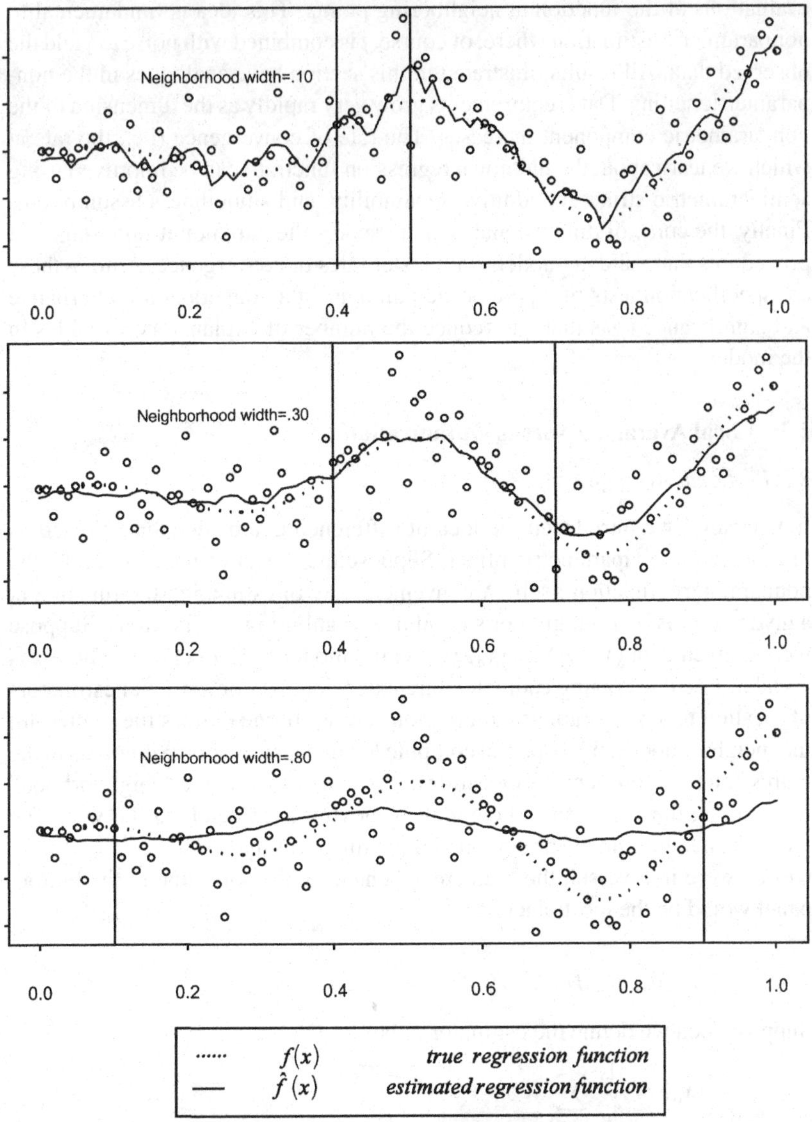

Data-generating mechanism $y_i = x_i \cos(4\pi x_i) + \varepsilon_i \quad \varepsilon_i \sim N(0, .09) \quad x_i \in [0, 1], \quad n = 100.$
Observations are averaged over neighborhoods of the indicated width.

Figure 2.2. Naive local averaging.

The mean-squared error (i.e., the bias squared plus the variance) is given by

$$E[\hat{f}(x_o) - f(x_o)]^2 = \left(\frac{1}{n_o} \sum_{N(x_o)} f(x_i) - f(x_o) \right)^2 + \frac{\sigma_\varepsilon^2}{n_o}. \qquad (2.3.2)$$

Mean-squared error can be minimized by widening the neighborhood $N(x_o)$ until the increase in bias squared is offset by the reduction in variance. (The latter declines because n_o increases as the neighborhood widens.) This trade-off between bias and variance is illustrated in Figure 2.3, which continues the

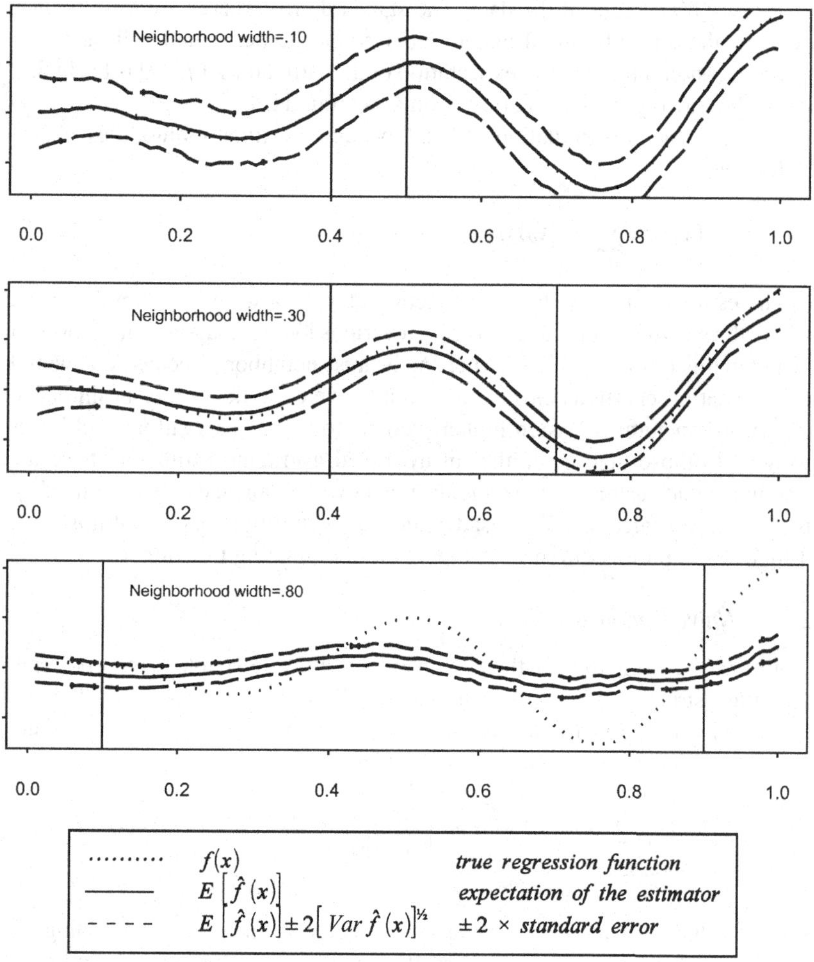

Data-generating mechanism $y_i = x_i \cos(4\pi x_i) + \varepsilon_i \quad \varepsilon_i \sim N(0, .09) \quad x_i \in [0, 1], \quad n = 100.$

Figure 2.3. Bias-variance trade-off.

example of Figure 2.2. In the first panel, local averaging is taking place using just 10 percent of the data at each point (of course, fewer observations are used as one approaches the boundaries of the domain). The solid line is $E[\hat{f}(x)]$ and the estimator exhibits little bias; it coincides almost perfectly with the true regression function (the dotted line). The broken lines on either side correspond to two times the standard errors of the estimator at each point: $2(Var[\hat{f}(x)])^{1/2}$. In the second panel the neighborhood is substantially broader; we are now averaging about 30 percent of the data at each point. The standard error curves are tighter, but some bias has been introduced. The $E[\hat{f}(x)]$ no longer coincides perfectly with the true regression curve. In the third panel, averaging is taking place over 80 percent of the data. The standard error curves are even tighter, but now there is substantial bias particularly at the peaks and valleys of the true regression function. The expectation of the estimator $E[\hat{f}(x)]$ is fairly flat, while the true regression function undulates around it.

A more general formulation of local averaging estimators modifies (2.3.1) as follows:

$$\hat{f}(x_o) = \sum_{1}^{n} w_i(x_o) y_i. \tag{2.3.3}$$

The estimate of the regression function at x_o is a weighted sum of the y_i, where the weights $w_i(x_o)$ depend on x_o. (Various local averaging estimators can be put in this form, including kernel and nearest-neighbor.) Because one would expect that observations close to x_o would have conditional means similar to $f(x_o)$, it is natural to assign higher weights to these observations and lower weights to those that are farther away. Local averaging estimators have the advantage that, as long as the weights are known or can be easily calculated, $\hat{f}$ is also easy to calculate. The disadvantage of such estimators is that it is often difficult to impose additional structure on the estimating function $\hat{f}$.

2.3.3 *Naive Optimization*

Optimization estimators, on the other hand, are more amenable to incorporating additional structure. As a prelude to our later discussion, consider the following naive estimator. Given data $(y_1, x_1) \ldots (y_n, x_n)$ on $y_i = f(x_i) + \varepsilon_i$, where $x_i \in [0, 1]$ and $|f'| \leq L$, suppose one solves

$$\min_{\hat{y}_1,\ldots,\hat{y}_n} \frac{1}{n} \sum_i (y_i - \hat{y}_i)^2 \quad \text{s.t.} \left| \frac{\hat{y}_i - \hat{y}_j}{x_i - x_j} \right| \leq L \qquad i, j = 1, \ldots, n. \tag{2.3.4}$$

Here $\hat{y}_i$ is the estimate of f at x_i and $\hat{f}$ is a piecewise linear function joining the $\hat{y}_i$ with slope not exceeding the derivative bound L. Under general conditions this estimator will be consistent. Furthermore, adding monotonicity or concavity constraints, at least at the points where we have data, is straightforward. As additional structure is imposed, the estimator becomes smoother, and its fit to the true regression function improves (see Figure 2.4).

2.4 A Bird's-Eye View of Important Theoretical Results

The non- and semiparametric literatures contain many theoretical results. Here we summarize – in crude form – the main categories of results that are of particular interest to the applied researcher.

2.4.1 *Computability of Estimators*

Our preliminary exposition of local averaging estimators suggests that their computation is generally straightforward. The naive optimization estimator considered in Section 2.3.3 can also be calculated easily even with additional constraints on the regression function. What is more surprising is that estimators minimizing the sum of squared residuals over (fairly general) infinite dimensional classes of smooth functions can be obtained by solving finite dimensional (often quadratic) optimization problems (see Sections 3.1 to 3.4).

2.4.2 *Consistency*

In nonparametric regression, smoothness conditions (in particular, the existence of bounded derivatives) play a central role in ensuring consistency of the estimator. They are also critical in determining the rate of convergence as well as certain distributional results.[2] With sufficient smoothness, derivatives of the regression function can be estimated consistently, sometimes by differentiating the estimator of the function itself (see Sections 3.1 to 3.4 and 3.7).

2.4.3 *Rate of Convergence*

How quickly does one "discover" the true regression function? In a parametric setting, the rate at which the variance of estimators goes to zero is typically $1/n$.[3]

[2] For example, in proving these results for minimization estimators, smoothness is used to ensure that uniform (over classes of functions) laws of large numbers and uniform central limit theorems apply (see Dudley 1984, Pollard 1984, and Andrews 1994a,b).

[3] In the location model $y = \mu + \varepsilon$, $Var(\bar{y}) = \sigma_y^2/n$; hence, $\mu - \bar{y} = O_P(n^{-1/2})$ and $(\mu - \bar{y})^2 = O_P(1/n)$. For the linear model $y = \alpha + \beta x + \varepsilon$ where the ordered pairs (y, x) are say i.i.d., we have

$$\int(\alpha + \beta x - \hat{\alpha} - \hat{\beta}x)^2 dx = (\alpha - \hat{\alpha})^2 \int dx + (\beta - \hat{\beta})^2 \int x^2 dx$$
$$+ 2(\alpha - \hat{\alpha})(\beta - \hat{\beta}) \int x dx = O_P(1/n)$$

because $\hat{\alpha}$, $\hat{\beta}$ are unbiased and $Var(\hat{\alpha})$, $Var(\hat{\beta})$ and $Cov(\hat{\alpha}, \hat{\beta})$ converge to 0 at $1/n$. The same rate of convergence usually applies to general parametric forms of the regression function.

Smoothness: $\min_{\hat{y}_1,\ldots,\hat{y}_n} \frac{1}{n}\sum_i (y_i - \hat{y}_i)^2$ s.t. $\left|\frac{\hat{y}_i - \hat{y}_j}{x_i - x_j}\right| \le 3 \quad i,j = 1,\ldots,25$

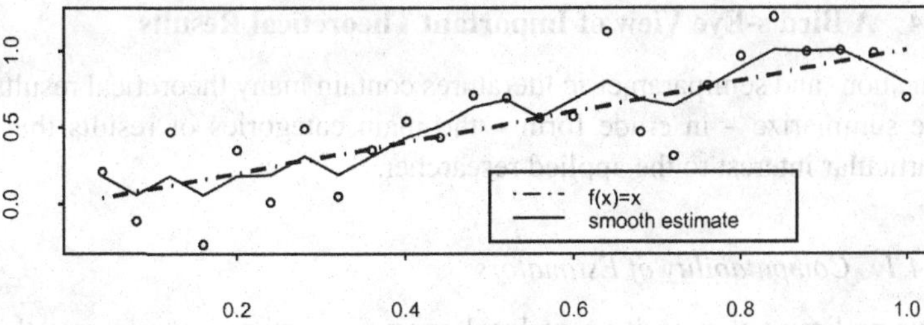

Smoothness and monotonicity: additional constraints $\hat{y}_i \le \hat{y}_j$ for all $x_i \le x_j$

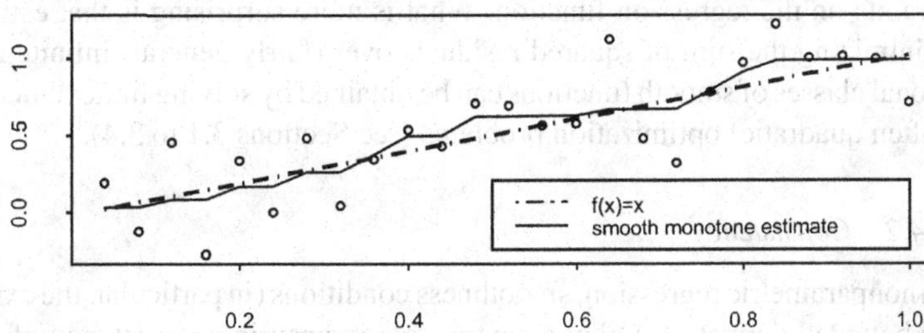

Smoothness, monotonicity, and concavity: additional constraints

$$\hat{y}_j \ge \frac{x_j - x_i}{x_k - x_i}\hat{y}_k + \frac{x_k - x_j}{x_k - x_i}\hat{y}_i \qquad i,j,k = 1,\ldots,n \quad x_i \le x_j \le x_k$$

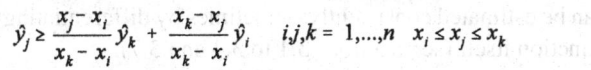

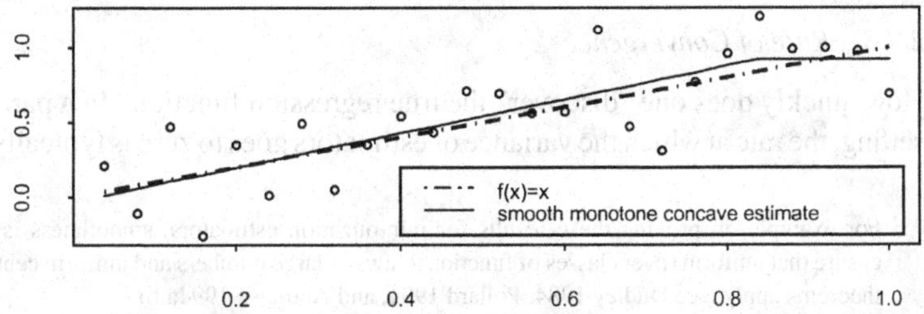

Data-generating mechanism $y_i = x_i + \varepsilon_i \quad \varepsilon_i \sim N(0, .04) \quad x_i \in [0,1]$. Simulations performed using GAMS – General Algebraic Modeling System (Brooke, Kendrick, and Meeraus 1992).

Figure 2.4. Naive nonparametric least squares.

It does not depend on the number of explanatory variables. For nonparametric estimators, convergence slows dramatically as the number of explanatory variables increases (recall our earlier discussion of the curse of dimensionality), but this is ameliorated somewhat if the function is differentiable. The optimal rate at which a nonparametric estimator can converge to the true regression function is given by (see Stone 1980, 1982)

$$\int [\hat{f}(x) - f(x)]^2 dx = O_P\left(\frac{1}{n^{2m/(2m+d)}}\right), \qquad (2.4.1)$$

where m is the degree of differentiability of f and d is the dimension of x. For a twice differentiable function of one variable, (2.4.1) implies an optimal rate of convergence of $O_P(n^{-4/5})$ (a case that will recur repeatedly). For a function of two variables, it is $O_P(n^{-2/3})$.

Local averaging and nonparametric least-squares estimators can be constructed that achieve the optimal rate of convergence (see Sections 3.1 through 3.3). Rate of convergence also plays an important role in test procedures.

If the model is additively separable or partially linear, then the rate of convergence of the optimal estimator depends on the nonparametric component of the model with the highest dimension (Stone 1985, 1986). For example, for the additively separable model $y = f_a(x_a) + f_b(x_b) + \varepsilon$, where x_a, x_b are scalars, the convergence rate is the same as if the regression function were a nonparametric function of one variable. The same is true for the partial linear model $y = z\beta + f(x) + \varepsilon$, where x and z are scalars.

Estimators of β in the partial linear model can be constructed that are $n^{1/2}$-consistent (i.e., for which the variance shrinks at the parametric rate $1/n$) and asymptotically normal. In Section 1.3, we have already seen a simple differencing estimator with this property (see Sections 3.6 and 4.5 for further discussion). Also, estimators of δ in the index model $y = f(x\delta) + \varepsilon$ can be constructed that are $n^{1/2}$-consistent asymptotically normal (see Chapter 7).

For the hybrid regression function $f(z, x_a, x_b, x_c) = z\beta + f_a(x_a) + f_b(x_b) + f_c(x_c)$, where x_a, x_b, x_c are of dimension d_a, d_b, d_c, respectively, the optimal rate of convergence for the regression as a whole is the same as for a nonparametric regression model with number of variables equal to $\max\{d_a, d_b, d_c\}$.

Constraints such as monotonicity or concavity do not enhance the (large sample) rate of convergence if enough smoothness is imposed on the model (see Section 6.6). They can improve performance of the estimator (such as the mean-squared error) if strong smoothness assumptions are not made or if the data set is of moderate size (recall Figure 2.4).

2.4.4 *Bias-Variance Trade-Off*

By increasing the number of observations over which averaging is taking place, one can reduce the variance of a local averaging estimator. But as progressively less similar observations are introduced, the estimator generally becomes more biased. The objective is to minimize the mean-squared error (variance plus bias squared). For nonparametric estimators that achieve optimal rates of convergence, the square of the bias and the variance converge to zero at the same rate (see Sections 3.1 and 3.2). (In parametric settings the former converges to zero much more quickly than the latter.) Unfortunately, this property can complicate the construction of confidence intervals and test procedures.

2.4.5 *Asymptotic Distributions of Estimators*

For a wide variety of nonparametric estimators, the estimate of the regression function at a point is approximately normally distributed. The joint distribution at a collection of points is joint normally distributed. Various functionals such as the average sum of squared residuals are also normally distributed (see Sections 3.1 through 3.3). In many cases, the bootstrap may be used to construct confidence intervals and critical values that are more accurate than those obtained using asymptotic methods (see Chapter 8).

2.4.6 *How Much to Smooth*

Smoothness parameters such as the size of the neighborhood over which averaging is being performed can be selected optimally by choosing the value that minimizes out-of-sample prediction error. The technique, known as cross-validation, will be discussed in Section 3.5.

2.4.7 *Testing Procedures*

A variety of specification tests of parametric or semiparametric null hypotheses against nonparametric or semiparametric alternatives are available.

Nonparametric tests of significance are also available as are tests of additive separability, monotonicity, homogeneity, concavity, and maximization hypotheses. A fairly unified testing theory can be constructed using either "goodness-of-fit" type tests or "residual regression" tests (see Chapters 6 and 8).

3 Introduction to Smoothing

3.1 A Simple Smoother

3.1.1 The Moving Average Smoother[1]

A wide variety of smoothing methods have been proposed. We will begin with a very simple moving average or "running mean" smoother. Suppose we are given data $(y_1, x_1) \ldots (y_n, x_n)$ on the model $y = f(x) + \varepsilon$. We continue to assume that x is scalar and that the data have been reordered so that $x_1 \leq \cdots \leq x_n$. For the time being, we will further assume that the x_i are equally spaced on the unit interval. Define the estimator of f at x_i to be the average of k consecutive observations centered at x_i. (To avoid ambiguity, it is convenient to choose k odd.) Formally, we define

$$\hat{f}(x_i) = \frac{1}{k} \sum_{j=\underline{i}}^{\bar{i}} y_j, \tag{3.1.1}$$

where $\underline{i} = i - (k-1)/2$ and $\bar{i} = i + (k-1)/2$ denote the lower and upper limits of summations. The estimator is of course equal to

$$\hat{f}(x_i) = \frac{1}{k} \sum_{j=\underline{i}}^{\bar{i}} f(x_j) + \frac{1}{k} \sum_{j=\underline{i}}^{\bar{i}} \varepsilon_j. \tag{3.1.2}$$

If k – the number of neighbors being averaged – increases with n, then by conventional central limit theorems the second term on the right-hand side will be approximately normal with mean 0 and variance σ_ε^2/k. If these neighbors cluster closer and closer to x_i – the point at which we are estimating the function – then the first term will converge to $f(x_i)$. Furthermore, if this

[1] The estimator is also sometimes called the "symmetric nearest-neighbor smoother."

convergence is fast enough, we will have

$$k^{1/2}(\hat{f}(x_i) - f(x_i)) \xrightarrow{D} N\left(0, \sigma_\varepsilon^2\right). \tag{3.1.3}$$

A 95 percent confidence interval for $f(x_i)$ is immediate

$$\hat{f}(x_i) \pm 1.96\frac{\sigma_\varepsilon}{k^{1/2}}, \tag{3.1.4}$$

and indeed quite familiar from the conventional estimation of a mean (σ_ε may be replaced by a consistent estimator). It is this simple kind of reasoning that we will now make more precise.

3.1.2 *A Basic Approximation*

Let us rewrite (3.1.2) as follows:

$$\begin{aligned}
\hat{f}(x_i) &= \frac{1}{k}\sum_{j=\underline{i}}^{\bar{i}} y_j \\
&= \frac{1}{k}\sum_{j=\underline{i}}^{\bar{i}} f(x_j) + \frac{1}{k}\sum_{j=\underline{i}}^{\bar{i}} \varepsilon_j \\
&\cong f(x_i) + \frac{f'(x_i)}{k}\sum_{j=\underline{i}}^{\bar{i}}(x_j - x_i) \\
&\quad + \frac{f''(x_i)}{2k}\sum_{j=\underline{i}}^{\bar{i}}(x_j - x_i)^2 + \frac{1}{k}\sum_{j=\underline{i}}^{\bar{i}} \varepsilon_j \\
&\cong f(x_i) + {}^1\!/\!_2 f''(x_i)\frac{1}{k}\sum_{j=\underline{i}}^{\bar{i}}(x_j - x_i)^2 + \frac{1}{k}\sum_{j=\underline{i}}^{\bar{i}} \varepsilon_j.
\end{aligned} \tag{3.1.5}$$

In the third and fourth lines, we have applied a second-order Taylor series.[2] Note that with the x_j symmetric around x_i, the second term in the third line is zero. So, we may rewrite (3.1.5) as[3]

$$\hat{f}(x_i) \cong f(x_i) + \frac{1}{24}\left(\frac{k}{n}\right)^2 f''(x_i) + \frac{1}{k}\sum_{j=\underline{i}}^{\bar{i}} \varepsilon_j. \tag{3.1.6}$$

[2] In particular, $f(x_j) = f(x_i) + f'(x_i)(x_j - x_i) + {}^1\!/\!_2 f''(x_i)(x_j - x_i)^2 + o(x_j - x_i)^2$. We are obviously assuming second-order derivatives exist.

[3] We have used the result ${}^1\!/\!_2 \frac{1}{k}\sum_{j=\underline{i}}^{\bar{i}}(x_j - x_i)^2 = \frac{1}{24}\frac{(k^2-1)}{n^2} \cong \frac{1}{24}\left(\frac{k}{n}\right)^2$. See the exercises for further details.

The last term is an average of k independent and identical random variables so that its variance is σ_ε^2/k and we have

$$\hat{f}(x_i) = f(x_i) + O\left(\frac{k}{n}\right)^2 + O_P\left(\frac{1}{k^{1/2}}\right). \tag{3.1.7}$$

The bias $E(\hat{f}(x_i) - f(x_i))$ is approximated by the second term of (3.1.6) and the $Var(\hat{f}(x_i))$ is approximately σ_ε^2/k, thus, the mean-squared error (the sum of the bias squared and the variance) at a point x_i is

$$E[\hat{f}(x_i) - f(x_i)]^2 = O\left(\frac{k}{n}\right)^4 + O\left(\frac{1}{k}\right). \tag{3.1.8}$$

3.1.3 *Consistency and Rate of Convergence*

The approximation embodied in (3.1.6) yields dividends immediately. As long as $k/n \to 0$ and $k \to \infty$, the second and third terms go to zero and we have a *consistent* estimator.

The *rate* at which $\hat{f}(x_i) - f(x_i) \to 0$ depends on which of the second or third terms in (3.1.6) converge to zero more slowly. Optimality is achieved when the bias squared and the variance shrink to zero at the same rate. Using (3.1.7), one can see that this occurs if $O(k^2/n^2) = O_P(1/k^{1/2})$, which implies that optimality can be achieved by choosing $k = O(n^{4/5})$. In this case,

$$\hat{f}(x_i) \cong f(x_i) + O\left(\frac{1}{n^{2/5}}\right) + O_P\left(\frac{1}{n^{2/5}}\right). \tag{3.1.9}$$

Equivalently, we could have solved for the optimal rate using (3.1.8). Setting $O(k^4/n^4) = O(1/k)$ and solving, we again obtain $k = O(n^{4/5})$. Substituting into (3.1.8) yields a rate of convergence of $E[\hat{f}(x_i) - f(x_i)]^2 = O(n^{-4/5})$ for the mean-squared error at a point x_i. This, in turn, underpins the following,

$$\int [\hat{f}(x) - f(x)]^2 dx = O_P\left(\frac{1}{n^{4/5}}\right), \tag{3.1.10}$$

which is a rather pleasant result in that it satisfies Stone's optimal rate of convergence, (2.4.1), where the order of differentiability $m = 2$ and the dimension $d = 1$.

3.1.4 *Asymptotic Normality and Confidence Intervals*

Applying a central limit theorem to the last term of (3.1.6), we have

$$k^{1/2}\left(\hat{f}(x_i) - f(x_i) - \frac{1}{24}\left(\frac{k}{n}\right)^2 f''(x_i)\right) \xrightarrow{D} N(0, \sigma_\varepsilon^2). \tag{3.1.11}$$

If we select k optimally, say, $k = n^{4/5}$, then $k^{1/2}(k/n)^2 = 1$ and the construction of a confidence interval for $f(x_i)$ is complicated by the presence of the term involving $f''(x_i)$, which would need to be estimated. However, if we require k to grow more slowly than $n^{4/5}$ (e.g., $k = n^{3/4}$), then $k^{1/2}(k/n)^2 \to 0$ and (3.1.11) becomes $k^{1/2}(\hat{f}(x_i) - f(x_i)) \overset{D}{\to} N(0, \sigma_\varepsilon^2)$. Intuitively, we are adding observations sufficiently slowly that they are rapidly clustering around the point of estimation. As a consequence, the bias is small relative to the variance (see (3.1.7)). In this case, a 95 percent confidence interval for $f(x_i)$ is approximately $\hat{f}(x_i) \pm 1.96\sigma_\varepsilon/k^{1/2}$. These are of course exactly the results we began with in (3.1.3) and (3.1.4).

Let us pause for a moment. In these last sections, we have illustrated three essential results for a simple moving average estimator: that it is consistent; that by allowing the number of terms in the average to grow at an appropriate rate, the optimal rate of convergence can be achieved; and, that it is asymptotically normal.

3.1.5 *Smoothing Matrix*

It is often convenient to write moving average (and other) smoothers in matrix notation. Let S be the smoother matrix defined by

$$\underset{(n-k+1)xn}{S} = \begin{bmatrix} \frac{1}{k}, \ldots \frac{1}{k}, 0, \ldots\ldots\ldots\ldots\ldots, 0 \\ 0, \frac{1}{k}, \ldots\ldots, \frac{1}{k}, 0, \ldots\ldots\ldots\ldots 0 \\ \vdots \quad \vdots \\ \vdots \quad \vdots \\ 0, \ldots\ldots\ldots\ldots 0, \frac{1}{k}, \ldots\ldots, \frac{1}{k}, 0 \\ 0, \ldots\ldots\ldots\ldots\ldots 0, \frac{1}{k}, \ldots\ldots, \frac{1}{k} \end{bmatrix}. \tag{3.1.12}$$

Then we may rewrite (3.1.1) in vector-matrix form as

$$\hat{y} = \hat{f}(x) = Sy, \tag{3.1.13}$$

where x, y, $\hat{y}$, $\hat{f}(x)$ are vectors.

3.1.6 *Empirical Application: Engel Curve Estimation*

A common problem in a variety of areas of economics is the estimation of Engel curves. Using South African household survey data (see Appendix E), we select the subset consisting of single individuals and plot the food share of total expenditure as a function of the log of total expenditure in Figure 3.1. The subset contains 1,109 observations.

We apply the moving average smoother with $k = 51$ to obtain the solid irregular line in the upper panel. The lack of smoothness is a feature of moving average smoothers. Note that the estimator does not quite extend to the boundaries of

Model: $y = f(x) + \varepsilon$, x is log of total expenditure and y is the food share of expenditure.
Data: The data consist of a sample of 1,109 single individuals ("Singles") from South Africa.

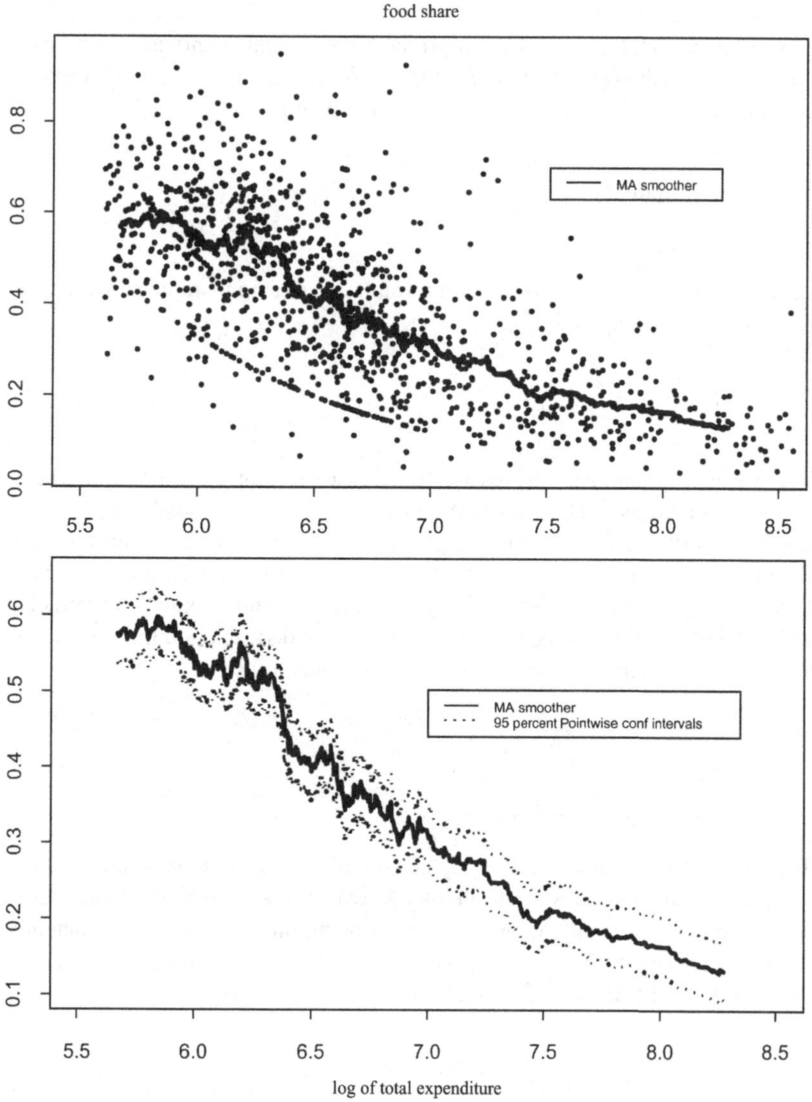

Figure 3.1. Engel curve estimation using moving average smoother.

the data because it drops observations at either end. This shortcoming will be remedied shortly, but boundary behavior is an important feature distinguishing nonparametric estimators.

The lower panel uses (3.1.3) to produce 95 percent pointwise confidence intervals. At median expenditure (*log* (*total expenditure*) = 6.54), the 95 percent confidence interval for food share is 38 to 46 percent.

3.2 Kernel Smoothers

3.2.1 *Estimator*

Let us return now to the more general formulation of a nonparametric estimator we proposed in Chapter 2:

$$\hat{f}(x_o) = \sum_1^n w_i(x_o) y_i. \tag{3.2.1}$$

Here we are estimating the regression function at the point x_o as a weighted sum of the y_i, where the weights $w_i(x_o)$ depend on x_o. A conceptually convenient way to construct local averaging weights is to use a unimodal function centered at zero that declines in either direction at a rate controlled by a scale parameter. Natural candidates for such functions, which are commonly known as kernels, are probability density functions. Let K be a bounded function that integrates to 1 and is symmetric around 0. Define the weights to be

$$w_i(x_o) = \frac{\frac{1}{\lambda n} K\left(\frac{x_i - x_o}{\lambda}\right)}{\frac{1}{\lambda n} \sum_1^n K\left(\frac{x_i - x_o}{\lambda}\right)}. \tag{3.2.2}$$

The shape of the weights (which, by construction, sum to 1) is determined by K, and their magnitude is controlled by λ, which is known as the bandwidth. A large value of λ results in greater weight being put on observations that are far from x_o. Using (3.2.1) the nonparametric regression function estimator, first suggested by Nadaraya (1964) and Watson (1964), becomes

$$\hat{f}(x_o) = \frac{\frac{1}{\lambda n} \sum_1^n K\left(\frac{x_i - x_o}{\lambda}\right) y_i}{\frac{1}{\lambda n} \sum_1^n K\left(\frac{x_i - x_o}{\lambda}\right)}. \tag{3.2.3}$$

A variety of other kernels are available (see Figure 3.2). Generally, selection of the kernel is less important than selection of the bandwidth over which observations are averaged. The simplest is the uniform kernel (also known as

Uniform ½ $u \in [-1,1]$
(Rectangular, box)

Triangular $(1 - |u|)$ $u \in [-1,1]$

Quartic $\dfrac{15}{16}(1 - u^2)^2$ $u \in [-1,1]$
(Biweight)

Epanechnikov $\dfrac{3}{4}(1 - u^2)$ $u \in [-1,1]$

Triweight $\dfrac{35}{32}(1 - u^2)^3$ $u \in [-1,1]$

Normal $\dfrac{1}{\sqrt{2\pi}}\exp\left(-\dfrac{1}{2}u^2\right)$ $u \in [-\infty,\infty]$

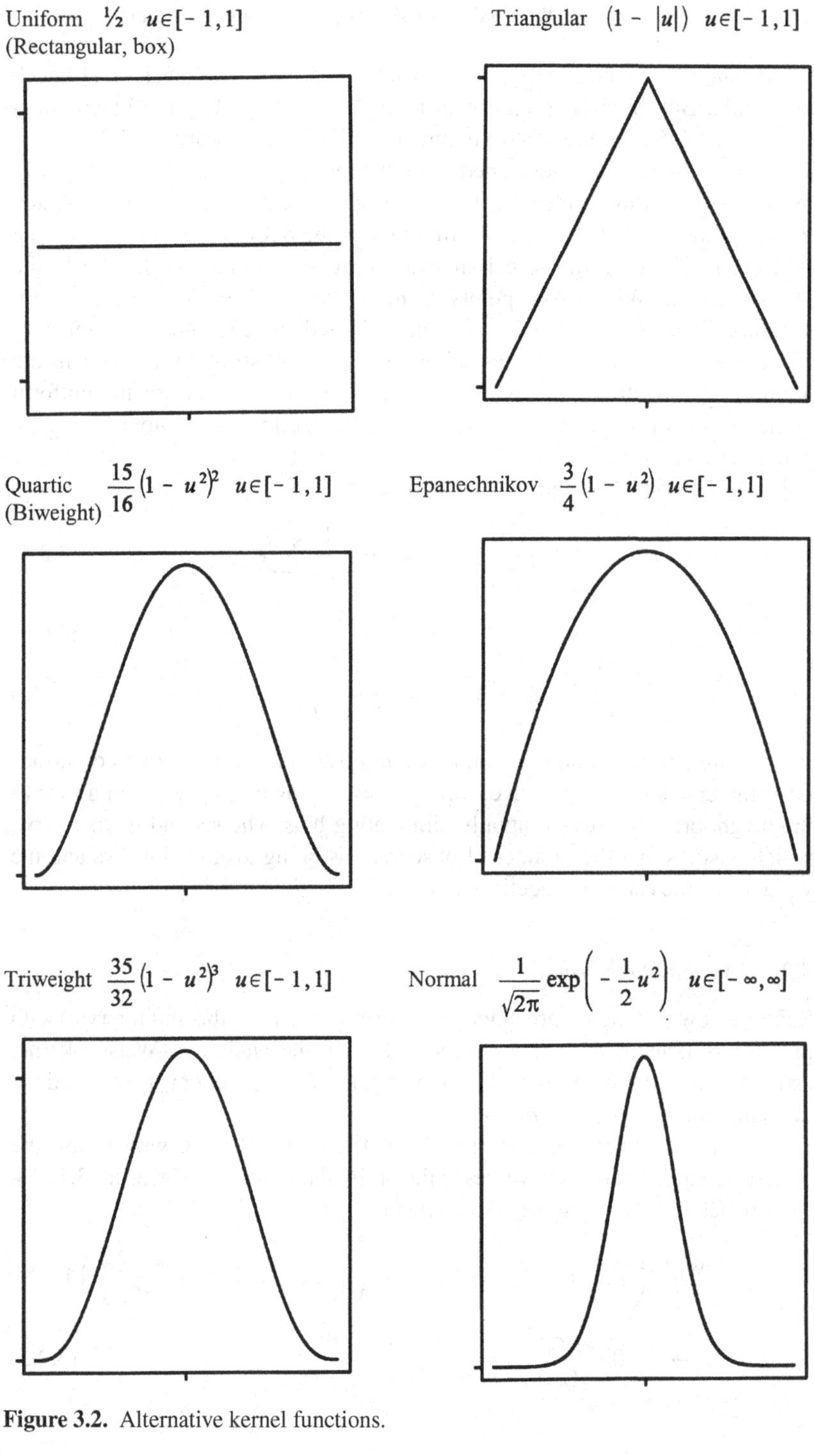

Figure 3.2. Alternative kernel functions.

the rectangular or box kernel), which takes a value of ½ on [−1,1] and 0 elsewhere. But the normal and other kernels are also widely used (see Wand and Jones 1995 for an extensive treatment of kernel smoothing).

Much of the intuition developed using the moving average smoother applies in the current setting. Indeed, with equally spaced x's on the unit interval, and the uniform kernel, the essential difference is the definition of the smoothing parameter. The uniform kernel simply averages observations that lie in the interval $x_o \pm \lambda$. With n data points in the unit interval, the proportion of observations falling in an interval of width 2λ will be 2λ, and the number of observations will be $2\lambda n$. Thus, if one uses the substitution $k = 2\lambda n$ in the arguments of Section 3.1, analogous results will be obtained for the uniform kernel estimator, which in this case is virtually identical to the moving average smoother.

In particular, (3.1.6) and (3.1.7) become

$$\hat{f}(x_i) \cong f(x_i) + \frac{1}{24}(2\lambda)^2 f''(x_i) + \frac{1}{2\lambda n}\sum_j \varepsilon_j \tag{3.2.4}$$

and

$$\hat{f}(x_i) \cong f(x_i) + O(\lambda^2) + O_P\left(\frac{1}{\lambda^{1/2} n^{1/2}}\right). \tag{3.2.4a}$$

Analogously to the conditions on k, we impose the following two conditions on λ: the first is $\lambda \to 0$, which ensures that averaging takes place over a shrinking neighborhood, thus eventually eliminating bias. The second is $\lambda n \to \infty$, which ensures that the number of observations being averaged grows and the variance of the estimator declines to 0.

3.2.2 *Asymptotic Normality*

Suppose now that the x's are randomly distributed (say on the unit interval) with probability density $p(x)$. For a general kernel, the Nadaraya–Watson kernel estimator (3.2.3) is consistent. The numerator converges to $f(x_o)p(x_o)$ and the denominator converges to $p(x_o)$.

The rate of convergence is optimized if $\lambda = O(n^{-1/5})$ in which case the integrated squared error converges at the optimal rate $O_P(n^{-4/5})$, as in (3.1.10). Confidence intervals may be constructed using

$$\lambda^{1/2} n^{1/2}\left(\hat{f}(x_o) - f(x_o) - \tfrac{1}{2} a_K \lambda^2 \left(f''(x_o) + 2f'(x_o)\frac{p'(x_o)}{p(x_o)}\right)\right)$$
$$\xrightarrow{D} N\left[0, \frac{b_K \sigma_\varepsilon^2}{p(x_o)}\right], \tag{3.2.5}$$

where $p\,(.)$ is the density of x and

$$a_K = \int u^2 K(u)du \qquad b_K = \int K^2(u)du. \tag{3.2.6}$$

Wand and Jones (1995, p. 176) provide the values of a_K and b_K for various kernels.

3.2.3 *Comparison to Moving Average Smoother*

Equation (3.2.5) requires estimation of the first and second derivatives of the regression function. However, if λ shrinks to zero faster than at the optimal rate, then the bias term disappears. Under such conditions, and assuming a uniform kernel for which $b_K = 1/2$, we may rewrite (3.2.5) as

$$\lambda^{1/2} n^{1/2}(\hat{f}(x_o) - f(x_o)) \xrightarrow{D} N\left[0, \frac{\sigma_\varepsilon^2}{2p(x_o)}\right]. \tag{3.2.7}$$

What is the probability that an observation will fall in the interval $x_o \pm \lambda$? It is roughly the height of the density times twice the bandwidth or $2\lambda p(x_o)$. Now consider the variance of $\hat{f}(x_o)$ implied by (3.2.7) – $\sigma_\varepsilon^2/2\lambda p(x_o)n$. The denominator is approximately the number of observations one can expect to be averaging when calculating the estimate of f at x_o. Compare this to the variance of the moving average estimator in Section 3.1, which is σ_ε^2/k.

3.2.4 *Confidence Intervals*

Again let us assume that the bias term is made to disappear asymptotically by permitting the bandwidth to shrink at a rate that is faster than the optimal rate. Applying (3.2.5), define the standard error of the estimated regression function at a point to be

$$s_{\hat{f}}(x_o) = \sqrt{\frac{b_K \hat{\sigma}_\varepsilon^2}{\lambda \hat{p}(x_o)n}}, \tag{3.2.8}$$

where

$$\hat{p}(x_o) = \frac{1}{\lambda n}\sum_1^n K\left(\frac{x_i - x_o}{\lambda}\right) \tag{3.2.9}$$

is the denominator of (3.2.3). (See footnote to Table 3.1 for values of b_K.) Then a 95 percent pointwise confidence interval can be constructed using

$$\hat{f}(x_o) \pm 1.96\, s_{\hat{f}}. \tag{3.2.10}$$

Table 3.1. *Asymptotic confidence intervals for kernel estimators – implementation.*

1. Select λ so that $n^{1/5}\lambda \to 0$, for example, $\lambda = O(n^{-1/4})$. This ensures that the bias term does not appear in (3.2.5).
2. Select a kernel K and obtain $b_K = \int K^2(u)du$. For the uniform kernel on $[-1,1]$ $b_K = 1/2$.[a]
3. Estimate f using the Nadaraya–Watson estimator (3.2.3).
4. Calculate $\hat{\sigma}_\varepsilon^2 = 1/n \sum (y_i - \hat{f}(x_i))^2$.
5. Estimate $p(x_o)$ using (3.2.9). If the uniform kernel is used, $\hat{p}(x_o)$ equals the proportion of x_i in the interval $x_o \pm \lambda$ divided by the width of the interval 2λ.
6. Calculate the confidence interval at $f(x_o)$ using $\hat{f}(x_o) \pm 1.96\sqrt{b_K \hat{\sigma}_\varepsilon^2 / \hat{p}(x_o)\lambda n}$
7. Repeat at other points if desired.

[a] For other kernels, the values of b_K are as follows: triangular, 2/3; quartic or biweight, 5/7; Epanechnikov, 3/5; triweight, 350/429; normal, $1/(2\pi^{1/2})$.

Table 3.1 provides implementation details. For confidence intervals when the residuals are heteroskedastic, see the bootstrap procedures in Chapter 8, Table 8.2.

3.2.5 *Uniform Confidence Bands*[4]

A potentially more interesting graphic for nonparametric estimation is a confidence band or ribbon around the estimated function. Its interpretation is that, in repeated samples, 95 percent of the estimated confidence bands will contain the entire true regression function f. The plausibility of an alternative specification (such as a parametric estimate, a monotone or concave estimate) can then be assessed by superimposing this specification on the graph to see if it falls within the band. Without loss of generality, assume that the domain of the nonparametric regression function is the unit interval. Returning to the assumption that $\lambda \to 0$ at a rate faster than optimal (but slowly enough to ensure consistency), a *uniform* 95 percent confidence band or ribbon can be constructed around the function f using

$$\hat{f}(x) \pm \left(\frac{c}{d} + d + \frac{1}{2d} \ln \left(\frac{\int (K'(u))^2}{4\pi^2 \int K^2(u)} \right) \right) s_{\hat{f}}, \qquad (3.2.11)$$

where $d = \sqrt{2\ln(1/\lambda)}$, c satisfies $\exp[-2\exp(-c)] = .95$, and $s_{\hat{f}}$ is the

[4] See Härdle and Linton (1994, p. 2317). See also Eubank and Speckman (1993) for an alternative approach to constructing uniform confidence bands for the case where the x's are equally spaced.

estimated standard error of the estimated regression function defined in (3.2.8).

3.2.6 *Empirical Application: Engel Curve Estimation*

We now apply kernel estimation to the South African data set on single individuals considered earlier. The upper panel of Figure 3.3 illustrates a kernel estimate (using a triangular kernel). It is considerably smoother than the simple moving average estimator in Figure 3.1. The lower panel of Figure 3.3 displays 95 percent pointwise confidence intervals as well as a 95 percent uniform confidence band around the estimate. Note that the uniform band – because it is designed to capture the entire function with 95 percent probability – is wider than the pointwise intervals.

3.3 Nonparametric Least-Squares and Spline Smoothers

3.3.1 *Estimation*

In Section 2.3.3, we introduced a primitive nonparametric least-squares estimator that imposed smoothness by bounding the slope of the estimating function. We will need a more tractable way to impose constraints on various order derivatives. Let C^m be the set of functions that have continuous derivatives up to order m. (For purposes of exposition we restrict these functions to the unit interval.) A measure of smoothness that is particularly convenient is given by the Sobolev norm

$$\|f\|_{Sob} = \left[\int f^2 + (f')^2 + (f'')^2 + \cdots + \left(f^{(m)}\right)^2 dx\right]^{1/2}, \qquad (3.3.1)$$

where $^{(m)}$ denotes the mth-order derivative. A small value of the norm implies that neither the function nor any of its derivatives up to order m can be too large over a significant portion of the domain. Indeed, bounding this norm implies that all lower-order derivatives are bounded in supnorm. Recall from Section 2.3.3 and Figure 2.4 that even bounding the first derivative produces a consistent nonparametric least-squares estimator.

Suppose we take our estimating set $\Im$ to be the set of functions in C^m for which the square of the Sobolev norm is bounded by say L, that is, $\Im = \{f \in C^m, \|f\|^2_{Sob} \le L\}$. The task of finding the function in $\Im$ that best fits the data appears to be daunting. After all, $\Im$ is an infinite dimensional family. What is remarkable is that the solution $\hat{f}$ that satisfies

$$s^2 = \min_f \frac{1}{n}\sum_i [y_i - f(x_i)]^2 \quad \text{s.t.} \quad \|f\|^2_{Sob} \le L \qquad (3.3.2)$$

Model: $y = f(x) + \varepsilon$, x is log total expenditure and y is the food share of expenditure.
Data: The data consist of a sample of 1,109 single individuals ("Singles") from South Africa.

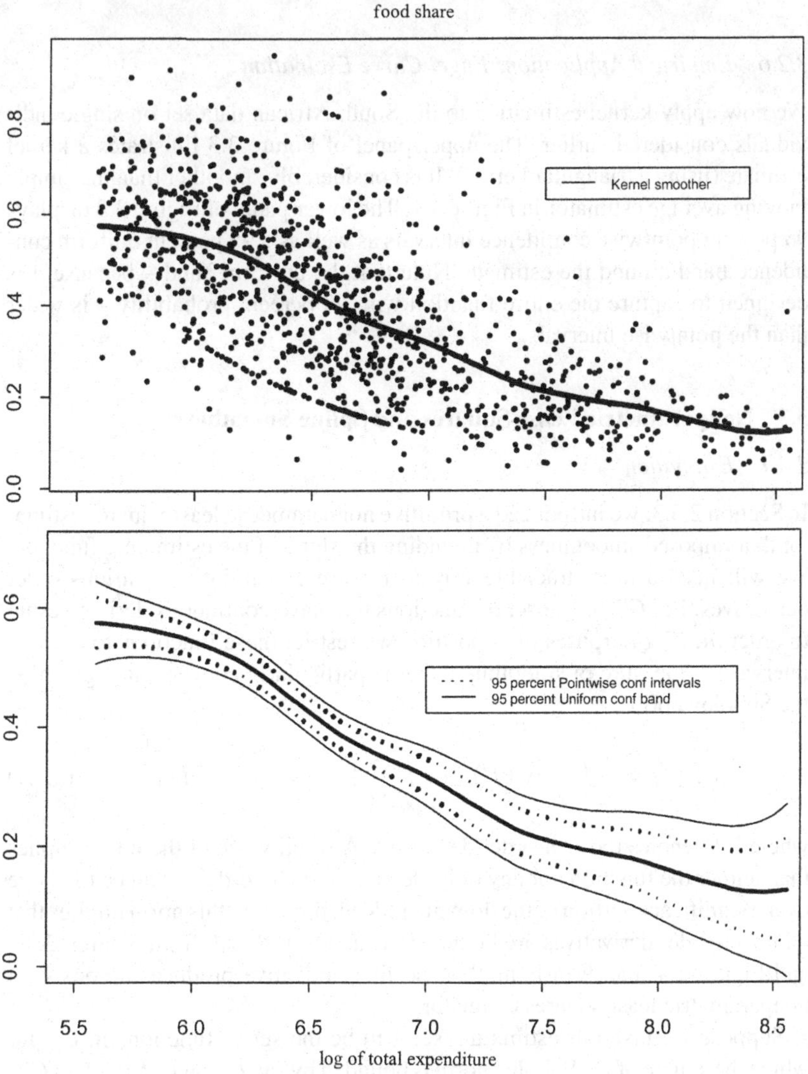

Figure 3.3. Engel curve estimation using kernel estimator.

can be obtained by minimizing a quadratic objective function subject to a quadratic constraint. The solution is of the form $\hat{f} = \sum_1^n \hat{c}_i r_{x_i}$, where $r_{x_1}, \ldots, r_{x_n}$ are functions computable from $x_1, \ldots, x_n$ and $\hat{c} = (\hat{c}_1, \ldots, \hat{c}_n)$ is obtained by solving

$$\min_c \frac{1}{n}[y - Rc]'[y - Rc] \quad \text{s.t. } c'Rc \leq L. \tag{3.3.3}$$

Here y is the $n \times 1$ vector of observations on the dependent variable, and R is an $n \times n$ matrix computable from $x_1, \ldots, x_n$. Note that even though one is estimating n parameters to fit n observations, the parameters are constrained; thus, there is no immediate reason to expect perfect fit.

The r_{x_i} are called representor functions and R, the matrix of inner products of the r_{x_i}, the representor matrix (see Wahba 1990, Yatchew and Bos 1997). Details of these computations are contained in Appendix D. An efficient algorithm for solving (3.3.3) may be found in Golub and Van Loan (1989, p. 564).

Furthermore, if x is a vector, the Sobolev norm (3.3.1) generalizes to include various order partial derivatives. The optimization problem has the same quadratic structure as in the one-dimensional case above, and the functions $r_{x_1}, \ldots, r_{x_n}$ as well as the matrix R are directly computable from the data $x_1, \ldots, x_n$. Further results may be found in Chapters 5 and 6 and Appendix D.

3.3.2 *Properties*[5]

The main statistical properties of the procedure are these: $\hat{f}$ is a consistent estimator of f; indeed, low-order derivatives of $\hat{f}$ consistently estimate the corresponding derivatives of f. The rate at which $\hat{f}$ converges to f satisfies the optimal rates given by Stone, (2.4.1). The optimal convergence result is useful in producing consistent tests of a broad range of hypotheses.

The average minimum sum of squared residuals s^2 is a consistent estimator of the residual variance σ_ε^2. Furthermore, in large samples, s^2 is indistinguishable from the true average sum of squared residuals in the sense that

$$n^{1/2}\left(s^2 - \frac{1}{n}\sum \varepsilon_i^2\right) \xrightarrow{P} 0. \tag{3.3.4}$$

Next, since $n^{1/2}(1/n \sum \varepsilon_i^2 - \sigma_\varepsilon^2) \rightarrow N(0, Var(\varepsilon^2))$ (just apply an ordinary central limit theorem), (3.3.4) implies that

$$n^{1/2}\left(s^2 - \sigma_\varepsilon^2\right) \xrightarrow{D} N(0, Var(\varepsilon^2)). \tag{3.3.5}$$

[5] These results are proved using empirical processes theory, as discussed in Dudley (1984) and Pollard (1984).

As explained in Section 3.6.2, this result lies at the heart of demonstrating that nonparametric least squares can be used to produce $n^{1/2}$-consistent normal estimators in the partial linear model.

3.3.3 *Spline Smoothers*

The nonparametric least-squares estimator is closely related to spline estimation. Assume for the moment $\eta > 0$ is a given constant,[6] and consider the "penalized" least-squares problem

$$\min_f \frac{1}{n} \sum_i [y_i - f(x_i)]^2 + \eta \| f \|^2_{Sob}. \tag{3.3.6}$$

The criterion function trades off fidelity to the data against smoothness of the function f. There is a penalty for selecting functions that fit the data extremely well but as a consequence are very rough (recall that the Sobolev norm measures the smoothness of a function and its derivatives). A larger η results in a smoother function being selected.

If one solves (3.3.2), our nonparametric least-squares problem, takes the Lagrangian multiplier, say $\hat{\eta}$ associated with the smoothness constraint, and then uses it in solving (3.3.6), the resulting $\hat{f}$ will be identical.

In their simplest incarnation, spline estimators use $\int (f'')^2$ as the measure of smoothness (see Eubank 1988, Wahba 1990). Equation (3.3.6) becomes

$$\min_f \frac{1}{n} \sum_i [y_i - f(x_i)]^2 + \eta \int (f'')^2. \tag{3.3.7}$$

As η increases, the estimate becomes progressively smoother. In the limit, f'' is forced to zero, producing a linear fit. At the other extreme, as η goes to zero, the estimator produces a function that interpolates the data points perfectly.

3.4 Local Polynomial Smoothers

3.4.1 *Local Linear Regression*

A natural extension of local averaging is the idea of local regression. Suppose one runs a linear regression using only observations that lie in a neighborhood of x_o which we will denote by $N(x_o)$. If included observations were given equal weight, one would solve

$$\min_{a,b} \sum_{x_i \in N(x_o)} [y_i - a(x_o) - b(x_o)x_i]^2 \tag{3.4.1}$$

[6] Actually, it is selected using cross-validation, which is a procedure we will discuss shortly.

where the dependence of the regression coefficients on x_o is emphasized by the notation. The estimate of f at x_o would be given by

$$\hat{f}(x_o) = \hat{a}(x_o) + \hat{b}(x_o)x_o. \tag{3.4.2}$$

Repeating this procedure at a series of points in the domain, one obtains a nonparametric estimator of the regression function f.

Alternatively, one could perform a weighted regression assigning higher weights to closer observations and lower ones to those that are farther away. (In the preceding procedure, one assigns a weight of 1 to observations in $N(x_o)$ and 0 to others.) A natural way to implement this is to let the weights be determined by a kernel function and controlled by the bandwidth parameter λ. The optimization problem may then conveniently be written as

$$\min_{a,b} \sum_i [y_i - a(x_o) - b(x_o)x_i]^2 \, K\left(\frac{x_i - x_o}{\lambda}\right). \tag{3.4.3}$$

Solutions are once again plugged into (3.4.2). This procedure is sometimes referred to as "kernel regression" because it applies kernel weights to a local regression. By replacing the linear function in (3.4.3) with a polynomial, the procedure generalizes to local polynomial regression.

Key references in this literature include Cleveland (1979), Cleveland and Devlin (1988), and Fan and Gijbels (1996). The latter is a monograph devoted to the subject and contains an extensive bibliography.

3.4.2 *Properties*

Under general conditions, local polynomial regression procedures are consistent, achieve optimal rates of convergence with suitable selection of the bandwidth, and yield point estimates that are asymptotically normal. For construction of confidence intervals, see Fan and Gijbels (1996, pp. 116–118). Furthermore, the behavior of local polynomial regression procedures at the boundary is often superior to kernel and spline estimation. An algorithm used to implement local polynomial regression proceeds as follows:

For a point x_o find the k nearest-neighbors. These will constitute the neighborhood $N(x_o)$. Define the *span* to be k/n. It is the fraction of total observations used in the local regression.

Let $\Delta(x_o)$ be the largest distance between x_o and any other point in the neighborhood $N(x_o)$. Assign weights to each point in the neighborhood using $K(|x_i - x_o|/\Delta(x_o))$, where K is the triweight kernel in Figure 3.2.

Calculate the weighted least-squares estimator using the observations in the neighborhood and produce the fitted value $\hat{f}(x_o)$. Repeat at the other values of x.

Model: $y = f(x) + \varepsilon$, x is log total expenditure and y is the food share of expenditure.
Data: The data consist of a sample of 1,109 single individuals ("Singles") from South Africa.

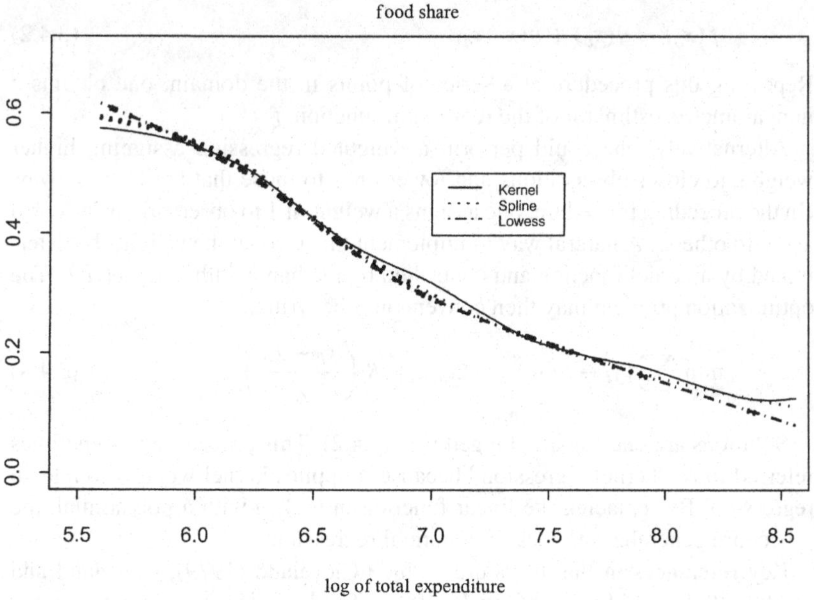

Figure 3.4. Engel curve estimation using kernel, spline, and lowess estimators.

Variants on these estimators include *loess* (*lo*cal regr*ess*ion;[7] Cleveland and Devlin 1988) and *lowess* (*lo*cally *we*ighted *s*catterplot *s*moothing; Cleveland 1979). After initial estimates using local regression, *lowess* seeks to increase robustness by assigning lower weights to those observations with large residuals and repeating the local regression procedure.

3.4.3 *Empirical Application: Engel Curve Estimation*

Figure 3.4 illustrates the application of kernel, spline, and *lowess* estimators to the data on single South Africans. Relative to the precision of estimation (as illustrated by the confidence intervals and bands in Figure 3.3), the estimators track each other closely. One should keep in mind that this is a sizable data set with over 1,000 observations.

[7] Evidently the name was chosen because a *loess* is a surface of loamy, silt, or clay deposits common in river valleys and usually formed by wind (see Chambers and Hastie 1993, p. 314).

3.5 Selection of Smoothing Parameter[8]

3.5.1 *Kernel Estimation*

We now turn to selection of smoothing parameters for kernel estimators. If the bandwidth λ is too large, then oversmoothing will exacerbate bias and eliminate important features of the regression function. Selection of a value of λ that is too small will cause the estimator to track the current data too closely, thus impairing the prediction accuracy of the estimated regression function when applied to new data (see Figures 2.2 and 2.3). To obtain a good estimate of f one would like to select λ to minimize the mean integrated squared error (*MISE*)

$$MISE(\lambda) = E\int[\hat{f}(x;\lambda) - f(x)]^2 dx, \tag{3.5.1}$$

where we write $\hat{f}(x;\lambda)$ to denote explicitly that the kernel estimator depends on the choice of λ. Of course we do not observe f, so the *MISE* cannot be minimized directly. Nor will selecting λ by minimizing the estimate of the residual variance

$$\hat{\sigma}_\varepsilon^2(\lambda) = \frac{1}{n}\sum_{i=1}^{n}[y_i - \hat{f}(x_i;\lambda)]^2 \tag{3.5.2}$$

lead to a useful result, for the minimum of (3.5.2) occurs when λ is reduced to the point where the data are fit perfectly. However, this idea can be modified to produce useful results. Consider a slight variation on (3.5.2) known as the cross-validation function

$$CV(\lambda) = \frac{1}{n}\sum_{i=1}^{n}[y_i - \hat{f}_{-i}(x_i;\lambda)]^2. \tag{3.5.3}$$

The only difference between (3.5.2) and (3.5.3) is that the kernel estimator is subscripted with a curious "$-i$" which is used to denote that $\hat{f}_{-i}$ is obtained by omitting the ith observation. The estimate of f at each point x_i is obtained by estimating the regression function using all other observations and then predicting the value of f at the omitted observation. (Thus, for a given value of λ, $CV(\lambda)$ requires calculation of n separate kernel estimates.)[9]

[8] Cross-validation was first proposed for the kernel estimator by Clark (1975) and for spline estimation by Wahba and Wold (1975).

[9] The notion that out-of-sample prediction is a useful criterion for estimation and testing is, of course, quite generally applied in statistics. In the simplest case, one can imagine dividing a sample in two, using one part to estimate the model and the other to assess its accuracy or validity. This naive approach, however, does not make optimal use of the data, a problem that is resolved through the cross-validation device.

This subtle change results in some extremely propitious properties, (see, e.g., Härdle and Marron 1985, and Härdle, Hall, and Marron 1988). In particular, suppose an optimal λ, say λ_{OPT}, could be chosen to minimize (3.5.1). Let $\hat{\lambda}$ be the value that minimizes (3.5.3). Then $MISE(\hat{\lambda})/MISE(\lambda_{OPT})$ converges in large samples to 1. That is, in large samples, selecting λ through cross-validation is as good as knowing the λ that minimizes the integrated mean-squared error.

3.5.2 *Nonparametric Least Squares*

The heuristics of smoothness bound selection for nonparametric least squares are similar. If one selects L in (3.3.2) to be much larger than the squared true norm of the function f, then the estimator will be less efficient though it will be consistent. If one selects a bound that is smaller, then the estimator will generally be inconsistent. The cross-validation function is defined as

$$CV(L) = \frac{1}{n}\sum_{i=1}^{n}[y_i - \hat{f}_{-i}(x_i)]^2, \tag{3.5.4}$$

where $\hat{f}_{-i}$ is obtained by solving

$$\min_f \frac{1}{n}\sum_{j\neq i}^{n}[y_j - f(x_j)]^2 \quad \text{s.t. } \|f\|^2_{Sob} \leq L. \tag{3.5.5}$$

The interpretation of the smoothing parameter is somewhat different. In kernel estimation it corresponds to the width of the interval over which averaging takes place; in nonparametric least squares it is the diameter of the set of functions over which estimation takes place.

Figure 3.5 illustrates the behavior of the cross-validation function for both kernel and nonparametric least-squares estimators. The data-generating mechanism is given by the model $y_i = x_i + \varepsilon_i$, $\varepsilon_i \sim N(0,.01)$, $i = 1,\ldots,25$ where the x_i are equally spaced on the interval [0,1]. The minimum of the cross-validation function for the kernel estimator is approximately at a bandwidth of .25.

For the nonparametric least-squares cross-validation function, note first that the square of the second-order Sobolev norm (3.3.1) of the true regression function is given by $\int_0^1 x^2 + 1 = 1\frac{1}{3}$ for $m \geq 2$. Thus, $L = 1\frac{1}{3}$ would be the smallest value that would ensure consistency of the nonparametric least-squares problem (3.3.2). In the simulations (Figure 3.5), the minimum of the cross-validation function is between 1.4 and 1.5.[10]

[10] For optimality results on cross-validation in a spline setting, see Li (1986, 1987), Wahba (1990, p. 47).

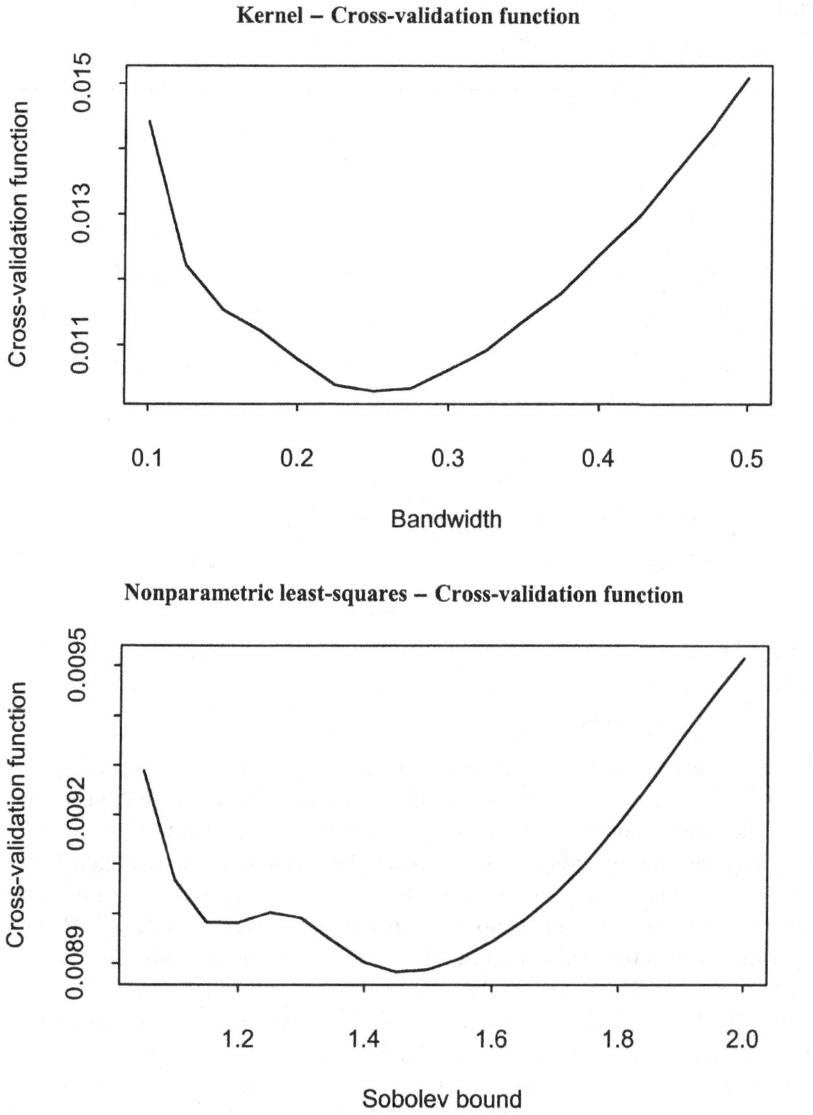

Data-generating mechanism: $y_i = x_i + \varepsilon_i$, $\varepsilon_i \sim N(0,.01)$, $i = 1, \ldots 25$, where x_i are equally spaced on the interval [0,1]. Kernel cross-validation performed using triangular kernel. Nonparametric least-squares cross-validation performed using Fortran code written by the author.

Figure 3.5. Selection of smoothing parameters.

Model: $y = f(x) + \varepsilon$, x is log total expenditure and y is the food share of expenditure.
Data: 1,109 single individuals ("Singles") from South Africa.
Kernel: triangular kernel

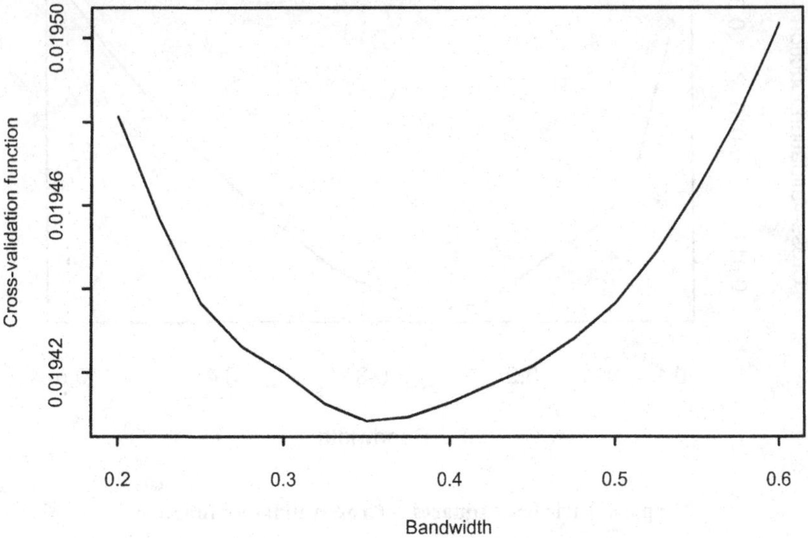

Figure 3.6. Cross-validation of bandwidth for Engel curve estimation.

3.5.3 *Implementation*

Various researchers have investigated alternate procedures for selecting the smoothing parameter. Unfortunately, unlike the case of kernel estimation of density functions, no convenient rules of thumb are available for kernel regression.[11] However, by simply trying different values for the smoothing parameter and visually examining the resulting estimate of the regression function, it is often possible to obtain a useful indication of whether one is over- or undersmoothing.

Furthermore, cross-validation can be automated relatively easily. The kernel cross-validation function in Figure 3.5 was obtained using the "regcvl" function in *XploRe*. *S-Plus* uses cross-validation to produce its spline estimates, and other automated procedures are also available.[12]

Figure 3.6 contains the cross-validation function for the data on food expenditures by South African singles (see Figures 3.1, 3.3, and 3.4). We have used a triangular kernel (because of the speed of computation). The minimum appears to be at about .35.

[11] For "rules of thumb" in a kernel density estimation setting, see Scott (1992). For alternatives to cross-validation in a nonparametric regression setting, see, for example, Simonoff (1996, p. 197) and references therein.

[12] See Venables and Ripley (1994, p. 250).

3.6 Partial Linear Model

3.6.1 *Kernel Estimation*

Given i.i.d. data $(y_1, x_1, z_1), \ldots, (y_n, x_n, z_n)$, consider the semiparametric regression model discussed in Chapter 1,

$$y = z\beta + f(x) + \varepsilon, \tag{3.6.1}$$

where $E(y \mid z, x) = z\beta + f(x), \sigma_\varepsilon^2 = Var[y \mid z, x]$. The function f is not known to lie in a particular parametric family. An early and important analysis of this model was that of Engle et al. (1986), who used it to study the impact of weather on electricity demand, which is an example that we too consider in Section 4.6.3.

Robinson's (1988) influential paper – one that was paralleled by Speckman (1988) in the statistics literature – demonstrates that β can be estimated at parametric rates, that is, $\hat{\beta} - \beta = O_P(n^{-1/2})$, despite the presence of the nonparametric function f. Specifically, Robinson rewrites (3.6.1) conditioning on the nonparametric variable x as follows:

$$y - E(y \mid x) = y - E(z \mid x)\beta - f(x) = (z - E(z \mid x))\beta + \varepsilon. \tag{3.6.2}$$

If $E(y \mid x)$ and $E(z \mid x)$ are known, then ordinary least squares on (3.6.2) yields an estimate of β, which is asymptotically normal with variance $\sigma_\varepsilon^2 / n\sigma_u^2$, where σ_u^2 is the variance of z conditional on x. (For the moment we will assume that this conditional variance is constant.)

Of course, the regression functions $E(y \mid x)$ and $E(z \mid x)$ are generally not even known to have particular parametric forms. Robinson then produces nonparametric (kernel) estimators of $h(x) = E(y \mid x)$ and $g(x) = E(z \mid x)$ that converge sufficiently quickly that their substitution in the OLS estimator does not affect its asymptotic distribution. The estimator is distributed as[13]

$$n^{1/2}(\hat{\beta} - \beta) \xrightarrow{D} N\left(0, \frac{\sigma_\varepsilon^2}{\sigma_u^2}\right). \tag{3.6.3}$$

It is often called the "double residual" estimator because it involves the residuals from initial nonparametric regressions of y on x and z on x, as may be seen from (3.6.2).

[13] For general results of this nature, see Newey (1994a). See also Linton (1995b) who has analyzed higher-order properties of $\hat{\beta}$. Bickel and Kwon (2001) have discussed inference for semiparametric models in a general setting.

3.6.2 *Nonparametric Least Squares*

Returning to (3.6.1), consider the conditional distribution of $y, z \mid x$

$$\begin{aligned} z &= E(z \mid x) + u = g(x) + u \\ y &= E(y \mid x) + v = h(x) + v = (g(x)\beta + f(x)) + (u\beta + \varepsilon) \end{aligned} \quad (3.6.4)$$

then,

$$Cov\begin{pmatrix} u \\ v \end{pmatrix} \equiv \begin{bmatrix} \sigma_u^2 & \sigma_{uv} \\ \dots & \sigma_v^2 \end{bmatrix} = \begin{bmatrix} \sigma_u^2 & \sigma_u^2\beta \\ \dots & \sigma_u^2\beta^2 + \sigma_\varepsilon^2 \end{bmatrix}. \quad (3.6.5)$$

Under sufficient smoothness assumptions, the nonparametric least-squares estimator (3.3.2) can be applied equation by equation. The sample variances $s_u^2 = \sum \hat{u}_i^2/n$, $s_v^2 = \sum \hat{v}_i^2/n$ are $n^{1/2}$-consistent, asymptotically normal estimators of the corresponding population variances σ_u^2, σ_v^2 (using (3.3.5)). It can also be demonstrated that $s_{uv} = \sum \hat{u}_i \hat{v}_i/n$ is a $n^{1/2}$-consistent, asymptotically normal estimator of σ_{uv}. In summary, the sample analogue to (3.6.5), that is, the matrix of estimated variances and covariances, is $n^{1/2}$-consistent asymptotically normal.

Now $\beta = \sigma_{uv}/\sigma_u^2$, so that it is fairly straightforward to show that its sample analogue, $\hat{\beta} = s_{uv}/s_u^2$, is also $n^{1/2}$-consistent, asymptotically normal. Furthermore, its variance is given by $\sigma_\varepsilon^2/n\sigma_u^2$, which is the same variance attained by the Robinson estimator. Inference may be conducted using (3.6.3).[14]

3.6.3 *The General Case*

Suppose one is given data $(y_1, x_1, z_1), \dots, (y_n, x_n, z_n)$, where z_i is a p-dimensional vector and x_i and y_i are scalars.[15] Let $z_i = g(x_i) + u_i$, where g is now a vector function with first derivatives bounded, $E(u_i \mid x_i) = 0$, and $E(Var(z_i \mid x_i)) = \sum_{z|x}$. Write the model as

$$\underset{n\times 1}{y} = \underset{n\times p}{Z}\,\underset{p\times 1}{\beta} + \underset{n\times 1}{f(x)} + \underset{n\times 1}{\varepsilon}, \quad (3.6.6)$$

where Z is the $n \times p$ matrix with ith row z_i. In this case, the double residual method requires that a separate nonparametric regression be performed for the dependent variable and for each parametric variable. Let $\underset{n\times 1}{\hat{h}(x)}$ be the estimates

[14] We note that one can perform semiparametric least squares on the model (3.6.1) by minimizing the sum of squared residuals with respect to β and f subject to a smoothness constraint on f, but the resulting estimator of β would not in general converge at $n^{1/2}$ (see Rice 1986 and Chen 1988).

[15] The case where x is also a vector requires nonparametric regression of several variables, which is covered in Chapter 5. Otherwise, the arguments of the current section apply directly. For proofs of the assertions below, see Robinson (1988) and Speckman (1988).

resulting from a nonparametric regression of y on x. Let $\hat{g}(x)$ be the estimates resulting from a nonparametric regression of each column of $\underset{n\times p}{Z}$ on x. (A kernel, spline, nonparametric least-squares, local polynomial, or other nonparametric smoother may be used). Write

$$y - \hat{h}(x) \cong (Z - \hat{g}(x))\beta + \varepsilon. \tag{3.6.7}$$

Then the double residual estimator of β is given by

$$\hat{\beta} = ((Z - \hat{g}(x))'(Z - \hat{g}(x)))^{-1}(Z - \hat{g}(x))'(y - \hat{h}(x)) \tag{3.6.8}$$

with large sample distribution

$$n^{1/2}(\hat{\beta} - \beta) \overset{D}{\rightarrow} N\left(0, \sigma_\varepsilon^2 \sum\nolimits_{z|x}^{-1}\right). \tag{3.6.9}$$

The residual variance may be estimated consistently using

$$s^2 = \frac{1}{n}(y - \hat{h}(x) - (Z - \hat{g}(x))\hat{\beta})'(y - \hat{h}(x) - (Z - \hat{g}(x))\hat{\beta}), \tag{3.6.10}$$

and a consistent estimate of the covariance matrix of $\hat{\beta}$ is given by

$$\hat{\sum}_{\hat{\beta}} = s^2((Z - \hat{g}(x))'(Z - \hat{g}(x)))^{-1}. \tag{3.6.11}$$

Equations (3.6.9) to (3.6.11) may be used to construct confidence intervals for β. Linear restrictions of the form $R\beta = r$ may be tested using the conventional statistic, which – if the null hypothesis is true – has the following distribution:

$$(R\hat{\beta} - r)'\left(R\hat{\sum}_{\hat{\beta}}R'\right)^{-1}(R\hat{\beta} - r) \overset{D}{\rightarrow} \chi^2_{rank(R)}. \tag{3.6.12}$$

Equivalently one may use

$$\frac{n\left(s^2_{res} - s^2\right)}{s^2} \overset{D}{\rightarrow} \chi^2_{rank(R)}, \tag{3.6.13}$$

where s^2 is the unrestricted estimator obtained in (3.6.10), and s^2_{res} is obtained by estimating the model (3.6.6) subject to the linear constraints[16] and then applying (3.6.10). Finally, one can perform a kernel regression of $y - Z\hat{\beta}$ on x to obtain $\hat{f}$.

[16] Recall that for a linear model, the restricted OLS estimator may be obtained by redefining variables. The "double-residual" model being estimated in (3.6.2) is linear.

3.6.4 *Heteroskedasticity*

Consider the basic linear regression model expressed in matrix notation $y = Z\beta + \varepsilon$, where coefficients are estimated using OLS: $\hat{\beta}_{ols} = (Z'Z)^{-1}Z'y$. If the observations have unknown covariance matrix Ω then

$$Var(\hat{\beta}_{ols}) = \frac{1}{n}\left(\frac{Z'Z}{n}\right)^{-1}\frac{Z'\Omega Z}{n}\left(\frac{Z'Z}{n}\right)^{-1}. \tag{3.6.14}$$

White (1980) demonstrated that to estimate this covariance matrix, one need only obtain a consistent estimator of *plim* $(Z'\Omega Z/n)$ and not of Ω itself. In the case of heteroskedasticity, he proposed $Z'\hat{\Omega}Z/n$ where the diagonal elements of $\hat{\Omega}$ are the squares of the estimated OLS residuals $\hat{\varepsilon}_i^2$. (Off-diagonal elements are zero.) He then showed that $Z'\Omega Z/n - Z'\hat{\Omega}Z/n \xrightarrow{P} 0$. Substitution into (3.6.14) yields a heteroskedasticity-consistent covariance matrix estimator fo $\hat{\beta}_{OLS}$.

Note that in the case of heteroskedasticity, the interior matrix of (3.6.14) may be written as

$$\frac{Z'\Omega Z}{n} = \frac{1}{n}\sum \sigma_i^2 z_i' z_i, \tag{3.6.15}$$

where σ_i^2 are the diagonal entries in Ω and z_i is the ith row of the Z matrix. The estimate may be computed using

$$\frac{Z'\hat{\Omega}Z}{n} = \frac{1}{n}\sum \hat{\varepsilon}_i^2 z_i' z_i. \tag{3.6.16}$$

Let us return to the partial linear model $y = Z\beta + f(x) + \varepsilon$ and suppose that the residuals have covariance matrix Ω. Then the covariance matrix of the OLS estimator (3.6.8) is approximately

$$Var(\hat{\beta}_{OLS}) \cong \frac{1}{n}\left(\frac{(Z-\hat{g}(x))'(Z-\hat{g}(x))}{n}\right)^{-1} \times \frac{(Z-\hat{g}(x))'\Omega(Z-\hat{g}(x))}{n}\left(\frac{(Z-\hat{g}(x))'(Z-\hat{g}(x))}{n}\right)^{-1}, \tag{3.6.17}$$

and in the case of heteroskedasticity, the interior matrix may be estimated using

$$\frac{(Z-\hat{g}(x))'\hat{\Omega}(Z-\hat{g}(x))}{n} = \frac{1}{n}\sum \hat{\varepsilon}_i^2 (z_i - \hat{g}(x_i))'(z_i - \hat{g}(x_i)), \tag{3.6.18}$$

where $\hat{\Omega}$ is a diagonal matrix with entries $\hat{\varepsilon}_i^2$, the estimated residuals from (3.6.7), and $\hat{g}(x_i)$ is the ith row of $\underset{n\times p}{\hat{g}(x)}$.[17]

3.6.5 *Heteroskedasticity and Autocorrelation*

Return once again to the pure linear regression model $y = Z\beta + \varepsilon$. Then for arbitrary residual covariance matrix Ω, the variance of the OLS estimator is given by (3.6.14). Furthermore, the interior matrix of (3.6.14) may be written as

$$\frac{Z'\Omega Z}{n} = \frac{1}{n}\sum_{i,j} \sigma_{ij} z_i' z_j, \qquad (3.6.19)$$

where σ_{ij} denotes elements of Ω and z_i, z_j are the ith and jth rows of the Z matrix. If the covariances are zero for observations that are more than say $\mathscr{L}$ periods apart, then (3.6.19) becomes

$$\frac{Z'\Omega Z}{n} = \frac{1}{n}\sum_{\substack{i,j\\|i-j|\le\mathscr{L}}} \sigma_{ij} z_i' z_j, \qquad (3.6.20)$$

which may be estimated using

$$\frac{Z'\hat{\Omega} Z}{n} = \frac{1}{n}\sum_{\substack{i,j\\|i-j|\le\mathscr{L}}} \hat{\varepsilon}_i \hat{\varepsilon}_j z_i' z_j. \qquad (3.6.21)$$

Here $\hat{\Omega}$ is the matrix $\hat{\varepsilon}\hat{\varepsilon}'$ with all terms whose expectation is known to be zero set to zero. (Thus, all entries more than $\mathscr{L}$ subdiagonals from the main diagonal are zero.) The results may be found in White (1985).

Consistency is retained even if distant correlations are never actually zero but die off sufficiently quickly. In this case, $\mathscr{L}$ is permitted to increase with sample size.

As a practical matter, however, (3.6.21) need not be positive definite. To resolve this, Newey and West (1987) proposed a modification as follows. Rewrite (3.6.21) as

$$\frac{1}{n}\sum_{\substack{i,j\\|i-j|\le\mathscr{L}}} \hat{\varepsilon}_i \hat{\varepsilon}_j z_i' z_j$$

$$= \frac{1}{n}\sum_i \hat{\varepsilon}_i^2 z_i' z_i + \frac{1}{n}\sum_{\ell=1}^{\mathscr{L}}\sum_{i=\ell+1}^{n} \hat{\varepsilon}_i \hat{\varepsilon}_{i-\ell}(z_i' z_{i-\ell} + z_{i-\ell}' z_i), \qquad (3.6.22)$$

[17] Here and in the next section it is convenient to think of $\hat{\Omega}$ as the matrix $\hat{\varepsilon}\hat{\varepsilon}'$ with all terms whose expectation is known to be zero set to zero (which in the case of pure heteroskedasticity means that all off-diagonal terms are set to zero).

but now insert weights to obtain

$$\frac{1}{n}\sum_i \hat{\varepsilon}_i^2 z_i' z_i + \frac{1}{n}\sum_{\ell=1}^{\mathscr{L}}\left(1-\frac{\ell}{\mathscr{L}+1}\right)\sum_{i=\ell+1}^{n}\hat{\varepsilon}_i\hat{\varepsilon}_{i-\ell}(z_i' z_{i-\ell} + z_{i-\ell}' z_i). \tag{3.6.23}$$

Thus, the matrix (3.6.20) may be estimated using either the White (1985) estimator in (3.6.21) or the Newey–West estimator in (3.6.23).

Return once again to the partial linear model. For arbitrary Ω, the OLS estimator (3.6.8) has a covariance matrix given by (3.6.17). Analogously to (3.6.21), the interior matrix may be estimated using (White 1985)

$$\frac{(Z-\hat{g}(x))'\hat{\Omega}(Z-\hat{g}(x))}{n} = \frac{1}{n}\sum_{\substack{i,j\\ |i-j|\le\mathscr{L}}}\hat{\varepsilon}_i\hat{\varepsilon}_j(z_i-\hat{g}(x_i))'(z_j-\hat{g}(x_j)), \tag{3.6.24}$$

where $\hat{\Omega}$ equals $\hat{\varepsilon}\hat{\varepsilon}'$ with all entries more than $\mathscr{L}$ subdiagonals from the main diagonal set to zero. Alternatively, following (3.6.23), the interior matrix may be estimated using the Newey–West approach as follows:

$$\begin{aligned}&\frac{1}{n}\sum_i \hat{\varepsilon}_i^2(z_i-\hat{g}(x_i))'(z_i-\hat{g}(x_i))\\ &+\frac{1}{n}\sum_{\ell=1}^{\mathscr{L}}\left(1-\frac{\ell}{\mathscr{L}+1}\right)\sum_{i=\ell+1}^{n}\hat{\varepsilon}_i\hat{\varepsilon}_{i-\ell}((z_i-\hat{g}(x_i))'(z_{i-\ell}-\hat{g}(x_{i-\ell}))\\ &+(z_{i-\ell}-\hat{g}(x_{i-\ell}))'(z_i-\hat{g}(x_i))).\end{aligned} \tag{3.6.25}$$

3.7 Derivative Estimation

3.7.1 Point Estimates

A variety of derivative estimators based on kernel procedures have been proposed. Conceptually, the simplest approach is to take derivatives of the kernel estimate. This may be done analytically or numerically. For example, suppose $\hat{f}$ is a kernel estimate of f, and let $h \to 0$ as sample size increases. Ullah (1988) and Rilstone and Ullah (1989) proposed

$$\hat{f}'(x) = \frac{1}{2h}(\hat{f}(x+h)-\hat{f}(x-h)) \tag{3.7.1}$$

and

$$\hat{f}''(x) = \frac{1}{(2h)^2}(\hat{f}(x+2h)-2\hat{f}(x)+\hat{f}(x-2h)). \tag{3.7.2}$$

However, the rate at which the optimal bandwidth goes to zero depends on the derivative being estimated. Generally, higher-order derivatives require greater smoothing of the function itself and hence a bandwidth that shrinks to zero more slowly.[18]

Nonparametric least-squares estimators of the kind discussed in Section 3.3 (and later in 5.1) can also be differentiated to produce estimates of derivatives. Generally it is required that the measure of smoothness incorporate at least two more derivatives than the derivative that is of interest. For example, if one is interested in the first derivative, than the Sobolev norm (3.3.1) should be of order three or more. If one is interested in the second derivative (as we will be later when estimating the state price density in an option pricing model), then the norm should be of order four or more.[19]

3.7.2 *Average Derivative Estimation*

Average derivatives or functionals of average derivatives are also frequently of interest. Consider

$$E(f'(x)) = \int f'(x)p(x)dx, \tag{3.7.3}$$

where $p(x)$ is the density function of x. Let $\hat{p}(x)$ be an estimate of $p(x)$. A simple "direct" estimator may be obtained using

$$\int \hat{f}'(x)\hat{p}(x)dx. \tag{3.7.4}$$

Or, one can use

$$\frac{1}{n}\sum_{i=1}^{n} \hat{f}'(x_i). \tag{3.7.5}$$

An alternative "indirect" estimator was proposed by Härdle and Stoker (1989). Suppose one is interested in the regression function on the interval $[a,b]$ and that the density function is zero at the endpoints, that is, $p(a) = p(b) = 0$. Let $s(x)$ be the negative of the score function, that is, $s(x) = -p'(x)/p(x)$. Then an alternative expression for the average derivative is given by

$$E(f'(x)) = E(s(x)y). \tag{3.7.6}$$

[18] See, for example, Härdle (1990, Proposition 3.1.2, p. 33), which imples that estimation of the first derivative has an associated optimal bandwidth of order $O(n^{-1/7})$; for the second derivative, it is $O(n^{-1/9})$. Recall that when estimating the function itself, the optimal bandwidth is $O(n^{-1/5})$.

[19] Thus, the usual spline estimators that penalize the second derivative (see, e.g., (3.3.7)) will not in general produce consistent estimators of first and second derivatives. For spline estimators that penalize higher-order derivatives, see Jim Ramsay's *S-Plus* routines available at www.psych.mcgill.ca/faculty/ramsay/ramsay.html.

The result is obtained using integration by parts, in particular

$$\begin{aligned} E(s(x)y) = E(s(x)f(x)) &= -\int p'(x)f(x)dx \\ &= -p(x)f(x)|_a^b + \int p(x)f'(x)dx \\ &= E(f'(x)) \end{aligned} \tag{3.7.7}$$

because the density of x is zero at the endpoints. The sample analogue of (3.7.6) is given by

$$-\frac{1}{n}\sum_{i=1}^{n}\frac{\hat{p}'(x_i)}{\hat{p}(x_i)}y_i. \tag{3.7.8}$$

In regions of sparse data, $\hat{f}'$, the estimate of the derivative used in (3.7.5) may be poor. Similarly, the estimated value of the density $\hat{p}(x_i)$ appearing in the denominator of (3.7.8) may be close to zero, leading to inaccurate estimates of the average derivative. To mitigate this problem, the estimators are usually modified to remove such observations. In particular, (3.7.5) becomes

$$\frac{1}{n}\sum_{i=1}^{n}\hat{f}'(x_i)I_i, \tag{3.7.5a}$$

and (3.7.8) becomes

$$-\frac{1}{n}\sum_{i=1}^{n}\frac{\hat{p}'(x_i)}{\hat{p}(x_i)}y_i I_i, \tag{3.7.8a}$$

where I_i is an indicator function that is zero if the density $\hat{p}(x_i)$ is close to zero.

3.8 Exercises[20]

1. Derive the approximation used in Footnote 3 to justify (3.1.5). In particular, prove that

$$\frac{1}{k}\sum_{j=\underline{i}}^{\bar{i}}(x_j - x_i)^2 = \frac{k^2-1}{12n^2},$$

where $x_1, \ldots, x_n$ are equally spaced on the unit interval.

[20] Data and sample programs for empirical exercises are available on the Web. See the Preface for details.

2. *Properties of Kernel Estimators*: Suppose x's are uniformly distributed on the unit interval and we are using the uniform kernel to estimate the model $y = f(x) + \varepsilon$. By adapting the results in (3.1.5)–(3.1.11),

(a) derive conditions under which the kernel estimator is consistent at a point, say x_o;
(b) derive the optimal rate of convergence for the bandwidth parameter λ;
(c) derive a 95 percent confidence interval for $f(x_o)$.

3. *Moving Average Estimation*: The purpose of this exercise is to perform a nonparametric regression using the simple moving average estimator and to construct pointwise confidence intervals.

(a) Open the South African survey data and select the subset of the data where the number of adults is 1 and the number of children 0. You will need data on the food share of total expenditure (*FoodShr*) and the log of total expenditure (*ltexp*). The number of observations will be 1,109.
(b) Sort the data so that *ltexp* is in increasing order and produce a scatterplot of the data.
(c) Using $k = 51$, apply the moving average estimator (3.1.1). You will obtain an estimate of the food share function f for observations 26 through 1,084. Superimpose the results on your scatterplot.
(d) Calculate 95 percent pointwise confidence intervals using (3.1.4) and superimpose these on a plot of the estimated regression function. Your results should be similar to those in Figure 3.1.

4. *Kernel Estimation, Confidence Intervals, and Bands*: The purpose of this exercise is to perform a kernel regression and to construct pointwise confidence intervals and a uniform confidence band for the South African food share data on single individuals (see Exercise 3).

(a) We will use the triangular kernel (Figure 3.2). Show that $\int K^2(u) = 2/3$ and that $\int K'(u)^2 = 2$.
(b) Estimate the share function f using the triangular kernel and a bandwidth of .5.
(c) Estimate the residual variance σ_ε^2 using the average sum of squared residuals from this regression.
(d) Calculate $s_{\hat{f}}$ at all the points at which you have data using (3.2.8).
(e) Plot $\hat{f}$ and the 95 percent pointwise confidence intervals using (3.2.10).
(f) Calculate the 95 percent uniform confidence band and superimpose it on your previous plot. Your results should be similar to those in Figure 3.3.

5. *Estimation Using Spline and Lowess Estimators*: The purpose of this exercise is to produce spline and *lowess* estimates using the South African food share data on single individuals (see Exercise 3).

(a) Estimate the share function f using a spline estimator (e.g., *smooth.spline* in *S-Plus*).
(b) Estimate f using a *lowess* estimator (e.g., *lowess* in *S-Plus*).

(c) Plot the kernel estimator of f from Exercise 4(b) above. Superimpose the spline and *lowess* estimates. Your results should be similar to Figure 3.4.

6. *Estimation Using the Super-smoother*: A smoother related to our simple moving average in Section 3.1 is the super-smoother. However, rather than taking a moving average, one performs least squares on k consecutive observations. Furthermore, at each point, cross-validation is used to select k. By allowing variability in the *span* (defined to be k/n), regions where the function has greater fluctuation will be estimated using observations that tend to be closer together, thus reducing bias. We will use the South African food share data on single individuals (see Exercise 3).

(a) Estimate the share function f using the super-smoother (e.g., *supsmu* in *S-Plus*) and plot the results.

(b) Superimpose the moving average estimate from Exercise 3(c) and the kernel estimate from Exercise 4(b) above.

7. *Cross-Validation Simulation*: Let $y_i = x_i + \varepsilon_i$, $\varepsilon_i \sim N(0,.01)$, $i = 1, \ldots, 25$, where the x_i are equally spaced on the interval [0,1]. Generate a data set using this model. Using a triangular kernel, calculate the cross-validation function (3.5.3) for values of the bandwidth λ in the range [.1,.5] in increments of say .025. Plot the cross-validation function, which should be similar to the upper panel of Figure 3.5.

8. *Cross-Validation and Engel Curve Estimation*: Open the South African food share data on single individuals (see Exercise 3). Using a triangular kernel, calculate the cross-validation function (3.5.3) for values of the bandwidth λ in the range [.2,.6] in increments of say .025. Plot the cross-validation function, which should be similar to that of Figure 3.6.

9. *Engel Curves with Heteroskedastic Variance*

(a) Using South African food share data on single individuals, apply a nonparametric smoother (such as kernel or *loess*) to estimate the Engel curve $y = f(x) + \varepsilon$, where x is "log expenditure," and y is "food share."

(b) Calculate the residuals from this procedure $\hat{\varepsilon}_1, \ldots, \hat{\varepsilon}_n$, and use a nonparametric smoother to estimate the model $\hat{\varepsilon}^2 = g(x) + v$. You have estimated a model for the residual variance as a function of x. Plot your results.

4 Higher-Order Differencing Procedures

4.1 Differencing Matrices

4.1.1 Definitions

In the previous chapter we introduced the idea of smoothing, which was used to estimate a nonparametric regression function. Now we will return to the idea of differencing, which in Chapter 1 was used to remove the nonparametric effect from a regression model.

Let m be the order of differencing and $d_0, d_1, \ldots, d_m$ differencing weights that satisfy the conditions

$$\sum_{j=0}^{m} d_j = 0 \quad \sum_{j=0}^{m} d_j^2 = 1. \tag{4.1.1}$$

The purpose of these restrictions will be made clear shortly. Define the differencing matrix

$$\underset{n\times n}{D} = \begin{bmatrix} d_0, d_1, d_2, \ldots d_m, 0, \ldots\ldots\ldots\ldots, 0 \\ 0, d_0, d_1, d_2, \ldots d_m, 0, \ldots\ldots\ldots, 0 \\ \vdots \quad \vdots \\ 0, \ldots\ldots\ldots\ldots 0, d_0, d_1, d_2, \ldots d_m, 0 \\ 0, \ldots\ldots\ldots\ldots\ldots 0, d_0, d_1, d_2, \ldots d_m \\ 0, \ldots\ldots\ldots\ldots\ldots\ldots\ldots\ldots\ldots, 0 \\ \vdots \quad \vdots \\ 0, \ldots\ldots\ldots\ldots\ldots\ldots\ldots\ldots\ldots, 0 \end{bmatrix}. \tag{4.1.2}$$

The last m rows have been filled with zeros so that D is square. It will be convenient to use lag matrices L_i. For $i > 0$, define L_i to be a square matrix with 0's everywhere except on the ith diagonal below the main diagonal, where it has 1's. If $i < 0$, L_i has 1's on the ith diagonal above the main diagonal. The matrix L_0 is defined to be the usual identity matrix, $L_i' = L_{-i}$, and $L_i L_j \doteq L_{i+j}$. It is evident from (4.1.2) that (except for end effects, which we denote using $\doteq$) the differencing matrix of order m is a weighted sum of lag matrices, that is,

$$D \doteq d_0 L_0 + d_1 L_1' + \cdots + d_m L_m'. \tag{4.1.3}$$

4.1.2 *Basic Properties of Differencing and Related Matrices*

We will need the matrix $D'D$, which has a symmetric band structure with 1's on the main diagonal. Hence, $tr(D'D) \doteq n$. As one moves away from the main diagonal, consecutive diagonals take values $\sum_{j=0}^{m-k} d_j d_{j+k}$ $k = 1, \ldots, m$. The remainder of the matrix is zero. Equivalently, using (4.1.3) and the properties of lag matrices, one can obtain

$$D'D \doteq L_0 + (L_1 + L_1') \sum_{j=0}^{m-1} d_j d_{j+1} + (L_2 + L_2') \sum_{j=0}^{m-2} d_j d_{j+2} + \cdots$$

$$+ (L_{m-1} + L_{m-1}') \sum_{j=0}^{1} d_j d_{j+m-1} + (L_m + L_m')\, d_0 d_m. \tag{4.1.4}$$

Because band structure is preserved by matrix multiplication, the matrix $D'DD'D$ will also have this property as well as being symmetric. The value on the main diagonal may be determined by multiplying the expansion in (4.1.4) by itself. Note that only products of the form $L_k L_k'$ and $L_k' L_k$ yield (except for end effects) the identity matrix L_0. Thus, the common diagonal value of $D'DD'D$ will be the sum of the coefficients of L_0, $L_1' L_1$, $L_1 L_1'$, $L_2' L_2$, $L_2 L_2'$, $\ldots$, $L_m' L_m$, $L_m L_m'$, that is,

$$[D'DD'D]_{ii} \doteq 1 + 2 \sum_{k=1}^{m} \left(\sum_{j=0}^{m-k} d_j d_{j+k} \right)^2. \tag{4.1.5}$$

A particularly useful quantity will be

$$\delta = \sum_{k=1}^{m} \left(\sum_{j=0}^{m-k} d_j d_{j+k} \right)^2. \tag{4.1.6}$$

We now have $[D'DD'D]_{ii} \doteq 1 + 2\delta$ and $tr(D'DD'D) \doteq n(1 + 2\delta)$.[1]

4.2 Variance Estimation

4.2.1 *The mth-Order Differencing Estimator*

Let us return to the problem of estimating the residual variance in a pure non-parametric regression model $y_i = f(x_i) + \varepsilon_i$, where $\varepsilon \,|\, x$ is distributed with

[1] The trace of $D'DD'D$ may be obtained alternatively as follows. Because for any symmetric matrix A, $tr\,(AA)$ is the sum of squares of elements of A, we may use (4.1.4) to conclude that $tr(D'DD'D) \doteq n(1 + 2\delta)$.

mean 0, variance σ_ε^2, and $E(\varepsilon^4 \mid x) = \eta_\varepsilon$, and f has first derivative bounded. Given observations on the model $(y_1, x_1) \ldots (y_n, x_n)$, where the x's have been reordered so that they are in increasing order, define $y' = (y_1, \ldots, y_n)$ and $f(x)' = (f(x_1), \ldots, f(x_n))$. In vector notation we have

$$y = f(x) + \varepsilon. \tag{4.2.1}$$

Applying the differencing matrix, we have

$$Dy = Df(x) + D\varepsilon. \tag{4.2.2}$$

A typical element of the vector Dy is of the form

$$\begin{aligned} d_0 y_i + \cdots + d_m y_{i+m} &= d_0 f(x_i) + \cdots + d_m f(x_{i+m}) \\ &\quad + d_0 \varepsilon_i + \cdots + d_m \varepsilon_{i+m}, \end{aligned} \tag{4.2.3}$$

and thus the role of the constraints (4.1.1) is now evident. The first condition ensures that, as the x's become close, the nonparametric effect is removed. The second condition ensures that the variance of the weighted sum of the residuals remains equal to σ_ε^2.

The mth-order differencing estimator of the residual variance is now defined to be

$$s_{diff}^2 = \frac{1}{n} \sum_{i=1}^{n-m} (d_0 y_i + d_1 y_{i+1} + \cdots + d_m y_{i+m})^2 = \frac{1}{n} y' D' D y. \tag{4.2.4}$$

4.2.2 *Properties*

Because differencing removes the nonparametric effect, in large samples we have

$$s_{diff}^2 \cong \frac{1}{n} \varepsilon' D' D \varepsilon. \tag{4.2.5}$$

Using the mean and variance of a quadratic form (see Appendix B, Lemma B.1), we have

$$E\left(s_{diff}^2\right) \cong \sigma_\varepsilon^2 \frac{1}{n} tr(D'D) \doteq \sigma_\varepsilon^2 \tag{4.2.6}$$

and

$$\begin{aligned} Var\left(s_{diff}^2\right) &\cong \frac{1}{n}\left[\left(\eta_\varepsilon - 3\sigma_\varepsilon^4\right) + \sigma_\varepsilon^4 \frac{2}{n} tr(D'DD'D)\right] \\ &= \frac{1}{n}\left[Var(\varepsilon^2) + 4\sigma_\varepsilon^4 \delta\right], \end{aligned} \tag{4.2.7}$$

where δ is defined in (4.1.6) and $\eta_\varepsilon = E(\varepsilon^4 \mid x)$.

4.2.3 *Optimal Differencing Coefficients*

From (4.2.7) it is evident that, to minimize the large sample variance of the differencing estimator, one needs to make δ as small as possible. Using time series techniques, Hall et al. (1990) have shown that if the d_j are selected to minimize δ, then

$$\sum_{j=0}^{m-k} d_j d_{j+k} = -\frac{1}{2m}, k = 1, 2, \ldots, m \quad \text{and} \quad \delta = \frac{1}{4m}. \tag{4.2.8}$$

In this case, matrix $D'D$ has (except for end effects) 1's on the main diagonal, $-\frac{1}{2m}$ on the m adjacent diagonals, and 0's elsewhere. That is,

$$D'D \doteq L_0 - \frac{1}{2m}(L_1 + L_1' + \cdots + L_m + L_m'), \tag{4.2.9}$$

so that $tr(D'D) \doteq n$.[2] Using (4.25) yields,

$$s_{diff}^2 \cong \frac{\varepsilon'\varepsilon}{n} - \frac{1}{2mn}\varepsilon'(L_1 + L_1' + \cdots + L_m + L_m')\varepsilon. \tag{4.2.10a}$$

Applying (4.2.7) and $\delta = 1/4m$ from (4.2.8), we have

$$Var\left(s_{diff}^2\right) \cong \frac{1}{n}\left(Var\left(\varepsilon^2\right) + \frac{\sigma_\varepsilon^4}{m}\right). \tag{4.2.10b}$$

On the other hand, if the regression function were parametric (e.g., if it were known to be linear and we used a conventional OLS estimator), then

$$s_{OLS}^2 = \frac{1}{n}\sum_{i=1}^{n}(y_i - \hat{\gamma}_1 - \hat{\gamma}_2 x_i)^2 \cong \frac{1}{n}\sum_{i=1}^{n}\varepsilon_i^2 + O_P\left(\frac{1}{n}\right), \tag{4.2.11a}$$

in which case

$$Var\left(s_{OLS}^2\right) \cong \frac{1}{n}Var(\varepsilon^2). \tag{4.2.11b}$$

Comparing the variances of the two residual estimators (4.2.10b) and (4.2.11b), we see that, as the order of differencing m increases, the variance of the differencing estimator approaches that of parametric estimators.

Optimal differencing weights do not have analytic expressions but may be calculated easily using standard optimization techniques. Hall et al. (1990) present weights to order $m = 10$. With minor modifications, these are reproduced in Table 4.1. Appendix C discusses calculation of optimal weights and contains weights for certain higher values of m.

[2] The matrix $D'DD'D$ has a symmetric band structure with $1 + 1/2m$ on the main diagonal so that $tr(D'DD'D) \doteq n(1 + 1/2m)$.

Table 4.1. *Optimal differencing weights.*[a]

m	$(d_0, d_1, \ldots, d_m)$
1	(0.7071,–.0.7071)
2	(0.8090,–0.5000,–0.3090)
3	(0.8582,–0.3832,–0.2809,–0.1942)
4	(0.8873,–0.3099,–0.2464,–0.1901,–0.1409)
5	(0.9064,–0.2600,–0.2167,–0.1774,–0.1420,–0.1103)
6	(0.9200,–0.2238,–0.1925,–0.1635,–0.1369,–0.1126,–0.0906)
7	(0.9302,–0.1965,–0.1728,–0.1506,–0.1299,–0.1107,–0.0930,–0.0768)
8	(0.9380,–0.1751,–0.1565,–0.1389,–0.1224,–0.1069,–0.0925,–0.0791,–0.0666)
9	(0.9443,–0.1578,–0.1429,–0.1287,–0.1152,–0.1025,–0.0905,–0.0792,–0.0687,–0.0588)
10	(0.9494,–0.1437,–0.1314,–0.1197,–0.1085,–0.0978,–0.0877,–0.0782,–0.0691,–0.0606,–.0527)

[a] In contrast to those in Hall et al. (1990), all the optimal weight sequences provided here decline in absolute value toward zero.

4.2.4 *Moving Average Differencing Coefficients*

Recall that our objective is to remove the nonparametric effect at a point, say x_i. Suppose we average consecutive observations centered at x_i (omitting the one at x_i) and subtract the average from y_i. In this case, the differencing matrix will have the form

$$\underset{n\times n}{D} = \frac{1}{\sqrt{1+\frac{1}{m}}} \times \begin{bmatrix} -\frac{1}{m},\ldots,-\frac{1}{m},1,-\frac{1}{m}\cdots-\frac{1}{m},0,\ldots\ldots\ldots\ldots,0 \\ 0,-\frac{1}{m},\ldots,-\frac{1}{m},1,-\frac{1}{m}\cdots-\frac{1}{m},0,\ldots\ldots\ldots\ldots,0 \\ \vdots \quad \vdots \\ 0,\ldots\ldots\ldots\ldots 0,-\frac{1}{m},\ldots,-\frac{1}{m},1,-\frac{1}{m}\cdots-\frac{1}{m},0 \\ 0,\ldots\ldots\ldots\ldots\ldots 0,-\frac{1}{m},\ldots,-\frac{1}{m},1,-\frac{1}{m}\cdots-\frac{1}{m} \\ 0,\ldots\ldots\ldots\ldots\ldots\ldots\ldots\ldots\ldots\ldots,0 \\ \vdots \quad \vdots \\ 0,\ldots\ldots\ldots\ldots\ldots\ldots\ldots\ldots\ldots\ldots,0 \end{bmatrix}. \tag{4.1.2a}$$

Again we have filled the last m rows with zeros so that D is square.

The differencing weights sum to zero and the constant multiplying the matrix ensures that their sum of squares is 1. The value of δ – which through (4.2.7) plays an important role in large sample efficiency – does not have a simple closed-form solution such as the one available for optimal differencing

Table 4.2. *Values of δ for alternate differencing coefficients.*[a]

m	Optimal	Moving average
2	.12500	.47222
4	.06250	.22500
6	.04167	.14683
8	.03125	.10880
10	.02500	.08636
20	.01250	.04246
50	.00500	.01680
100	.00250	.00837
200	.00125	.00418
500	.00050	.00167

[a]See (4.1.6) for definition of δ.

coefficients. (In that case it is $1/4m$.) Nevertheless, its value can be computed directly using (4.1.6). Table 4.2 lists values of δ for moving average and optimal differencing weights. The moving average values are larger. On the other hand, symmetry of the moving average weights is likely to reduce bias relative to the optimal weights which decline monotonically in one direction. We compare alternative differencing weights in Section 4.10.

4.2.5 *Asymptotic Normality*

Proposition 4.2.1: Let $d_0, d_1, \ldots, d_m$ be arbitrary differencing weights satisfying (4.1.1); then,

$$\begin{aligned} n^{1/2}\left(s^2_{diff} - \sigma^2_\varepsilon\right) &\sim N\left(0, \eta_\varepsilon - \sigma^4_\varepsilon + 4\sigma^4_\varepsilon \delta\right) \\ &= N\left(0, \eta_\varepsilon - 3\sigma^4_\varepsilon + 2\sigma^4_\varepsilon(1 + 2\delta)\right), \end{aligned} \tag{4.2.12a}$$

which, if one uses optimal differencing weights, becomes

$$n^{1/2}\left(s^2_{diff} - \sigma^2_\varepsilon\right) \sim N\left(0, \eta_\varepsilon - \sigma^4_\varepsilon + \frac{\sigma^4_\varepsilon}{m}\right). \tag{4.2.12b}$$

To make use of these results, we will need a consistent estimator of $\eta_\varepsilon = E(\varepsilon^4)$ for which we will use fourth-order powers of the differenced data. To motivate the estimator, it is convenient to establish the following:

$$E(d_0\varepsilon_i + \cdots + d_m\varepsilon_{i+m})^4 = \eta_\varepsilon\left(\sum_{i=0}^{m} d_i^4\right) + 6\sigma^4_\varepsilon\left(\sum_{i=0}^{m-1} d_i^2 \sum_{j=i+1}^{m} d_j^2\right). \tag{4.2.13}$$

This result may be obtained by first noting that, when the left-hand side is expanded, only two types of terms will have nonzero expectations: those that involve the fourth power of a residual (e.g., $E\varepsilon_i^4 = \eta_\varepsilon$) and those that involve products of squares of residuals (e.g., $E\varepsilon_i^2\varepsilon_{i+j}^2 = \sigma_\varepsilon^4$, $j \neq 0$). Equation (4.2.13) is then obtained by summing the coefficients of such terms. We now have the following result.

Proposition 4.2.2: Let

$$\hat{\eta}_\varepsilon = \frac{\frac{1}{n}\sum_{i=1}^{n-m}(d_0 y_i + \cdots + d_m y_{i+m})^4 - 6\left(s_{diff}^2\right)^2\left(\sum_{i=0}^{m-1} d_i^2 \sum_{j=i+1}^{m} d_j^2\right)}{\sum_{i=0}^{m} d_i^4}; \tag{4.2.14a}$$

then, $\hat{\eta}_\varepsilon \xrightarrow{P} \eta_\varepsilon$.

Equations (4.2.13) and (4.2.14a) are valid for arbitrary differencing weights. If the order of differencing is large (say $m \geq 25$), then the denominator approaches 1 and the right-hand side of the numerator approaches 0; thus

$$\hat{\eta}_\varepsilon \cong \frac{1}{n}\sum_{i=1}^{n-m}(d_0 y_i + \cdots + d_m y_{i+m})^4. \tag{4.2.14b}$$

These results may be used to test equality of residual variances for two possibly different regression models: $y_A = f_A(x_A) + \varepsilon_A$ and $y_B = f_B(x_B) + \varepsilon_B$. Let s_A^2, $\hat{\eta}_A$, s_B^2, $\hat{\eta}_B$ be optimal differencing estimators of the residual variances and fourth-order moments obtained using (4.2.4) and (4.2.14a). Then, Propositions 4.2.1 and 4.2.2 imply that, under the null hypothesis,

$$\frac{s_A^2 - s_B^2}{\left(\frac{\hat{\eta}_A + (1/m - 1)s_A^4}{n_A} + \frac{\hat{\eta}_B + (1/m - 1)s_B^4}{n_B}\right)^{1/2}} \sim N(0, 1). \tag{4.2.15}$$

4.3 Specification Test[3]

4.3.1 A Simple Statistic

We remain with the pure nonparametric model $y = f(x) + \varepsilon$, where f has first derivative bounded, $E(\varepsilon \mid x) = 0$, and $Var(\varepsilon \mid x) = \sigma_\varepsilon^2$. Let $h(x, \gamma)$ be a known

[3] A variety of procedures are available for testing a parametric null against a nonparametric alternative. See Chapter 6.

function of x and an unknown parameter γ (h can of course be linear). We wish to test the null hypothesis that the regression function has the parametric form $h(x, \gamma)$ against the nonparametric alternative $f(x)$. Let $\hat{\gamma}_{LS}$ be obtained using, for example, parametric nonlinear least squares. Define the restricted estimator of the residual variance

$$s_{res}^2 = \frac{1}{n} \sum (y_i - h(x_i, \hat{\gamma}_{LS}))^2. \tag{4.3.1}$$

Proposition 4.3.1: Suppose $H_0 : f(x) = h(x, \gamma)$ is true, where h is a known function. Define s_{res}^2 as in (4.3.1). For arbitrary differencing weights satisfying (4.1.1) we have

$$\left(\frac{n}{4\delta}\right)^{1/2} \frac{\left(s_{res}^2 - s_{diff}^2\right)}{s_{diff}^2} \xrightarrow{D} N(0, 1). \tag{4.3.2a}$$

If one uses optimal differencing weights, the statistic becomes

$$(mn)^{1/2} \frac{\left(s_{res}^2 - s_{diff}^2\right)}{s_{diff}^2} \xrightarrow{D} N(0, 1). \tag{4.3.2b}$$

In the denominator, s_{diff}^2 may be replaced by s_{res}^2 because, under the null, both estimators of the residual variance are consistent.

A test of the significance of x is a special case of the preceding procedure. In this case, f is a constant function; thus, the restricted estimator of the regression function is just the sample mean of the y_i.

4.3.2 *Heteroskedasticity*

Suppose now the residuals are independent but heteroskedastic with unknown covariance matrix Ω and one uses optimal differencing weights to obtain s_{diff}^2. The specification test in Proposition 4.3.1 may be extended as follows. If the null hypothesis is true and optimal differencing coefficients are used, then

$$(mn)^{1/2} \frac{\left(s_{res}^2 - s_{diff}^2\right)}{\hat{\xi}^{1/2}} \xrightarrow{D} N(0, 1), \tag{4.3.2c}$$

where

$$\hat{\xi} = \frac{1}{m} \left(\frac{1}{n} \sum \hat{\varepsilon}_i^2 \hat{\varepsilon}_{i-1}^2 + \cdots + \frac{1}{n} \sum \hat{\varepsilon}_i^2 \hat{\varepsilon}_{i-m}^2 \right). \tag{4.3.2d}$$

As in Proposition 4.3.1, the result is readily modified for arbitrary differencing coefficients.

4.3.3 Empirical Application: Log-Linearity of Engel Curves

We return to our South African data on single individuals and ask whether a model that is linear in the log of expenditures provides an adequate representation. There is a considerable body of evidence in the empirical literature to support the proposition that food Engel curves are approximately linear. On the other hand, as we will see later, nonlinearities in Engel curves are important in identifying equivalence scales. Figure 4.1 displays a kernel estimate and the linear OLS estimate. The kernel estimate lies close to the linear model except at the right tail of the income distribution. (At the left tail there also appears to be a departure from linearity, but it is modest.) Furthermore, there are relatively few observations in the right tail of the distribution, and, as a consequence, the nonparametric model is not being estimated precisely (see the confidence intervals in Figure 3.3). Suppose we compare the fit of the linear and kernel models. The former has an R^2 of .477. If we estimate the residual variance

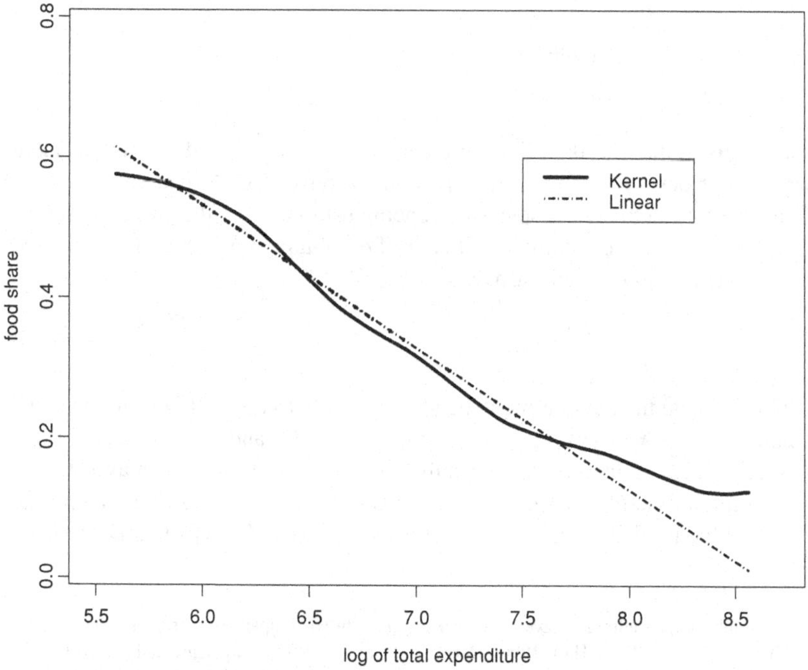

Optimal differencing estimate of residual variance using $m = 25$: $s^2_{diff} = .01941$. Implied $R^2 = .490$. Linear model: $FoodShr = \underset{(.043)}{1.75} - \underset{(.0064)}{.203} * ltexp$. Standard errors in parentheses. $s^2_{res} = .01993$, $R^2 = .477$.

Figure 4.1. Testing linearity of Engel curves.

using $m = 25$ and optimal differencing coefficients (see (4.2.4)), then the R^2, which we define to be $1 - s^2_{diff}/s^2_y$, increases to .490. This is not a dramatic increase in explanatory power. A formal test of the linear specification may be implemented using (4.3.2b), yielding a value of 4.45, which suggests rejection of the null. In contrast, a test of significance of the expenditure variable using (4.3.2b) yields an overwhelming rejection of the null with a statistic of 160.2.

4.4 Test of Equality of Regression Functions[4]

4.4.1 A Simplified Test Procedure

Suppose one has data $(y_{A1}, x_{A1}), \ldots, (y_{An_A}, x_{An_A})$ and $(y_{B1}, x_{B1}), \ldots, (y_{Bn_B}, x_{Bn_B})$ from two possibly different regression models A and B. We emphasize that the data have already been ordered so that within each subpopulation the x's are in increasing order. Let $n = n_A + n_B$ be the total number of observations. The basic models are

$$\begin{aligned} y_{Ai} &= f_A(x_{Ai}) + \varepsilon_{Ai} \\ y_{Bi} &= f_B(x_{Bi}) + \varepsilon_{Bi} \end{aligned} \tag{4.4.1}$$

where, given the x's, the ε's have mean 0, variance σ^2_ε, and are independent within and between populations; f_A and f_B have first derivatives bounded. Using (4.2.4), define consistent differencing estimators of the variance, say s^2_A and s^2_B. Let s^2_w be the "within" estimator of σ^2_ε obtained by taking the weighted sum of the two individual estimates:

$$s^2_w = \frac{n_A}{n} s^2_A + \frac{n_B}{n} s^2_B. \tag{4.4.2}$$

Concatenate the data on the dependent variable to obtain the n-dimensional column vectors $x = (x_{A1}, \ldots, x_{An_A}, x_{B1}, \ldots, x_{Bn_B})'$ and $y = (y_{A1}, \ldots, y_{An_A}, y_{B1}, \ldots, y_{Bn_B})'$. Since under the null hypothesis $f_A = f_B$, we may estimate the common function using, say, a kernel smoother. Furthermore, if an optimal bandwidth is used, then the average sum of squared residuals from this restricted

[4] A number of procedures are available for testing equality of nonparametric regression functions. These include Hall and Hart (1990), Härdle and Marron (1990), King, Hart, and Wehrly (1991), Delgado (1993), Kulasekera (1995), Pinkse and Robinson (1995), Young and Bowman (1995), Baltagi, Hidalgo, and Li (1996), Kulasekera and Wang (1997), Koul and Schick (1997), Fan and Lin (1998), Munk and Dette (1998), Lavergne (2001) and Hall and Yatchew (2002). See also Hart (1997, p. 236).

regression will satisfy

$$n^{1/2}\left(s_{res}^2 - \frac{1}{n}\sum_{i=2}^{n}\varepsilon_i^2\right) \xrightarrow{P} 0. \tag{4.4.3}$$

This is true because the estimator satisfies the optimal rate of convergence (3.1.10). Thus, for fixed order of differencing m, we may apply the specification test in Proposition 4.3.1, setting $s_{diff}^2 = s_w^2$.

4.4.2 *The Differencing Estimator Applied to the Pooled Data*

An alternative test procedure applies the differencing estimator to the pooled data. Define P_p, the "pooled" permutation matrix, to be the matrix that reorders the pooled data so that the x's are in increasing order. Thus, if $x^* = P_p x$, then the consecutive elements of the reordered vector x^* are in increasing order. Apply the differencing estimator of the variance (4.2.4) to the reordered data to obtain

$$s_p^2 = \frac{1}{n} y' P_p' D' D P_p y, \tag{4.4.4}$$

the pooled estimator of the residual variance.

Proposition 4.4.1: For arbitrary differencing coefficients satisfying (4.1.1), we have $n^{1/2}(s_{diff}^2 - \sigma_\varepsilon^2) \xrightarrow{D} N(0, \eta_\varepsilon - 3\sigma_\varepsilon^4 + 2\sigma_\varepsilon^4(1+2\delta))$. If, in addition, $f_A = f_B$, then $n^{1/2}(s_p^2 - \sigma_\varepsilon^2)$ has the same approximate distribution. If optimal differencing coefficients are used, then the approximate distribution becomes $N(0, \eta_\varepsilon + (1/m - 1)\sigma_\varepsilon^4)$.

The asymptotic variances of s_w^2, s_p^2 may be obtained using (4.2.7) and (4.2.10b) (see also Appendix B, Lemma B.1, or Hall et al. 1990). Asymptotic normality follows from finitely dependent central limit theory.

We will now consider a statistic based on the difference of the pooled and within estimates of the variance. Define

$$\Upsilon \equiv n^{1/2}\left(s_p^2 - s_w^2\right) \doteq \frac{1}{n^{1/2}} y'[P_p' D' D P_p - D' D] y. \tag{4.4.5}$$

The second occurrence of $D'D$ corresponds to the within estimator and is – more precisely – a block diagonal matrix with two $D'D$ matrices, one for each of the two subpopulations. (Except for end effects, a block diagonal $D'D$ matrix is identical to the second such matrix in (4.4.5).)

Proposition 4.4.2: Let $Q_\Upsilon = P_p' D' D P_p - D' D$ and $\hat{\pi}_\Upsilon = tr(Q_\Upsilon Q_\Upsilon)/n$. Suppose $\hat{\pi}_\Upsilon \xrightarrow{P} \pi_\Upsilon > 0$. Then, under the null hypothesis that $f_A = f_B$,

$$\Upsilon = n^{1/2}\left(s_p^2 - s_w^2\right) \xrightarrow{D} N\left(0, 2\pi_\Upsilon \sigma_\varepsilon^4\right). \tag{4.4.6}$$

Thus, $\Upsilon / s_w^2 (2\hat{\pi}_\Upsilon)^{1/2} \xrightarrow{D} N(0, 1)$, and one would reject for large positive values of the test statistic. The quantity π_Υ no longer admits the simple interpretation associated with π in Chapter 1; however, it remains between 0 and 1 (see Yatchew 1999). The condition $\pi_\Upsilon > 0$ ensures that, in the pooled reordered data, the proportion of observations that are near observations from a different probability law does not go to 0. (Heuristically, this requires that the data intermingle upon pooling and that neither n_A/n nor n_B/n converge to zero.) Ideally, of course, one would like the pooled x's to be well intermingled so that s_p^2 contains many terms incorporating $f_s(x_j^*) - f_t(x_{j-1}^*)$, where $s \neq t$ and * denotes data reordered after pooling.

4.4.3 *Properties*

The test procedure described in the last subsection is consistent. For example, suppose we use first-order differencing ($m = 1$), x_A and x_B are independently and uniformly distributed on the unit interval, and an equal number of observations are taken from each subpopulation (i.e., $n_A = n_B = \frac{1}{2}n$). If $f_A \neq f_B$, then the within estimator in (4.4.2) remains consistent, whereas the pooled estimator in (4.4.4) converges as follows

$$s_p^2 \to \sigma_\varepsilon^2 + \tfrac{1}{4} \int (f_A(x) - f_B(x))^2 dx \tag{4.4.7}$$

so that the mean of Υ defined in (4.4.6) diverges (see Yatchew 1999). In general, power depends not only on the difference between the two regression functions but also on the degree to which data are generated from both populations at points where the difference is large. For fixed differencing of order m, the procedure will detect local alternatives that converge to the null at a rate close to $n^{-1/4}$. The rate may be improved by permitting the order of differencing to grow with sample size. Nonconstant variances across equations can readily be incorporated (see Yatchew 1999).

The test procedure may be applied to the partial linear model. Consider $y_A = z_A \beta_A + f_A(x_A) + \varepsilon_A$ and $y_B = z_B \beta_B + f_B(x_B) + \varepsilon_B$. Suppose one obtains $n^{1/2}$-consistent estimators of β_A and β_B (e.g., by using the differencing estimator in Section 4.5). To test $f_A = f_B$ one can apply (4.4.2), (4.4.4), and (4.4.5) to $y_A - z_A \hat{\beta}_A \cong f_A(x_A) + \varepsilon_A$ and $y_B - z_B \hat{\beta}_B \cong f_B(x_B) + \varepsilon_B$ without altering the asymptotic properties of the procedure. Alternatively, one can apply the simplified procedure outlined in Section 4.4.1 that uses Proposition 4.3.1.

4.4.4 *Empirical Application: Testing Equality of Engel Curves*

Equivalence scales are used to compare the welfare of families of different composition. For example, if a single person spends $50,000 and a couple needs $82,500 to achieve the same standard of living, we say the equivalence scale is 1.65. Engel's method for constructing equivalence scales is premised on the idea that two households are equally well off if they spend the same proportion of their total expenditures on food. The existence of equivalence scales and how to calculate them have been a matter of much debate, and we will devote considerable effort later to their estimation.

The upper panel of Figure 4.2 illustrates the food Engel curves for singles and couples with no children. There are 1,109 observations in the first group and 890 in the second. Geometrically, Engel's method asks whether a leftward horizontal shift of the "couples" Engel curve would cause it to be superimposed on the "singles" Engel curve. The magnitude of the shift measures the *log* of the equivalence scale. (Keep in mind that the horizontal variable is the *log* of total expenditures.) Later – in the context of index model estimation – we will show how to estimate that shift, but assume for the moment that it is .5, in which case the equivalence scale is $1.65 = \exp(.5)$.

The lower panel of Figure 4.2 illustrates the two Engel curves following a horizontal shift of the couples Engel curve. They seem to track each other fairly closely, and we can now ask whether the two Engel curves coincide. (If they do not, there is no single equivalence scale that works at all levels of income.)

Let y_A and y_B be the food shares for singles and couples. Let x_A be the *log* of total expenditures for singles. Define x_B to be the log (*total expenditures*/1.65), which equals log (*total expenditures*) – .5.

To apply the simplified procedure based on the specification test in Proposition 4.3.1, we first estimate the common regression function using a kernel estimator. The average sum of squared residuals s^2_{res} is .018356. Using $m = 25$, we calculate s^2_w to be .018033 and substitute this quantity for s^2_{diff} in (4.3.2b) to obtain a statistic of 4.01. Next we apply the test of equality of regression functions in Proposition 4.4.2. For $m = 25$, the standardized test statistic $\Upsilon / s^2_w (2\hat{\pi}_\Upsilon)^{1/2}$ takes a value of 1.76. Thus, there is some evidence against the hypothesis that the two Engel curves coincide. However, the rejection – given the size of the data set – is hardly overwhelming.

In performing these tests it is useful to compare implied values of $R^2 = 1 - s^2_\varepsilon / s^2_y$, where $s^2_y = .04106$ is the variance of the food share variable across all 1,999 observations. We can take s^2_w to be an unconstrained estimator of the residual variance. The implied "unrestricted" fit is 56.1 percent. Both s^2_{res}, the estimated residual variance from the kernel regression, and s^2_p, the pooled estimator of the residual variance, impose the restriction of equality of regression functions. The corresponding implied fits are 55.5 and 55.8 percent,

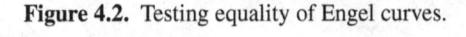

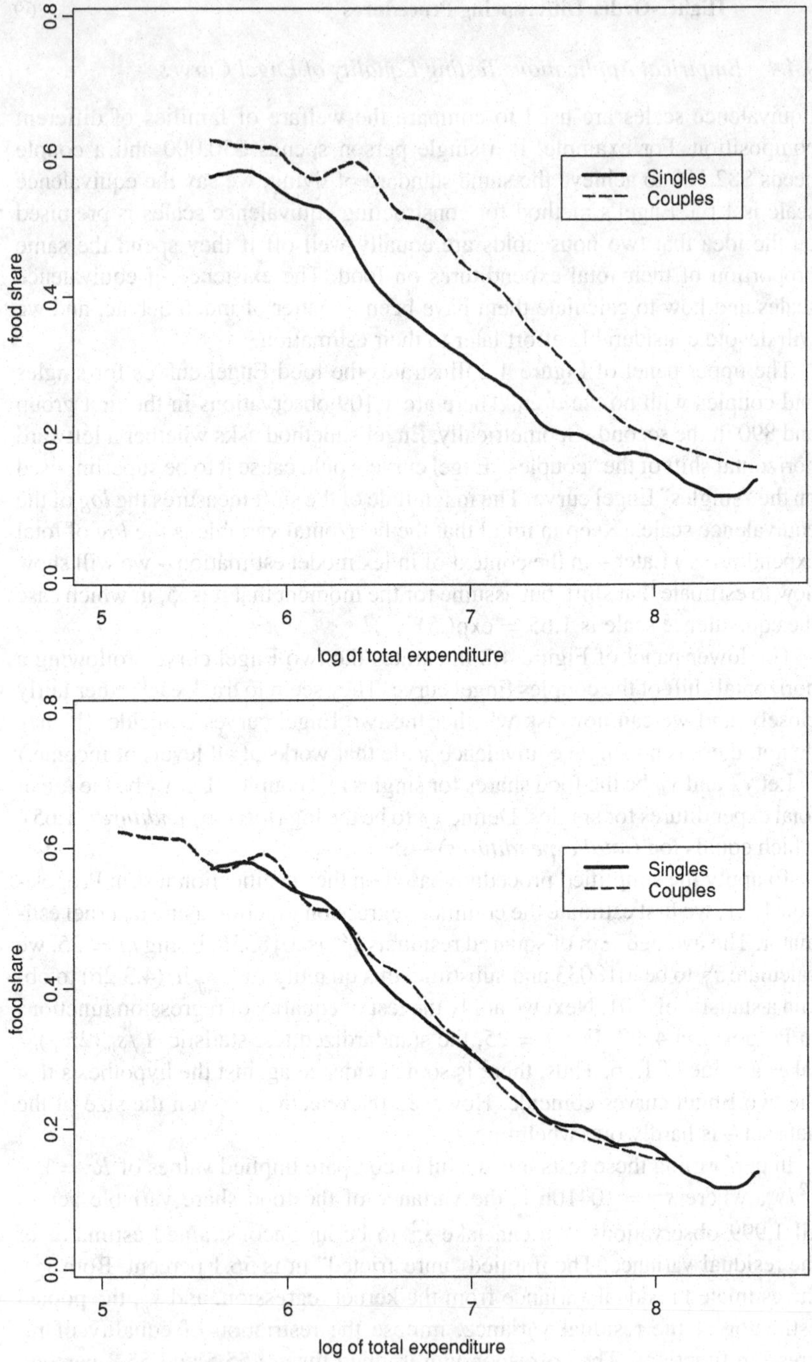

Figure 4.2. Testing equality of Engel curves.

respectively. Thus, the imposition of the constraint results in a modest deterioration in fit.

4.5 Partial Linear Model

4.5.1 Estimator

Let us return to estimation of the partial linear model $y_i = z_i\beta + f(x_i) + \varepsilon_i$, where x_i is a scalar, z_i is a p-dimensional row vector, $\varepsilon_i \mid x_i, z_i$ is distributed with mean 0, variance σ_ε^2, and f has a bounded first derivative. We will also assume that the vector of parametric variables z has a smooth regression relationship with the nonparametric variable x. Thus, we may write $z_i = g(x_i) + u_i$, where g is a vector function with first derivatives bounded, $E(u_i \mid x_i) = 0$, and $E(Var(z_i \mid x_i)) = \sum_{z|x}$. Assume that each observation is independently drawn and that the data $(y_1, x_1, z_1), \ldots, (y_n, x_n, z_n)$ have been reordered so that the x's are in increasing order. Define $y' = (y_1, \ldots, y_n)$, $f(x)' = (f(x_1), \ldots, f(x_n))$, and Z as the $n \times p$ matrix with ith row z_i. In matrix notation, we have

$$y = Z\beta + f(x) + \varepsilon. \tag{4.5.1}$$

Applying the differencing matrix, we have

$$Dy = DZ\beta + Df(x) + D\varepsilon \cong DZ\beta + D\varepsilon. \tag{4.5.2}$$

The following proposition contains our main result.

Proposition 4.5.1: For arbitrary differencing coefficients satisfying (4.1.1), define $\hat{\beta}_{diff} = [(DZ)'DZ]^{-1}(DZ)'Dy$. Then,

$$n^{1/2}(\hat{\beta}_{diff} - \beta) \xrightarrow{D} N\left(0, (1+2\delta)\sigma_\varepsilon^2 \textstyle\sum_{z|x}^{-1}\right) \tag{4.5.3}$$

$$s_{diff}^2 = \frac{1}{n}(Dy - DZ\hat{\beta}_{diff})'(Dy - DZ\hat{\beta}_{diff}) \xrightarrow{P} \sigma_\varepsilon^2 \tag{4.5.4}$$

$$\hat{\textstyle\sum}_{z|x} = \frac{1}{n}(DZ)'DZ \xrightarrow{P} \textstyle\sum_{z|x}. \tag{4.5.5}$$

For optimal differencing coefficients, replace $1 + 2\delta$ in (4.5.3) with $1 + \frac{1}{2m}$.

The covariance matrix of the differencing estimator of β may be estimated using

$$\hat{\textstyle\sum}_{\hat{\beta}} = (1+2\delta)\frac{s_{diff}^2}{n}\hat{\textstyle\sum}_{z|x}^{-1}. \tag{4.5.6}$$

Proposition 4.5.2: Linear restrictions of the form $R\beta = r$ may be tested using the conventional statistic which – if the null hypothesis is true – has the following distribution:

$$(R\hat{\beta} - r)'\left(R\hat{\sum}_{\beta} R'\right)^{-1}(R\hat{\beta} - r) \xrightarrow{D} \chi^2_{rank(R)}. \tag{4.5.7a}$$

Equivalently, one may use

$$\frac{n\left(s^2_{diff\,res} - s^2_{diff}\right)}{s^2_{diff}(1 + 2\delta)} \xrightarrow{D} \chi^2_{rank(R)}, \tag{4.5.7b}$$

where s^2_{diff} is the unrestricted differencing estimator in (4.5.4) and $s^2_{diff\,res}$ is obtained by estimating the differenced model (4.5.2) subject to the linear constraints[5] and then applying (4.5.4).

The statistic in (4.5.7b) is but a thinly disguised version of its analogue in the usual analysis of linear models, which compares restricted and unrestricted sum of squares.

A heuristic proof of Proposition 4.5.1 in the case in which all variables are scalars is provided in Chapter 1. More detailed proofs of Propositions 4.5.1 and 4.5.2 may be found in Appendix B. As is evident from (4.5.3), the estimator is $n^{1/2}$-consistent and asymptotically normal. It is close to being asymptotically efficient for moderate values of m. For example, at $m = 10$, it has a relative efficiency of 95 percent. By increasing the order of differencing as sample size increases, the estimator becomes asymptotically efficient.

4.5.2 *Heteroskedasticity*

Suppose now that $Var(\varepsilon\varepsilon') = \Omega$; then, the residual vector in (4.5.2) has covariance matrix $D\Omega D'$, and

$$Var(\hat{\beta}_{diff}) \cong \frac{1}{n}\left(\frac{Z'D'DZ}{n}\right)^{-1}\frac{Z'D'D\Omega D'DZ}{n}\left(\frac{Z'D'DZ}{n}\right)^{-1}. \tag{4.5.8}$$

If the order of differencing is large or, better still, if m increases with sample size, then we may estimate the interior matrix using

$$\frac{Z'D'\hat{\Omega}DZ}{n}, \tag{4.5.9}$$

where $\hat{\Omega}$ is a diagonal matrix of squared estimated residuals from (4.5.2).

[5] Recall that for a linear model the restricted OLS estimator may be obtained by redefining variables. The model we are estimating in (4.5.2) is approximately linear since, as a result of differencing, $Df(x)$ is close to zero.

Suppose, on the other hand, that the order of differencing m is fixed at some low level. Now consider the structure of $D\Omega D'$. Because Ω is diagonal, the nonzero elements of $D\Omega D'$ consist of the main diagonal and the m adjacent diagonals (m is the order of differencing). This is because differencing introduces a moving average process of order m into the residuals.[6] White's (1985) generalizations may then be applied to our differenced model $Dy \cong DZ\beta + D\varepsilon$, where, as usual, differencing has (approximately) removed the nonparametric effect. To mimic the structure of $D\Omega D'$ we define $\widehat{D\Omega D'}$ to be the matrix $\widehat{D\varepsilon}\widehat{D\varepsilon}'$ with all terms more than m diagonals away from the main diagonal set to zero. In this case we may estimate the interior matrix of (4.5.8) using

$$\frac{Z'D'\widehat{D\Omega D'}DZ}{n}. \tag{4.5.10}$$

With some additional effort, autocorrelation-consistent standard errors may also be constructed for differencing estimators, though the double residual method outlined in Section 3.6 generally results in simpler implementation.

4.6 Empirical Applications

4.6.1 Household Gasoline Demand in Canada

In a recent paper, Yatchew and No (2001) estimated a partial linear model of household demand for gasoline in Canada – a model very similar to those estimated by Hausman and Newey (1995) and Schmalensee and Stoker (1999). The basic specification is given by

$$\begin{aligned} dist = f(price) + \beta_1 income + \beta_2 drivers + \beta_3 hhsize + \beta_4 youngsingle \\ + \beta_5 age + \beta_6 retire + \beta_7 urban + monthly\ dummies + \varepsilon, \end{aligned} \tag{4.6.1}$$

where *dist* is the log of distance traveled per month by the household, *price* is the log of price of a liter of gasoline, *drivers* is the log of the number of licensed drivers in the household, *hhsize* is the log of the size of the household, *youngsingle* is a dummy for singles up to age of 35, *age* is the log of age, *retire* is a dummy for those households where the head is over the age of 65, and *urban* is a dummy for urban dwellers. Figure 4.3 summarizes the results. The "parametric estimates" refer to a model in which price enters log-linearly. The "double residual estimates" use Robinson (1988) (see Section 3.6). That procedure requires one to estimate regression functions of the dependent variable and each of the parametric independent variables on the nonparametric variable.

[6] Alternatively, note that $D\Omega D' = (d_0L_0 + \cdots + d_mL_m)\Omega(d_0L_0' + \cdots + d_mL_m')$. The lag matrices L_i, L_i' shift the main diagonal of Ω to the ith off-diagonals.

Variable	Parametric estimates		Robinson double-residual estimates			Differencing estimates	
	Coef	SE	Coef	SE	HCSE	Coef	SE
price	−0.9170	0.0960	–	–	–	–	–
income	0.2890	0.0200	0.3000	0.0200	0.0201	0.2816	0.0209
drivers	0.5610	0.0330	0.5650	0.0330	0.0318	0.5686	0.0338
hhsize	0.1000	0.0260	0.0940	0.0260	0.0256	0.0892	0.0274
youngsingle	0.1930	0.0610	0.1980	0.0610	0.0651	0.2099	0.0622
age	−0.0780	0.0440	−0.0750	0.0440	0.0419	−0.1171	0.0555
retire	−0.2070	0.0320	−0.1980	0.0320	0.0342	−0.2113	0.0387
urban	−0.3310	0.0200	−0.3250	0.0200	0.0195	−0.3331	0.0203
Monthly Effects (see Figure 4.4)							
s_ε^2	.5003		.5053			.4997	
R^2	.2635		.2563			.2644	

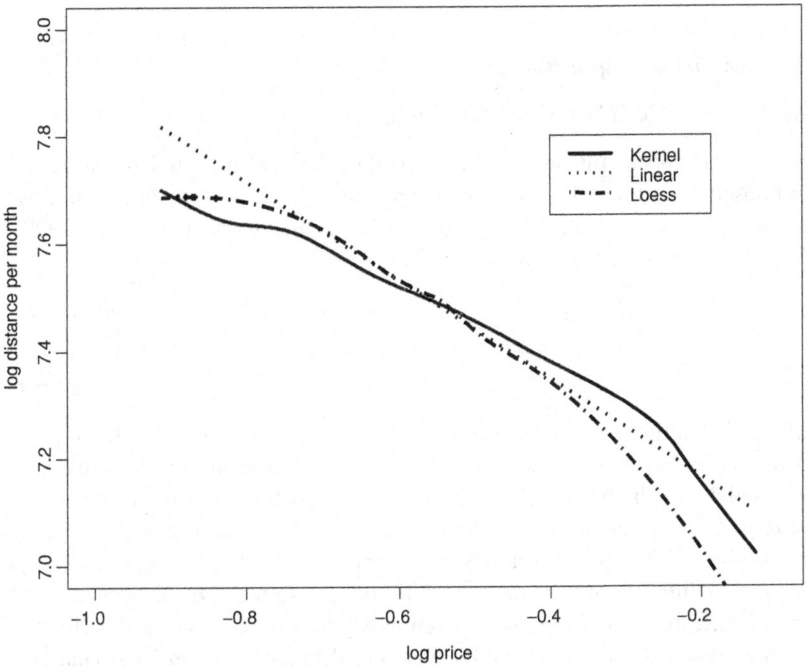

Variance of dependent variable is .6794. Order of differencing $m = 10$. Number of observations is 6230. Robinson estimates of parametric effects produced using kernel procedure *ksmooth* in *S-Plus*. Solid line is kernel estimate applied to data after removal of estimated parametric effect. Dotted line is parametric estimate of price effect. Specification test of log-linear model for price effect yields value of .3089. Nonparametric significance test for price effect yields test statistic of 3.964.

Figure 4.3. Household demand for gasoline.

The residuals are then used to estimate the parametric effects. We implement Robinson's method using *ksmooth*, a kernel regression estimation procedure in *S-Plus*.

The "differencing estimates" use tenth-order differencing and Proposition 4.5.1 to estimate the parametric effects. The three sets of estimates are very similar except that the standard errors of the differencing estimates are marginally larger.

The estimated parametric effects, which have been estimated by differencing, are then removed, and kernel regression is applied to obtain a nonparametric estimate of the price effect (the solid line in Figure 4.3). Applying the specification test in Proposition 4.3.1 yields a value of .31, suggesting that the log-linear specification is adequate. A test of the significance of the price effect using the same proposition yields a value of 4.0, which indicates that the price variable is significant. Figure 4.4 displays seasonal effects.

Figure 4.3 also contains heteroskedasticity-consistent standard errors (HCSE) for the double residual estimates. The HCSE were computed using (3.6.17) and (3.6.18). There is very little difference in standard errors relative to the homoskedastic case.

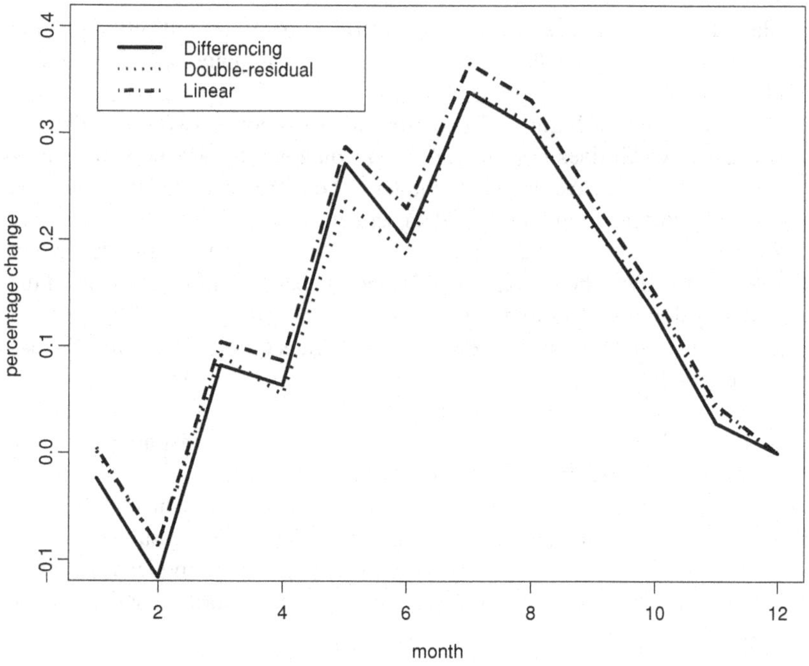

Figure 4.4. Household demand for gasoline: Monthly effects.

4.6.2 *Scale Economies in Electricity Distribution*[7]

We now consider the example of Section 1.6 in considerably more detail. Suppose we have a slightly more general specification that is a semiparametric variant of the translog model (variable definitions may be found in Appendix E):

$$\begin{aligned} tc = {} & f(cust) + \beta_1 wage + \beta_2 pcap + \tfrac{1}{2}\beta_{11} wage^2 + \tfrac{1}{2}\beta_{22} pcap^2 \\ & + \beta_{12} wage \cdot pcap + \beta_{31} cust \cdot wage + \beta_{32} cust \cdot pcap + \beta_4 PUC \\ & + \beta_5 kwh + \beta_6 life + \beta_7 lf + \beta_8 kmwire + \varepsilon. \end{aligned} \tag{4.6.2}$$

Note that, in addition to appearing nonparametrically, the scale variable *cust* interacts parametrically with wages and the price of capital. One can readily verify that, if these interaction terms are zero (i.e., $\beta_{31} = \beta_{32} = 0$), then the cost function is homothetic. If in addition $\beta_{11} = \beta_{22} = \beta_{12} = 0$, then the model reduces to the log-linear specification of Section 1.6.

Differencing estimates of the parametric component of (4.6.2) are presented in Figure 4.5. (We use third-order optimal differencing coefficients, in which case $m = 3$.) Applying Proposition 4.5.2, we do not find significant statistical evidence against either the homothetic or the log-linear models. For example, the statistic testing the full version (4.6.2) against the log-linear specification, which sets five parameters to zero and is distributed χ^2_5 under the null, takes a value of 3.23. Estimates of nonprice covariate effects exhibit little variation as one moves from the full translog model to the homothetic and log-linear models.

The last column of Figure 4.5 contains HCSEs reported two ways: the first uses (4.5.9), which does not incorporate off-diagonal terms; the second uses (4.5.10), which does. We believe the latter to be more accurate here given the low order of differencing the small data set permits.

We may now remove the estimated parametric effect from the dependent variable and analyze the nonparametric effect. In particular, for purposes of the tests that follow, the approximation $y_i - z_i\hat{\beta} = z_i(\beta - \hat{\beta}) + f(x_i) + \varepsilon_i \cong f(x_i) + \varepsilon_i$ does not alter the large sample properties of the procedures. We use the estimates of the log-linear model to remove the parametric effect.

Figure 4.5 displays the ordered pairs $(y_i - z_i\hat{\beta}_{diff}, x_i)$ as well as a kernel estimate of *f*. Parametric null hypotheses may be tested against nonparametric alternatives using the specification test in Section 4.3. If we insert a constant function for f, then the procedure constitutes a test of significance of the scale variable x against a nonparametric alternative. The resulting statistic is 9.8, indicating a strong scale effect. Next we test a quadratic model for output. The resulting test statistic is 2.4, suggesting that the quadratic model may be inadequate.

[7] For a detailed treatment of these data, see Yatchew (2000).

Variable	Full model: semi-parametric translog		Homothetic model: semi-parametric homothetic		Log-linear model: semi-parametric Cobb–Douglas			
	Coef	SE	Coef	SE	Coef	SE	HCSE Eqn. 4.5.9	HCSE Eqn. 4.5.10
wage	−5.917	13.297	−6.298	12.453	0.623	0.320	0.343	0.361
pcap	−2.512	2.107	−1.393	1.600	0.545	0.068	0.078	0.112
$\frac{1}{2} wage^2$	0.311	2.342	0.720	2.130	–	–	–	–
$\frac{1}{2} pcap^2$	0.073	0.083	0.032	0.066	–	–	–	–
$wage \cdot pcap$	0.886	0.738	0.534	0.599	–	–	–	–
$cust \cdot wage$	0.054	0.086	–	–	–	–	–	–
$cust \cdot pcap$	−0.039	0.049	–	–	–	–	–	–
PUC	−0.083	0.039	−0.086	0.039	−0.075	0.038	0.034	0.033
kwh	0.031	0.086	0.033	0.086	0.008	0.086	0.074	0.089
life	−0.630	0.117	−0.634	0.115	−0.628	0.113	0.095	0.097
lf	1.200	0.450	1.249	0.436	1.327	0.434	0.326	0.304
kmwire	0.396	0.087	0.399	0.087	0.413	0.084	0.090	0.115
s_ε^2	.01830		.0185		.01915			
R^2	.668		.665		.653			

Estimated scale effect

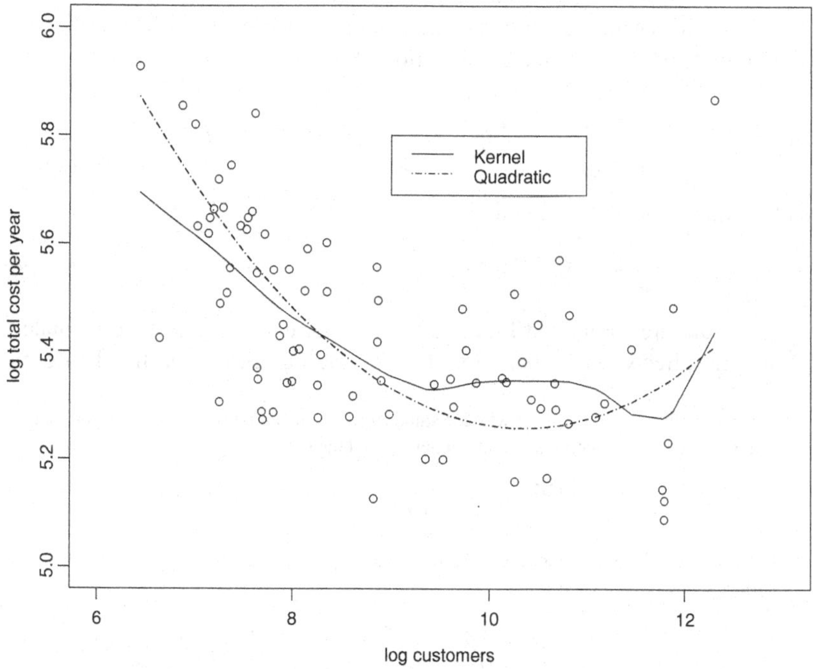

Test of full (translog) model versus log-linear (Cobb–Douglas) model: χ_5^2 under H_o : 3.23. Test of quadratic versus nonparametric specification of scale effect: $V = (mn)^{1/2}(s_{res}^2 - s_{diff}^2)/s_{diff}^2 = (3*81)^{1/2}(.0211 - .0183)/.0183 = 2.4$ where V is $N(0,1)$. Kernel estimate produced using *ksmooth* function in *S-Plus*. The last two columns of the table contain heteroskedasticity-consistent standard errors (HCSEs).

Figure 4.5. Scale economies in electricity distribution.

To provide further illustrations of differencing procedures we divide our data into two subpopulations: those that deliver additional services besides electricity, that is, public utility commissions (PUC), and those that are pure electricity distribution utilities (non-PUC). The numbers of observations in the two subpopulations are $n_{PUC} = 37$ and $n_{nonPUC} = 44$. We denote differencing estimates of parametric effects and of residual variances as $\hat{\beta}_{PUC}$, $\hat{\beta}_{nonPUC}$, s^2_{PUC}, and s^2_{nonPUC}. For each subpopulation, we estimate the log-linear model using the differencing estimator and report the results in Figure 4.6.

To test whether PUC and non-PUC entities experience the same parametric effects, we use

$$(\hat{\beta}_{PUC} - \hat{\beta}_{nonPUC})' \left(\hat{\Sigma}_{\hat{\beta}_{PUC}} + \hat{\Sigma}_{\hat{\beta}_{nonPUC}}\right)^{-1} \times (\hat{\beta}_{PUC} - \hat{\beta}_{nonPUC}) \xrightarrow{D} \chi^2_{dim(\beta)}. \tag{4.6.3}$$

The computed value of the χ^2_6 test statistic is 6.4, and thus the null is not rejected. Next, we constrain the parametric effects to be equal across the two types of utilities while permitting distinct nonparametric effects. This is accomplished by taking a weighted combination of the two estimates

$$\hat{\beta}_{weighted} = \left[\hat{\Sigma}^{-1}_{\hat{\beta}_{PUC}} + \hat{\Sigma}^{-1}_{\hat{\beta}_{nonPUC}}\right]^{-1} \left[\hat{\Sigma}^{-1}_{\hat{\beta}_{PUC}} \cdot \hat{\beta}_{PUC} + \hat{\Sigma}^{-1}_{\hat{\beta}_{nonPUC}} \cdot \hat{\beta}_{nonPUC}\right] \tag{4.6.4}$$

with estimated covariance matrix

$$\hat{\Sigma}_{\hat{\beta}_{weighted}} = \left[\hat{\Sigma}^{-1}_{\hat{\beta}_{PUC}} + \hat{\Sigma}^{-1}_{\hat{\beta}_{nonPUC}}\right]^{-1}. \tag{4.6.5}$$

The results are reported in Table 4.3.[8] The data can be purged of the estimated parametric effects, and separate nonparametric curves can be fitted to each

[8] A numerically similar estimator with the same large sample properties may be constructed by differencing the data within each subpopulation and then stacking as follows

$$\begin{bmatrix} Dy_{PUC} \\ Dy_{nonPUC} \end{bmatrix} = \begin{bmatrix} DZ_{PUC} \\ DZ_{nonPUC} \end{bmatrix} \beta + \begin{bmatrix} Df_{PUC}(x_{PUC}) \\ Df_{nonPUC}(x_{nonPUC}) \end{bmatrix} + \begin{bmatrix} D\varepsilon_{PUC} \\ D\varepsilon_{nonPUC} \end{bmatrix}.$$

Let $\hat{\beta}$ be the OLS estimator applied to the preceding equation. Then, the common residual variance may be estimated using

$$s^2 = \frac{1}{n}\left(\begin{bmatrix} Dy_{PUC} \\ Dy_{nonPUC} \end{bmatrix} - \begin{bmatrix} DZ_{PUC} \\ DZ_{nonPUC} \end{bmatrix}\hat{\beta}\right)' \left(\begin{bmatrix} Dy_{PUC} \\ Dy_{nonPUC} \end{bmatrix} - \begin{bmatrix} DZ_{PUC} \\ DZ_{nonPUC} \end{bmatrix}\hat{\beta}\right),$$

and the covariance matrix of $\hat{\beta}$ may be estimated using

$$\hat{\sum}_{\hat{\beta}} = \left(1 + \frac{1}{2m}\right) \frac{s^2}{n} \left[(DZ_{PUC})'(DZ_{PUC}) + (DZ_{nonPUC})'(DZ_{nonPUC})\right]^{-1},$$

where m is the order of (optimal) differencing.

	Partial linear model[a]			
Variable	PUC		non-PUC	
	Coef	SE	Coef	SE
wage	0.65	0.348	1.514	0.684
pcap	0.424	0.090	0.632	0.113
kwh	0.108	0.121	0.079	0.123
life	−0.495	0.131	−0.650	0.199
lf	1.944	0.546	0.453	0.702
kmwire	0.297	0.109	0.464	0.123
s_ε^2	0.013		0.023	

Estimated scale effect

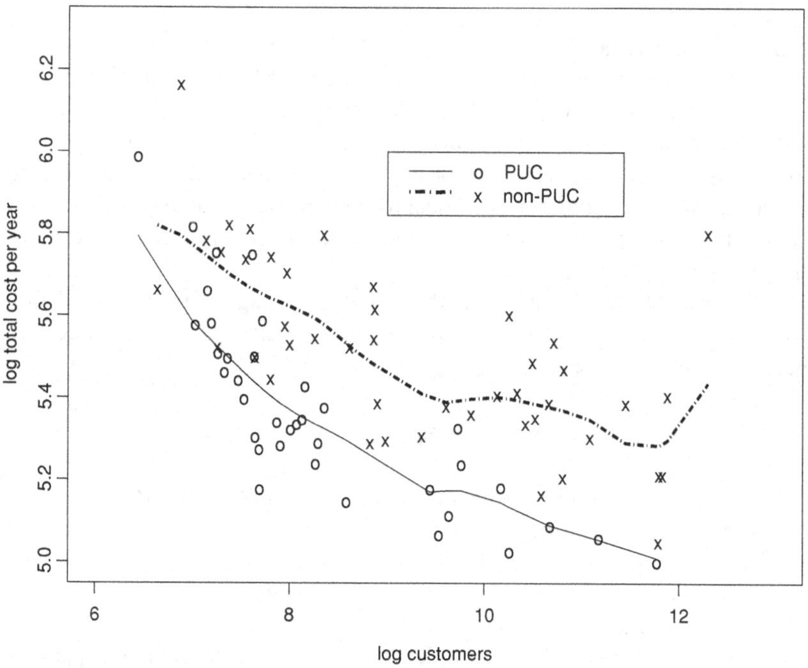

[a] Order of differencing $m = 3$.

Figure 4.6. Scale economies in electricity distribution: PUC and non-PUC analysis.

Table 4.3. *Mixed estimation of PUC/non-PUC effects: Scale economies in electricity distribution.*[a]

Variable	Coef	SE
wage	0.875	0.304
pcap	0.526	0.067
kwh	0.066	0.086
life	−0.547	0.107
lf	1.328	0.422
kmwire	0.398	0.078

[a]Estimates of parametric effects are obtained separately for PUC and non-PUC subpopulations. Hence, no PUC effect is estimated. The estimates above are obtained using (4.6.4) and (4.6.5).

subset of the data, as in the bottom panel of Figure 4.6. The PUC curve lies below the non-PUC curve consistent with our earlier finding that PUC entities have lower costs (see PUC coefficients in Figure 4.5).

We may now adapt our test of equality of regression functions in Section 4.4.2 to test whether the curves in Figure 4.6 are parallel, that is, whether one can be superimposed on the other by a vertical translation. This may be accomplished simply by removing the mean of the purged dependent variable from each of the two subpopulations.

Define the within estimate to be the weighted average of the subpopulation variance estimates, keeping in mind that the estimated parametric effect has been removed using, say, $\hat{\beta}_{weighted}$:

$$s_w^2 = \frac{n_{PUC}}{n} s_{PUC}^2 + \frac{n_{nonPUC}}{n} s_{nonPUC}^2. \tag{4.6.6}$$

Let y_{PUC}^{purge} be the vector of data on the dependent variable for PUCs with the estimated parametric effect removed and then centered around 0 and define y_{nonPUC}^{purge} similarly.[9] Now stack these two vectors and the corresponding data on the nonparametric variable x to obtain the ordered pairs $(y_i^{purge}, x_i)\ i = 1, \ldots, n$. Let P_p be the permutation matrix that reorders these data so that the nonparametric variable x is in increasing order. Note that, because separate equations

[9] Because the hypothesis that the parametric effects are the same across the two populations has not been rejected, one may use subpopulation estimates β_{PUC}^2 and β_{nonPUC}^2 or the weighted estimate $\hat{\beta}_{weighted}$ when computing s_{PUC}^2, s_{nonPUC}^2, and s_p^2.

were estimated for the two subpopulations, z does not contain the PUC dummy. Define

$$s_p^2 = \frac{1}{n} y^{purge'} P_p' D' D P_p y^{purge}. \qquad (4.6.7)$$

If the null hypothesis is true, then differencing will still remove the nonparametric effect in the pooled data and s_p^2 will converge to σ_ε^2. Otherwise, it will generally converge to some larger value. Applying Proposition 4.4.2 with $m = 1$, we obtain a value of 1.77 for $\Upsilon / s_w^2 (2\hat{\pi}_\Upsilon)^{1/2}$, which, noting that this is a one-sided test, suggests that there is some evidence against the hypothesis that the scale effects are parallel. Finally, we note that, given the size of the two subsamples, one must view the asymptotic inferences with some caution. An alternative approach that generally provides better inference in moderately sized samples would be based on the bootstrap, which is discussed in Chapter 8.

4.6.3 Weather and Electricity Demand

In a classic paper, Engle et al. (1986) used the partial linear model to study the impact of weather and other variables on electricity demand. We estimate a similar model in which weather enters nonparametrically and other variables enter parametrically. Our data consist of 288 quarterly observations in Ontario for the period 1971 to 1994. The specification is

$$elec_t = f(temp_t) + \beta_1 relprice_t + \beta_2 gdp_t + \varepsilon, \qquad (4.6.8)$$

where *elec* is the log of electricity sales, *temp* is heating and cooling degree days measured relative to 68 °F, *relprice* is the log of the ratio of the price of electricity to the price of natural gas, and *gdp* is the log of gross provincial product. We begin by testing whether electricity sales and *gdp* are cointegrated under the assumption that *relprice* and *temp* are stationary (setting aside issues of global warming). The Johansen test indicates a strong cointegrating relationship. We therefore reestimate the model in the form

$$elec_t - gdp_t = f(temp_t) + \beta_1 relprice_t + \varepsilon. \qquad (4.6.9)$$

Figure 4.7 contains estimates of a pure parametric specification for which the temperature effect is modeled using a quadratic as well as estimates of the partial linear model (4.6.9). The price of electricity relative to natural gas is negative and quite strongly significant. In the partial linear model, the

Variable	Quadratic model		Partial linear model[a]	
	Coef	Newey–West SE	Coef	Newey–West SE
constant	−1.707	0.0286	–	–
temp	-1.29×10^{-4}	3.80×10^{-5}	–	–
temp^2	4.07×10^{-7}	5.08×10^{-8}	–	–
relprice	−0.0695	0.0255	−0.073	.0252
s^2	.00312		.00282	
R^2	.788		.809	

Estimated temperature effect

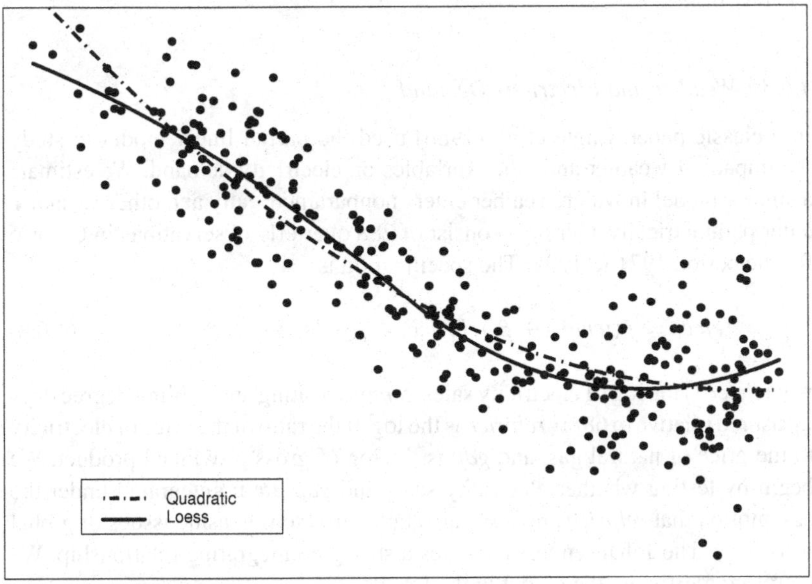

[a] The partial linear model was estimated using the double residual procedure with *loess* as the smoother. The scatterplot consists of points with the parametric (relative price) effect removed.

Figure 4.7. Weather and electricity demand.

ratio of the coefficient estimate to the Newey–West standard error is −2.9 (see Section 3.6).

4.7 Partial Parametric Model

4.7.1 Estimator

A natural generalization of the partial linear model replaces the linear portion with a nonlinear parametric specification $y_i = f(x_i) + r(z_i, \beta) + \varepsilon_i$, where the regression function r is known and β is a p-dimensional vector. Suppose that the data $(y_1, x_1, z_1), \ldots, (y_n, x_n, z_n)$ have been reordered so that the x's are in increasing order. Let $x' = (x_1, \ldots, x_n)$, $y' = (y_1, \ldots, y_n)$, and Z be the $n \times p$ matrix with ith row z_i.

Define $f(x)' = (f(x_1), \ldots, f(x_n))$ to be the column vector of nonparametric effects and $r(Z, \beta) = (r(z_1, \beta), \ldots, r(z_n, \beta))'$ to be the column vector of parametric effects. Let $\partial r(z, \beta)/\partial\beta$ be the $p \times 1$ column vector of partial derivatives of r with respect to β and $\partial r(Z, \beta)/\partial\beta$ the $p \times n$ matrix of partials of $r(z_1, \beta), \ldots, r(z_n, \beta)$ with respect to β. In matrix notation we may write the model as

$$y = f(x) + r(Z, \beta) + \varepsilon. \tag{4.7.1}$$

Applying the differencing matrix, we have

$$Dy = Df(x) + Dr(Z, \beta) + D\varepsilon. \tag{4.7.2}$$

Proposition 4.7.1: For arbitrary differencing weights satisfying (4.1.1), let $\hat{\beta}_{diffnls}$ satisfy

$$\min_{\beta} \frac{1}{n}(Dy - Dr(Z, \beta))'(Dy - Dr(Z, \beta)); \tag{4.7.3}$$

then,

$$\hat{\beta}_{diffnls} \overset{A}{\sim} N\left(\beta, (1 + 2\delta)\frac{\sigma_\varepsilon^2}{n} \sum\nolimits_{\frac{\partial r}{\partial \beta}|x}^{-1}\right), \tag{4.7.4}$$

where

$$\sum\nolimits_{\frac{\partial r}{\partial \beta}|x} = E\left(Var\left(\frac{\partial r}{\partial \beta} \mid x\right)\right). \tag{4.7.5}$$

Furthermore,

$$s_{diffnls}^2 = \frac{1}{n}(Dy - Dr(Z, \hat{\beta}_{nls}))'(Dy - Dr(Z, \hat{\beta}_{nls})) \xrightarrow{P} \sigma_\varepsilon^2, \tag{4.7.6}$$

and

$$\hat{\sum}_{\frac{\partial r}{\partial \beta}|x} = \frac{1}{n}\frac{\partial r(Z,\hat{\beta})}{\partial \beta} D'D \frac{\partial r(Z,\hat{\beta})}{\partial \beta'} \xrightarrow{P} \sum_{\frac{\partial r}{\partial \beta}|x}. \tag{4.7.7}$$

For optimal differencing weights, replace $1 + 2\delta$ with $1 + 1/2m$ in (4.7.4).

As will be illustrated in Section 4.7.2, nonlinear least-squares procedures (e.g., in *S-Plus*) may be applied to (4.7.2) to obtain estimates of β. However, the covariance matrix produced by such programs needs to be multiplied by $1 + 2\delta$ as indicated by (4.7.4) (see also Footnote to Table 4.4.)

4.7.2 *Empirical Application: CES Cost Function*

We continue with our example on electricity distribution costs. Consider a conventional constant elasticity of substitution (CES) cost function (see, e.g., Varian 1992, p. 56)

$$tc = \beta_0 + \frac{1}{\rho}\log(\beta_1 WAGE^{\rho} + (1-\beta_1)PCAP^{\rho}), \tag{4.7.8}$$

where tc is the log of total cost per customer and *WAGE* and *PCAP* denote factor prices in levels. (Elsewhere we use *wage* and *pcap* to denote logs of factor prices. See Appendix E for variable definitions.) We are interested in assessing whether cost per customer is affected by the scale of operation, that is, the number of customers. We therefore introduce a nonparametric scale effect (as well as several covariates)

$$\begin{aligned} tc = {} & f(cust) + \frac{1}{\rho}\log(\beta_1 WAGE^{\rho} + (1-\beta_1)PCAP^{\rho}) \\ & + \beta_2 PUC + \beta_3 kwh + \beta_4 life + \beta_5 lf + \beta_6\, kmwire + \varepsilon. \end{aligned} \tag{4.7.9}$$

First differencing and dividing by $\sqrt{2}$ so that the variance of the residual remains the same yields

$$\begin{aligned} & [tc_i - tc_{i-1}]/\sqrt{2} \\ & \cong \frac{1}{\rho}\big[\log\big(\beta_1 WAGE_i^{\rho} + (1-\beta_1)PCAP_i^{\rho}\big) \\ & \quad - \log\big(\beta_1 WAGE_{i-1}^{\rho} + (1-\beta_1)PCAP_{i-1}^{\rho}\big)\big]/\sqrt{2} \\ & \quad + \beta_2[PUC_i - PUC_{i-1}]/\sqrt{2} + \beta_3[kwh_i - kwh_{i-1}]/\sqrt{2} \\ & \quad + \beta_4[life_i - life_{i-1}]/\sqrt{2} + \beta_5[lf_i - lf_{i-1}]/\sqrt{2} \\ & \quad + \beta_6[kmwire_i - kmwire_{i-1}]/\sqrt{2} + [\varepsilon_i - \varepsilon_{i-1}]/\sqrt{2}. \end{aligned} \tag{4.7.10}$$

Table 4.4. *Scale economies in electricity distribution: CES cost function.*

	Parametric model		Partial parametric model[a]	
Variable	Coef	SE	Coef	SE
cust	−0.739	0.177	—	—
$cust^2$	0.036	0.010	—	—
WAGE	0.544	0.221	0.701	0.200
PCAP	1 − .544	—	1 − .701	—
ρ	0.197	0.560	0.467	0.585
PUC	−0.082	0.038	−0.081	0.047
kwh	0.001	0.087	−0.008	0.092
life	−0.594	0.122	−0.492	0.149
lf	1.144	0.433	1.241	0.479
kmwire	0.4293	0.086	0.371	0.096
s_ε^2	.0214		.0177	
R^2	.611		.678	

[a]Order of differencing $m = 1$. Model estimated using nonlinear least squares in *S-Plus*. Standard errors produced by *S-Plus* multiplied by $\sqrt{1.5}$ as per (4.7.4). Test of quadratic versus nonparametric specification of scale effect using the differencing test statistic in (4.3.2b) yields $V = (mn)^{1/2}(s_{res}^2 - s_{diff}^2)/s_{diff}^2 = 81^{1/2}(.0214 - .0177)/.0177 = 1.88$.

Our parametric null consists of a quadratic specification for the scale effect, that is, $f(cust) = \gamma_0 + \gamma_1 cust + \gamma_2 cust^2$ in (4.7.9). Results for this parametric specification and for (4.7.10) are presented in Table 4.4. The model was estimated using nonlinear least squares in *S-Plus*. Applying the differencing specification test yields an asymptotically $N(0, 1)$ statistic of 1.88.

The effects of covariates (*PUC*, *kwh*, *life*, *lf*, and *kmwire*) remain fairly similar across the various parametric and semiparametric specifications contained in Figures 1.2 and 4.5. Variants of the Leontief model may be implemented by imposing the restriction $\rho = 1$, which is a parameter that is estimated quite imprecisely in this specification.

4.8 Endogenous Parametric Variables in the Partial Linear Model

4.8.1 Instrumental Variables

We return to the framework of Section 4.5, the partial linear model. Suppose one or more of the p parametric variables in Z are correlated with the residual and suppose W is an $n \times q$ matrix of observations on instruments for Z. We will assume that there are at least as many instruments as parametric variables, that is, $q \geq p$, and that each instrument has a smooth regression function on x, the nonparametric variable. Let $\widehat{DZ}$ be the predicted values of DZ:

$$\widehat{DZ} = DW((DW)'DW)^{-1}(DW)'DZ. \tag{4.8.1}$$

As is the case for the conventional linear model, instrumental variable estimation may be motivated by multiplying (4.5.2) by $(\widehat{DZ})'$:

$$(\widehat{DZ})'Dy = (\widehat{DZ})'Df(x) + (\widehat{DZ})'DZ\beta + (\widehat{DZ})'D\varepsilon. \tag{4.8.2}$$

Because differencing removes the nonparametric effect in large samples, this suggests the two-stage-least-squares estimator $((\widehat{DZ})'DZ)^{-1}(\widehat{DZ})'Dy$. Define the conditional moment matrices: $\sum_{w\,|\,x} = E_x Var(w \,|\, x)$ and $\sum_{zw\,|\,x} = E_x Cov(z, w \,|\, x)$, where $Cov(z, w \,|\, x)$ is the $p \times q$ matrix of covariances between the z and w variables conditional on x.

Proposition 4.8.1: For arbitrary differencing weights satisfying (4.1.1),

$$\hat{\beta}_{diff2sls} = [(\widehat{DZ})'DZ]^{-1}(\widehat{DZ})'Dy$$

$$\xrightarrow{D} N\left(\beta, (1+2\delta)\frac{\sigma_\varepsilon^2}{n}\left[\sum_{zw|x}\sum_{w|x}^{-1}\sum_{zw|x}'\right]^{-1}\right) \tag{4.8.3}$$

$$s^2_{diff2sls} = \frac{1}{n}(Dy - DZ\hat{\beta}_{diff2sls})'(Dy - DZ\hat{\beta}_{diff2sls}) \xrightarrow{P} \sigma_\varepsilon^2 \tag{4.8.4}$$

$$\hat{\sum}_{w|x} = \frac{1}{n}(DW)'DW \xrightarrow{P} \sum_{w|x} \tag{4.8.5}$$

$$\hat{\sum}_{zw|x} = \frac{1}{n}(DZ)'DW \xrightarrow{P} \sum_{zw|x}. \tag{4.8.6}$$

For optimal differencing weights, replace $1 + 2\delta$ with $1 + 1/2m$ in (4.8.3).

4.8.2 *Hausman Test*

We can now produce a Hausman-type test (Hausman 1978) of endogeneity. The covariance matrices of each of the two estimators may be replaced by consistent estimates.

Proposition 4.8.2: Let $\sum_{\hat{\beta}_{diff}}$ be the large sample covariance matrix of $\hat{\beta}_{diff}$ (Eq. (4.5.3)) and $\sum_{\hat{\beta}_{diff2sls}}$ the corresponding covariance matrix for $\hat{\beta}_{diff2sls}$ (Eq. (4.8.3)); then, under the null hypothesis that z is uncorrelated with ε,

$$(\hat{\beta}_{diff} - \hat{\beta}_{diff2sls})' \left[\Sigma_{\hat{\beta}_{diff2sls}} - \Sigma_{\hat{\beta}_{diff}}\right]^{-1} (\hat{\beta}_{diff} - \hat{\beta}_{diff2sls}) \xrightarrow{D} \chi^2_p, \tag{4.8.7}$$

where p is the dimension of β.

4.9 Endogenous Nonparametric Variable

4.9.1 Estimation

Suppose that in the pure nonparametric regression model, the explanatory variable x is correlated with the residual. That is,

$$y = f(x) + \varepsilon \quad E(\varepsilon \mid x) \neq 0. \tag{4.9.1}$$

In general, this model is difficult to estimate because conventional instrumental variable techniques are not directly transferable to a nonlinear or nonparametric setting. However, suppose an instrument w exists for x that is uncorrelated with the residual

$$x = w\pi + u \quad E(u \mid w) = 0 \quad E(\varepsilon \mid w) = 0. \tag{4.9.2}$$

Suppose further that $E(\varepsilon \mid x, u) = \rho u$, in which case we may write $\varepsilon = \rho u + v$. This is a fairly strong assumption, but in this case we have

$$y = f(x) + u\rho + v \quad E(v \mid x, u) = 0. \tag{4.9.3}$$

Equation (4.9.3) is a partial linear model. To estimate it we need to perform the linear regression in (4.9.2), and save the residuals and insert them into (4.9.3), from which we may estimate ρ. If $\hat{\rho}$ is significantly different from zero, then x is endogenous.

The model generalizes readily to the case of the partial linear model $y = f(x) + z\beta + \varepsilon$. In this case, if x is correlated with the residual we need to perform the first-stage regression (4.9.2). We then rewrite the model as $y = f(x) + \rho u + z\beta + v$, reorder so that x is in increasing order, and regress the differenced values of y on the differenced values of $\hat{u}$ and z.

The approach described here originates with Hausman (1978). See also Holly and Sargan (1982) and Blundell and Duncan (1998). Generalizations may be found in Newey, Powell, and Vella (1999). The model may of course also be estimated using the double residual method in Section 3.6.

4.9.2 *Empirical Application: Household Gasoline Demand and Price Endogeneity*

Earlier we have estimated household demand for gasoline using Canadian microdata (see Section 4.6.1). The price variable, which enters nonparametrically, has a significant and negative effect on consumption, as illustrated in Figure 4.3.

However, the interpretation of the price effect is in question. If one examines the variation in prices within a given urban area, the coefficient of variation may be found to be as much as 5 percent or higher for regular gasoline.[10] Thus, individuals who drive more are likely to encounter a broader range of prices; hence, their search and transaction costs for cheap gasoline are lower. Furthermore, these same individuals derive greater benefit from cheap gas and therefore would be willing to incur higher search and transactions costs. Thus, one might expect price to be negatively correlated with the residual in an equation in which the dependent variable is distance traveled or the level of gasoline consumption. In this case the price coefficient would overestimate the true responsiveness of consumption to price.[11] To separate these two effects one should ideally have much more precise data on location. One could then instrument the observed price variable with the average price over a relatively small geographic area (such as the average intracity price). This level of detail is not available in these (public) data; however, as a check on our estimates we can instrument our price variable with the five provincial or regional dummies. These will serve the role of w in (4.9.2). Following (4.9.3), (4.6.1) may be rewritten as

$$y = f(price) + u\rho + z\beta + v, \tag{4.9.4}$$

where z is the collection of parametric variables, u is the residual in the instrumental variable equation $price = regional\ dummies \cdot \pi + u$, and $E(v \mid price, u, z) = 0$. After estimating u from an OLS regression, (4.9.4) was estimated using differencing. The coefficient of u was .31 with a standard

[10] The coefficient of variation of the price of regular gasoline is about 9 percent in our complete data set. After adjusting for geographic and time-of-year effects, the coefficient falls to about 7 percent.

[11] In the extreme case, demand could be perfectly inelastic at the same time that the estimated price effect is significantly negative.

error of .25, which, given the available instruments, does not suggest endogeneity.

4.10 Alternative Differencing Coefficients

Hall et al. (1990, p. 515, Table 2), henceforth HKT, compared the relative efficiency of alternative differencing estimators of the residual variance. They found that, for small m, optimal weights performed substantially better than a "spike" sequence in which the differencing weight near the middle of the sequence was close to unity whereas others were equal and close to zero. This is essentially equivalent to using a running mean smoother. For large m, they found both types of weights to have similar properties.

They also compared optimal weights to the usual weights used for numerical differentiation. (These are equivalent to mth-order divided differences for equally spaced data.) They found that these weights become progressively less efficient relative to optimal weights as m increases.

Seifert et al. (1993) studied the mean-squared error of various differencing-type estimators of the residual variance. They found that the bias resulting from the use of HKT optimal weights can be substantial in some cases, particularly if sample size is small and the signal-to-noise ratio is high. The mean-squared error of differencing estimators of the partial linear model has apparently not been studied.

Because HKT differencing weights put maximum weight at the extreme of a sequence, one would expect that in some cases bias would be exacerbated. On the other hand, weights that are symmetric about a midpoint and decline as one moves away might have better bias properties. In particular, for even m (so that the number of weights is odd), we solve the optimization problem given by

$$
\begin{aligned}
&\min_{d_0,\ldots,d_m} \delta = \sum_{k=1}^{m}\left(\sum_{j=0}^{m-k} d_j d_{j+k}\right)^2 \\
&\text{s.t.} \sum_{j=0}^{m} d_j = 0 \quad \sum_{j=0}^{m} d_j^2 = 1 \qquad (4.10.1)\\
&d_0 = d_m \quad d_1 = d_{m-1} \quad d_2 = d_{m-2} \ldots\ldots d_{m/2-1} = d_{m/2+1} \\
&d_{m/2+1} \le d_{m/2+2} \cdots \le d_m.
\end{aligned}
$$

The constraints impose (4.1.1), symmetry, and monotonicity toward zero as one moves away from the centermost weight. Optimal values are presented in Table 4.5.

The optimization problems were solved using GAMS (see Brooke et al. 1992). Table 4.6 compares the efficiency of optimal weights to symmetric

Table 4.5. *Symmetric optimal differencing weights.*

m	$(d_0, d_1, \ldots, d_m)$
2	(−0.4082, 0.8165, −0.4082)
4	(−0.1872, −0.2588, 0.8921, −0.2588, −0.1872)
6	(−0.1191, −0.1561, −0.1867, 0.9237, −0.1867, −0.1561, −0.1191)
8	(−0.0868, −0.1091, −0.1292, −0.1454, 0.9410, −0.1454, −0.1292, −0.1091, −0.0868)
10	(−0.0681, −0.0830, −0.0969, −0.1091, −0.1189, 0.9519, −0.1189, −0.1091, −0.0969, −0.0830, −0.0681)

Table 4.6. *Relative efficiency of alternative differencing sequences.*

	$(1 + 2\delta)$		
m	Optimal	Symmetric optimal	Moving average
2	1.250	1.940	1.944
4	1.125	1.430	1.450
6	1.083	1.276	1.294
8	1.063	1.204	1.218
10	1.050	1.161	1.173
20	1.025	1.079	1.085
100	1.005	1.015	1.017
200	1.003	1.008	1.008
500	1.001	1.003	1.003

optimal weights. It is not surprising that symmetric optimal weights are substantially less efficient (since we are free to choose only about half as many coefficients). For discussion of HKT optimal weights, see Section 4.2.3 and Appendix C.

4.11 The Relationship of Differencing to Smoothing

Chapter 3 focused on smoothing techniques. The essential objective was to produce good estimates of a nonparametric regression function. Take, for example, the basic model

$$y = f(x) + \varepsilon. \tag{4.11.1}$$

If one smooths the data by applying a smoother S that takes local averages, then one can expect a reasonable approximation to the function f

$$Sy = Sf(x) + S\varepsilon \cong Sf \cong f, \tag{4.11.2}$$

where $S\varepsilon \cong 0$ because smoothing random noise produces the zero function.

The present chapter has discussed differencing procedures. The objective has been to remove a nonparametric effect

$$Dy = Df(x) + D\varepsilon \cong D\varepsilon. \tag{4.11.3}$$

The essence of the relationship between smoothing and differencing is this. A smoothing procedure can always be used to remove a nonparametric effect. For example, using (4.11.2) we may write

$$(I - S)y = (I - S)f(x) + (I - S)\varepsilon \cong (I - S)\varepsilon, \tag{4.11.4}$$

and we may think of $D = I - S$ as a differencing procedure.

Differencing, on the other hand, will not in general contain an implicit useful estimate of the nonparametric effect. This is because there is no requirement for the order of differencing to increase with sample size. It is, however, a convenient device for producing test procedures, as we have seen in Section 4.3. (We will make use of this device in Chapter 6 to produce a general class of goodness-of-fit tests.)

As we have seen, differencing also yields a simple estimator of the partial linear model

$$\begin{aligned} Dy &= Df(x) + DZ\beta + D\varepsilon \\ &\cong DZ\beta + D\varepsilon, \end{aligned} \tag{4.11.5}$$

where D is applied to data that have been reordered so that the x's (but not necessarily the z's) are close. The asymptotic properties of the differencing estimator are similar to those produced by the double residual method

$$\begin{aligned} (I - S)y &= (I - S)f(x) + (I - S)Z\beta + (I - S)\varepsilon \\ &\cong (I - S)Z\beta + (I - S)\varepsilon \\ &\cong (I - S)Z\beta + \varepsilon, \end{aligned} \tag{4.11.6}$$

where S smooths data by a nonparametric regression on the x variable. The residuals in the differenced model (4.11.5) are $D\varepsilon$ and are approximately equal to ε only if the order of differencing is large. There is an additional distinction between smoothing and differencing obscured by the preceding notation but one we have emphasized earlier. When applying differencing, we use a single differencing matrix D and apply it to all the data. However, when smoothing is applied in the double residual procedure, it is common to run separate nonparametric regressions for y and each column of Z on the nonparametric variable x. This implies that the smoothing matrix S will in general be different in each of these regressions.

4.12 Combining Differencing and Smoothing

4.12.1 *Modular Approach to Analysis of the Partial Linear Model*

Our applications of the partial linear model $y = z\beta + f(x) + \varepsilon$ leave some untidy loose ends. Typically, our analysis is divided into two components: first we obtain a differencing estimate of β and undertake inference procedures on β as if f were not present in the model. Then we analyze f by performing nonparametric estimation and inference on the newly constructed data $(y_i - z_i\hat{\beta}_{diff}, x_i)$ as if β were known. Is such a modular approach valid? Separate analysis of the parametric portion is justified by virtue of results like Proposition 4.5.1. However, a little more justification is necessary with respect to the appropriateness of our analysis of the nonparametric part.[12]

In the following we will provide justification for various modular procedures we have already implemented – whether they involve combining differencing procedures in sequence or combining differencing and smoothing procedures.

4.12.2 *Combining Differencing Procedures in Sequence*

Recall the estimator of the residual variance in the partial linear model $y = z\beta + f(x) + \varepsilon$ as defined in (4.5.4):

$$\begin{aligned} s^2_{diff} &= \frac{1}{n}(Dy - DZ\hat{\beta}_{diff})'(Dy - DZ\hat{\beta}_{diff}) \\ &= \frac{1}{n}(y - Z\hat{\beta}_{diff})'D'D(y - Z\hat{\beta}_{diff}). \end{aligned} \tag{4.12.1}$$

It is easy to show that $\hat{\beta}$ converges to β sufficiently quickly so that the approximation $y_i - z_i\hat{\beta}_{diff} \cong f(x_i) + \varepsilon_i$ remains valid. In particular, we have

$$\begin{aligned} n^{1/2} \Bigg(& \frac{1}{n}(y - Z\hat{\beta}_{diff})'D'D(y - Z\hat{\beta}_{diff}) \\ & - \frac{1}{n}(f(x) + \varepsilon)'D'D(f(x) + \varepsilon) \Bigg) \xrightarrow{P} 0. \end{aligned} \tag{4.12.2}$$

This in turn implies that inference on the residual variance (Propositions 4.2.1 and 4.2.2 and Equation (4.2.15)), specification testing (Proposition 4.3.1), and tests of equality of regression functions (Propositions 4.4.1 and 4.4.2) may be applied to the data with the estimated parametric effect removed. In each case, differencing is used first to estimate the parametric effect and then to perform a specific inference procedure.

[12] For example, we have applied tests of specification, tests of equality of nonparametric regression functions, and conventional kernel and spline estimation procedures after removing estimated parametric effects.

4.12.3 *Combining Differencing and Smoothing*

Suppose we perform a kernel regression of $y_i - z_i\hat{\beta}_{diff}$ on x_i. For simplicity, assume the x's to be uniformly distributed on the unit interval and that the uniform kernel is used. Define λ as the bandwidth and $N(x_o) = \{x_i \mid x_i \in x_o \pm \lambda\}$ to be the neighborhood of x_o over which smoothing is being performed. Using a Taylor approximation (see Sections 3.1 and 3.2), we have

$$\begin{aligned}\hat{f}(x_o) &\cong \frac{1}{2\lambda n}\sum_{N(x_o)} y_i - z_i\hat{\beta}_{diff}\\ &= \frac{1}{2\lambda n}\sum_{N(x_o)} f(x_i) + \frac{1}{2\lambda n}\sum_{N(x_o)} \varepsilon_i + (\beta - \hat{\beta}_{diff})\frac{1}{2\lambda n}\sum_{N(x_o)} z_i\\ &\cong f(x_o) + \tfrac{1}{2} f''(x_o)\frac{1}{2\lambda n}\sum_{N(x_o)}(x_i - x_o)^2\\ &\quad + \frac{1}{2\lambda n}\sum_{N(x_o)} \varepsilon_i + (\beta - \hat{\beta}_{diff})\frac{1}{2\lambda n}\sum_{N(x_o)} z_i. \end{aligned} \tag{4.12.3}$$

The neighborhood $N(x_o)$ will have close to $2\lambda n$ terms so that in each summation we are calculating a simple average.

Consider the term involving the second derivative, which corresponds to the bias: $\sum_{N(x_o)}(x_i - x_o)^2/2\lambda n$ is like the variance of a uniform variable on an interval of width 2λ centered at x_o, in which case it is $O_P(\lambda^2)$.

The next term corresponds to the variance term: it has mean 0 and variance $\sigma_\varepsilon^2/2\lambda n$ so that it is $O_P((\lambda n)^{1/2})$. The last term arises out of the removal of the estimated parametric effect, where β has been estimated $n^{1/2}$-consistently so it is of order $O_P(n^{-1/2})O_P(1)$. Summarizing, we have

$$\hat{f}(x_o) - f(x_o) = O_P(\lambda^2) + O_P((\lambda n)^{-1/2}) + O_P(n^{-1/2})O_P(1). \tag{4.12.4}$$

So long as $\lambda \to 0$ and $\lambda n \to \infty$, consistency of the kernel estimator is unaffected because all three terms converge to zero. Furthermore, $\lambda = O(n^{-1/5})$ still minimizes the rate at which the (sum of the) three terms converge to zero.

$$\hat{f}(x_o) - f(x_o) = O_P(n^{-2/5}) + O_P(n^{-2/5}) + O_P(n^{-1/2})O_P(1), \tag{4.12.5}$$

so that the optimal rate of convergence is unaffected. The order of the first two terms is $O_P(n^{-2/5})$, whereas the third term converges to zero more quickly and independently of λ. Confidence intervals may also be constructed in the usual way, for applying (4.12.4) we have

$$\begin{aligned}(\lambda n)^{1/2}(\hat{f}(x_o) - f(x_o)) &= O_P((\lambda n)^{1/2}\lambda^2) + O_P(1) + O_P(\lambda^{1/2}) \\ &= O_P(1) + O_P(1) + O_P(n^{-1/10}) \qquad \text{if } \lambda = O(n^{-1/5}), \qquad (4.12.6)\end{aligned}$$

and the third term goes to zero, albeit slowly. If the optimal bandwidth $\lambda = O(n^{-1/5})$ is selected, then confidence intervals must correct for a bias term.

Similar arguments apply to other nonparametric estimators. For example, if one uses a nonparametric least-squares or spline estimator in a regression of $y_i - z_i\hat{\beta}_{diff}$ on x_i, then the estimator $\hat{f}$ remains consistent and its rate of convergence is unchanged.

4.12.4 *Reprise*

The practical point of this section is that for the partial linear model $y = z\beta + f(x) + \varepsilon$ (or more generally the partial parametric model), we can separate the analysis of the parametric portion from the analysis of the nonparametric portion. Given a differencing estimate of β (or for that matter, any $n^{1/2}$-consistent estimate), we may construct the new dependent variable $y_i^* = y_i - z_i\hat{\beta}_{diff}$, set aside the original y_i, and analyze the data (y_i^*, x_i) as if they came from the pure nonparametric model $y_i^* = f(x_i) + \varepsilon_i$. None of the large sample properties we have discussed will be affected. This holds true regardless of the dimension of the parametric variable z.

This idea – that so long as the rate of convergence of an estimator is fast enough we can treat it as known – will be used extensively to simplify testing and inference procedures in later chapters. Indeed, we have already used it to derive a simple specification test (Sections 1.4 and 4.3). In the specification test setting, the parametric model estimates converged fast enough so that we could replace the estimated sum of squared residuals with the actual sum of squared residuals when deriving an approximate distribution for the test statistic (see, e.g., (1.4.1)).

4.13 Exercises[13]

1. (a) Suppose the components of $\vartheta = (\vartheta_1, \ldots, \vartheta_\xi)'$ are i.i.d. with $E\vartheta_i = 0$, $Var(\vartheta_i) = \sigma_\vartheta^2$, $E\vartheta_i^4 = \eta_\vartheta$, and covariance matrix $\sigma_\vartheta^2 I_\xi$. If A is a symmetric matrix, show that $E(\vartheta' A\vartheta) = \sigma_\vartheta^2 trA$ and $Var(\vartheta' A\vartheta) = (\eta_\vartheta - 3\sigma_\vartheta^4)trA \odot A + \sigma_\vartheta^4 trAA$. (If A, B are matrices of identical dimension, define $[A \odot B]_{ij} = A_{ij}B_{ij}$.)

[13] Data and sample programs for empirical exercises are available on the Web. See the Preface for details.

(b) Consider the heteroskedastic case where $Var(\vartheta_i) = \sigma_i^2$, $E\vartheta_i^4 = \eta_i$, ϑ has the diagonal covariance matrix Ω, and η is the diagonal matrix with entries η_i. Then $E(\vartheta' A\vartheta) = trA\Omega$ and $Var(\vartheta' A\vartheta) = tr(\eta \odot A \odot A - 3\Omega^2 \odot A \odot A) + 2tr(\Omega A \Omega A)$.

2. (a) Suppose x has support the unit interval with density bounded away from 0. Given n observations on x, reorder them so that they are in increasing order: $x_1 \leq \cdots \leq x_n$. Then for any ϵ positive and arbitrarily close to 0, $1/n \sum (x_i - x_{i-1})^2 = O_P(n^{-2(1-\epsilon)})$.[14]

(b) For an arbitrary collection of points in the unit interval, prove that the maximum value that $1/n \sum (x_i - x_{i-1})^2$ can take is $1/n$. (This occurs when all observations are at one of the two endpoints of the interval.)

3. (a) Using the results of Exercise 2, prove that

$$n^{1/2}\left(s_{diff}^2 - \frac{1}{n}\varepsilon' D' D\varepsilon\right) \xrightarrow{P} 0.$$

(b) Using Exercise 1, derive the mean and variance of s_{diff}^2 as in (4.2.6) and (4.2.7).

(c) Now assemble the results and use a finitely dependent central limit theorem to prove Proposition 4.2.1.

4. Derive (4.2.13) and use it to prove Proposition 4.2.2.

5. Prove Proposition 4.3.1.

6. Prove Proposition 4.4.1.

7. Prove Proposition 4.4.2.

8. (a) Suppose an equal number of observations are drawn from two populations A and B with differing regression functions $f_A \neq f_B$. Furthermore, suppose the data are such that upon pooling and reordering, the x's become perfectly interleaved. That is, an observation from subpopulation A is always followed by an observation from subpopulation B. Show that the pooled estimator in (4.4.4) with first-order differencing converges as follows:

$$s_p^2 \to \sigma_\varepsilon^2 + 1/2 \int (f_A(x) - f_B(x))^2 dx.$$

(b) Suppose, more generally, that x_A and x_B are independently and uniformly distributed on the unit interval and an equal number of observations are taken from each subpopulation (i.e., $n_A = n_B = 1/2\, n$). Show that the pooled estimator in (4.4.4) with first-order differencing converges as in (4.4.7).

9. *South African Food Share Engel Curves – Testing Parametric Specifications.* Results should be similar to Figure 4.1.

(a) Using South African food share data on single individuals, fit a linear regression model of the form $FoodShr = \alpha + \beta ltexp + \varepsilon$, where $FoodShr$ is the food share

[14] Because ϵ may be chosen arbitrarily close to zero, we will write $1/n \sum (x_i - x_{i-1})^2 \cong O_P(n^{-2})$. Note also that for fixed j, $1/n \sum (x_i - x_{i-j})^2 \cong O_P(n^{-2})$.

and *ltexp* is the log of total expenditure. Obtain the estimate of the residual variance and the R^2.

(b) Fit a kernel smooth $\hat{f}$ to the data and plot the linear and kernel fits on one graph. Estimate the residual variance using the kernel fit by applying

$$s_{ker}^2 = \frac{1}{n}\sum(y_i - \hat{f}(x_i))^2.$$

(c) Estimate the residual variance using the optimal differencing estimator (4.2.4) for $m = 5, 10, 25$.

(d) Test the linear fit by applying Proposition 4.3.1.

10. *South African Food Share Data – Testing Similarity of Shape of Engel Curves.* Results should be similar to Figure 4.2.

(a) From the South African food share data, select two subsets: the first consisting of single individuals and the second consisting of couples with no children.

(b) Fit kernel smooths to the model $FoodShr = f(ltexp) + \varepsilon$ for each of the two subsets and plot these on a single graph.

(c) For the couples data, subtract .5 from *ltexp*, the *log* of total expenditure (which is equivalent to dividing total expenditure by 1.65). Replot the kernel smooths from Part (b).

(d) Using the "singles" data and the translated "couples" data, apply Proposition 4.4.2 to test equality of regression functions.

11. *Household Gasoline Consumption*: The objective of this problem is to apply differencing and double residual methods. The results should be similar to those in Figures 4.3 and 4.4.

(a) Using the data on household gasoline consumption, estimate (4.6.1) under the assumption that f is linear. Calculate the $R^2 = 1 - s_\varepsilon^2/s_y^2$.

(b) Reorder the data so that the price variable is in increasing order. Use optimal differencing coefficients (say $m = 10$) to remove the nonparametric effect and estimate the parametric effects in (4.6.1). Estimate the residual variance using (4.5.4). Estimate the standard errors using (4.5.5) and (4.5.6). Calculate $R^2 = 1 - s_{diff}^2/s_y^2$.

(c) Apply the double residual method outlined in Section 3.6 by first doing a kernel regression of the dependent variable and each of the parametric variables in (4.6.1) on the log of price. (You will perform 18 plus 1 regressions.) Save the residuals from each and apply ordinary least squares. The OLS procedure will produce the estimated standard errors for the parametric effects. Calculate the average sum of squared residuals from this OLS regression and use this as the estimate of the residual variance. Calculate $R^2 = 1 - s_\varepsilon^2/s_y^2$.

(d) Using the estimates from the differencing procedure in Part (b), remove the estimated parametric effect from the dependent variable and perform a kernel regression of this purged variable on the log of price. Plot this and the estimated parametric effect of price from Part (a).

(e) Apply Proposition 4.3.1 to test linearity of the price effect. Run a linear regression of model (4.6.1), omitting the price variable. Using the estimated residual variance, apply Proposition 4.3.1 to test the significance of the price effect.
(f) Estimate the heteroskedasticity-consistent standard errors using (3.6.17) and (3.6.18).

12. *Scale Economies in Electricity Distribution*: The results should be similar to those in Figures 4.5 and 4.6 and Table 4.3.

(a) Using the electricity distribution data and (4.6.2), estimate semiparametric variants of translog, homothetic, and Cobb–Douglas models. In each case the scale variable (number of customers) is nonparametric and other variables are parametric.
(b) Test the semiparametric Cobb–Douglas variant against the full semiparametric translog using Proposition 4.5.2.
(c) Divide your data into two subsets consisting of public utility commissions (PUC) and non-PUC. Using the Cobb–Douglas variant of (4.6.2), apply the differencing estimator of Proposition 4.5.1 to estimate the separate parametric effects for each subpopulation. Apply (4.6.3) to test the null that the parametric effects are the same.
(d) Calculate the weighted combination of these two estimates $\hat{\beta}_{weighted}$ using (4.6.4) and (4.6.5). For each subpopulation, use $\hat{\beta}_{weighted}$ to remove the estimated parametric effects by subtracting $\hat{\beta}_{weighted}(z - \bar{z})$ from the dependent variable. The vector mean of the independent variables $\bar{z}$ should be calculated separately within each subpopulation.
(e) Test whether the nonparametric regression effects for the two subpopulations are parallel.
(f) Estimate heteroskedasticity-consistent standard errors using the two methods outlined in Section 4.5 (in particular see (4.5.9) and (4.5.10)).

13. *Weather and Electricity Demand*: Results should be similar to Figure 4.7.

(a) Estimate the relationship between electricity consumption, the price of electricity relative to natural gas, and a quadratic temperature effect. Obtain Newey–West standard errors for the coefficients of this parametric specification.
(b) Estimate the partial linear model (4.6.9) using the double residual method and the *loess* estimator. Obtain heteroskedasticity- and autocorrelation-consistent standard errors using the procedures outlined in Section 3.6.5 (assume $\mathcal{L} = 5$).

14. *CES Cost Function and Scale Economies in Electricity Distribution:* Results should be similar to those in Table 4.4.

(a) Using the electricity distribution data and a nonlinear least-squares procedure, estimate (4.7.9) assuming the function f that measures the scale effect is quadratic.

(b) After ensuring that the data are reordered so that the scale effect is increasing, first difference the specification as indicated in (4.7.10) and apply nonlinear least squares. Rescale the estimated standard errors by $\sqrt{1.5}$.
(c) Using the estimated residual variances from the two preceding procedures, apply the specification test in Section 4.3 to assess the quality of the quadratic fit.

15. *Endogeneity of Observed Price of Gasoline*

(a) Regress the *log* of price on the Regional Dummies and save the residuals $\hat{u}$.
(b) Estimate (4.9.4) where z consists of all parametric variables appearing in (4.6.1). Test the endogenity of price by determining whether the coefficient of $\hat{u}$ is significantly different from zero.

5 Nonparametric Functions of Several Variables

5.1 Smoothing

5.1.1 Introduction

In economics it is rarely the case that one is interested in a function of a single variable. Moreover, even if one is comfortable incorporating most of the explanatory variables parametrically (e.g., within a partial linear model), more than one variable may enter nonparametrically. The effects of geographic location – a two-dimensional variable – provides a good example. (Indeed, in Section 5.4.1 we estimate the effects of location on housing prices nonparametrically while permitting other housing characteristics to be modeled parametrically.)

In this chapter we therefore turn to models in which there are several nonparametric variables. A variety of techniques are available. We will focus primarily on kernel and nonparametric least-squares estimators. However, the elementary "moving average smoother" which we considered in Section 3.1 has a close multidimensional relative in nearest-neighbor estimation. Spline techniques have natural generalizations (see particularly Wahba 1990 and Green and Silverman 1994). Local linear and local polynomial smoothers also have multivariate counterparts (see Fan and Gijbels 1996).

5.1.2 Kernel Estimation of Functions of Several Variables

Suppose f is a function of two variables and one has data $(y_1, x_1), \ldots, (y_n, x_n)$ on the model $y_i = f(x_{i1}, x_{i2}) + \varepsilon_i$, where $x_i = (x_{i1}, x_{i2})$. We will assume f is a function on the unit square $[0,1]^2$. We want to estimate $f(x_o)$ by averaging nearby observations; in particular, we will average observations falling in a square of dimension $2\lambda \times 2\lambda$, which is centered at x_o. If the x_i are drawn from, say, a uniform distribution on the unit square, then there will be (approximately) $4\lambda^2 n$ observations in the neighborhood $N(x_o) = \{x_i | x_{i1} \in x_{o1} \pm \lambda, x_{i2} \in x_{o2} \pm \lambda\}$. For example, any square with sides $2\lambda = .5$ has area .25 and will capture about

25 percent of the observations. Consider then

$$\begin{aligned}\hat{f}(x_o) &= \frac{1}{4\lambda^2 n}\sum_{N(x_o)} y_i \\ &= \frac{1}{4\lambda^2 n}\sum_{N(x_o)} f(x_i) + \frac{1}{4\lambda^2 n}\sum_{N(x_o)} \varepsilon_i \\ &\cong f(x_o) + O(\lambda^2) + \frac{1}{4\lambda^2 n}\sum_{N(x_o)} \varepsilon_i \\ &\cong f(x_o) + O(\lambda^2) + O_P\left(\frac{1}{\lambda n^{1/2}}\right). \end{aligned} \tag{5.1.1}$$

We have mimicked the reasoning in Sections 3.1 and 3.2 but this time for the bivariate uniform kernel estimator. (As before, we have assumed that f is twice differentiable but spared the reader the details of the Taylor series expansion.) The last line of (5.1.1) may now be compared with its counterpart in the univariate case, (3.2.4a). Note the subtle difference. The bias term is still proportional to λ^2, but the variance term is now $O_P(1/\lambda n^{1/2})$ rather than $O_P(1/\lambda^{1/2} n^{1/2})$ since we are averaging approximately $4\lambda^2 n$ values of ε_i.

Hence, for consistency, we now need $\lambda \to 0$ and $\lambda n^{1/2} \to \infty$. As before, convergence of $\hat{f}(x_o)$ to $f(x_o)$ is fastest when the bias and variance terms go to zero at the same rate, that is, when $\lambda = O(n^{-1/6})$. The second and third terms of the last line of (5.1.1) are then $O(n^{-1/3})$ and $O_P(n^{-1/3})$, respectively. Furthermore, $\int[\hat{f}(x) - f(x)]^2 dx = O_P(n^{-2/3})$, which is optimal (see (2.4.1)).

More generally, if the x_i are d-dimensional with probability density $p(x)$ defined, say, on the unit cube in $\mathbb{R}^d$ and we are using a kernel K then the estimator becomes

$$\hat{f}(x_o) = \frac{\frac{1}{\lambda^d n}\sum_1^n y_i \prod_{j=1}^d K\left(\frac{x_{ij}-x_{oj}}{\lambda}\right)}{\frac{1}{\lambda^d n}\sum_1^n \prod_{j=1}^d K\left(\frac{x_{ij}-x_{oj}}{\lambda}\right)}. \tag{5.1.2}$$

Again, if K is the uniform kernel that takes the value ½ on [−1,1], then the product of the kernels (hence the term product kernel) is $\frac{1}{2}^d$ only if $x_{ij} \in [x_{oj} - \lambda, x_{oj} + \lambda]$ for $j = 1, \ldots, d$, that is, only if x_i falls in the d-dimensional cube centered at x_o with sides of length 2λ. The estimator is consistent if $\lambda \to 0$ and $\lambda^{d/2} n^{1/2} \to \infty$. Indeed, the numerator converges to $f(x_o)p(x_o)$ and the denominator converges to $p(x_o)$, where $p(x)$ is the density function of x. Confidence interval construction is simplified if the bias term converges to zero sufficiently quickly so that it does not affect the asymptotic distribution. For $d = 2$, one requires $\lambda = o(n^{-1/6})$; for $d = 3$, the condition is $\lambda = o(n^{-1/7})$.

In the preceding paragraph we have introduced a simple kernel estimator for functions of several variables that averages observations over a cube centered at x_o. A multitude of variations and alternatives exist. For example, one could select different bandwidths for each dimension so that averaging would take place over rectangular cubes rather than perfect cubes. Or, one might select different kernels for each dimension. Still more generally, one could average over nonrectangular regions such as spheres or ellipsoids.[1]

5.1.3 Loess

The *loess* estimator we described in Section 3.4 extends readily to the multivariate setting. To estimate the function at a point, say x_o, k nearest-neighbors are selected and a weighted local regression is performed. In *S-Plus*, one can choose between local linear and local quadratic regressions. In addition one can choose to rescale the explanatory variables by their standard deviations. For more details, see Chambers and Hastie (1993, pp. 309–376). In the applications to follow, we use *loess* to estimate the first-stage nonparametric regression in a double residual estimator of the partial linear model.

5.1.4 Nonparametric Least Squares

In Section 3.3 we introduced a nonparametric least-squares estimator for functions of one variable. The estimator is a linear combination of functions called representors, and it uses a measure of smoothness (3.3.1) that integrates the square of a function and two or more of its derivatives. Suppose we are given data $(y_1, x_1), \ldots, (y_n, x_n)$ on the model $y_i = f(x_{i1}, x_{i2}) + \varepsilon_i$, where $x_i = (x_{i1}, x_{i2})$. We will assume f is a function on the unit square $[0,1]^2$. Define the Sobolev norm $\|f\|_{Sob}$ as in Appendix D. Suppose $\hat{f}$ satisfies

$$s^2 = \min_f \frac{1}{n} \sum_i [y_i - f(x_i)]^2 \quad \text{s.t. } \|f\|^2_{Sob} \leq L. \tag{5.1.3}$$

Then the solution is of the form $\hat{f} = \sum_1^n \hat{c}_i r_{x_i}$, where $r_{x_1}, \ldots, r_{x_n}$ are functions computable from $x_1, \ldots, x_n$, and $\hat{c} = (\hat{c}_1, \ldots, \hat{c}_n)$ is obtained by solving

$$\min_c \frac{1}{n} [y - Rc]' \, [y - Rc] \quad \text{s.t. } c'Rc \leq L. \tag{5.1.4}$$

Here y is the $n \times 1$ vector of observations on the dependent variable, and R is the matrix of inner products of the representors r_{x_i}. The difference between the one-dimensional problem (3.3.3) and its two-dimensional counterpart is the calculation of the representor matrix. Fortunately, in our setup,

[1] See Scott (1992, pp. 149–155) and Wand and Jones (1995, pp. 103–105).

two-dimensional representors are products of one-dimensional representors. In particular, let $r_{x_i}(x_1, x_2)$ be the representor function at the point $x_i = (x_{i1}, x_{i2})$. Then $r_{x_i}(x_1, x_2) = r_{x_{i1}}(x_1) r_{x_{i2}}(x_2)$, where $r_{x_{i1}}(x_1)$ is the representor in the Sobolev space of functions of x_1, and $r_{x_{i2}}(x_2)$ is defined analogously. Theoretical and computational details are contained in Appendix D. See also Wahba (1990) and Yatchew and Bos (1997).

5.2 Additive Separability

5.2.1 *Backfitting*

The nonparametrics literature has devoted considerable attention to improving the rate of convergence of nonparametric estimators using additive models, which, in the simplest case, are of the form $f(x_a, x_b) = f_a(x_a) + f_b(x_b)$.[2] A powerful and general algorithm used to estimate additively separable models is motivated by the observation that

$$E[y - f_a(x_a) \mid x_b] = f_b(x_b) \quad \text{and} \quad E[y - f_b(x_b) \mid x_a] = f_a(x_a). \tag{5.2.1}$$

If $\hat{f}_a$ is a good estimate of f_a, then f_b may be estimated by nonparametric regression of $y - \hat{f}_a(x_a)$ on x_b. A parallel argument holds for estimation of f_a. Beginning with these observations, the algorithm in Table 5.1 has been widely studied.

The initial estimates f_a^0, f_b^0 in Table 5.1 may be set to zero or to the estimates from a parametric procedure (such as a linear regression).

The procedure may be generalized in the obvious fashion to additively separable models with more than two additive terms, where each term may be a function of several variables. Assuming that optimal nonparametric estimators are applied to each component, the rate of convergence of the estimated regression function equals the rate of convergence of the component with the largest number of explanatory variables.

For example, if $y = f_a(x_a) + f_b(x_b) + f_c(x_c) + \varepsilon$, where x_a, x_b, x_c are scalars, and optimal estimators are applied in the estimation of f_a, f_b, f_c, then the rate of convergence of $\hat{f}_a + \hat{f}_b + \hat{f}_c$ is the same as if the regression model were a function of only one variable. That is, $\int((\hat{f}_a + \hat{f}_b + \hat{f}_c) - (f_a + f_b + f_c))^2 = O_P(n^{-2m/(2m+1)})$, where m is the number of bounded derivatives.[3]

[2] See, for example, Stone (1985, 1986); Buja, Hastie, and Tibshirani (1989) Hastie and Tibshirani (1987, 1990); Linton (1997); Linton, Mammen, and Nielsen (1999); Linton (2000) and references therein.

[3] Applying (2.4.1) and assuming two bounded derivatives, we have $\int(\hat{f}_a + \hat{f}_b + \hat{f}_c)^2 = O_P(n^{-4/5})$ as compared with $O_P(n^{-4/7})$ for the model $f(x_a, x_b, x_c)$ or $O_P(n^{-1})$ for the parametric model.

Table 5.1. *The backfitting algorithm.*[a]

Initialization:	Select initial estimates f_a^0, f_b^0.
Iteration:	Obtain $\hat{f}_a^i$ by nonparametric regression of $y - \hat{f}_b^{i-1}(x_b)$ on x_a.
	Obtain $\hat{f}_b^i$ by nonparametric regression of $y - \hat{f}_a^{i-1}(x_a)$ on x_b.
Convergence:	Continue iteration until there is little change in individual function estimates.

[a] See Hastie and Tibshirani (1990), Chapter 4 and references therein.

More generally, if f is additively separable with parametric and nonparametric components, say $y = z\beta + f_a(x_a) + f_b(x_b) + \varepsilon$, where z, x_a, x_b are of dimension d_z, d_a, d_b, respectively, then the rate of convergence of the optimal estimator is given by[4]

$$\int ((z\hat{\beta} + \hat{f}_a(x_a) + \hat{f}_b(x_b)) - (z\beta + f_a(x_a) + f_b(x_b)))^2$$
$$= O_P\left(n^{\frac{-2m}{2m+\max\{d_a,d_b\}}}\right). \tag{5.2.2}$$

The result is very similar to (2.4.1) except that d has been replaced by $\max\{d_a,d_b\}$.

In performing the component nonparametric regressions, a variety of techniques may be used, including kernel, spline, and *loess* estimation. Indeed, the algorithm is particularly versatile in that different techniques may be selected for different components. For example, f_a may be estimated using kernel regression and f_b using nonparametric least squares (or even nonparametric least squares subject to constraints). The backfitting algorithm is available in *S-Plus* using the function *gam* (generalized additive model).

An alternative procedure for estimation of additive (and multiplicative) models based on marginal integration has been proposed by Newey (1994b) and Linton and Nielsen (1995). One of the major attractions to their approach is that, in contrast to backfitting, their estimator has simple statistical properties.

5.2.2 *Additively Separable Nonparametric Least Squares*

We turn now to nonparametric least-squares estimation of the additively separable model. The optimization problem in (5.1.3) becomes

$$\min_{f_a, f_b} \frac{1}{n} \sum_i [y_i - f_a(x_{ai}) - f_b(x_{bi})]^2 \quad \text{s.t. } \|f_a + f_b\|_{Sob}^2 \leq L, \tag{5.2.3}$$

[4] Again assuming two bounded derivatives and supposing that the dimensions d_z, d_a, d_b are 3, 2, 1, respectively, then the optimal rate of convergence is $O_P(n^{-2/3})$ as compared with $O_P(n^{-4/10})$ for the model $f(z, x_a, x_b)$ or $O_P(n^{-1})$ for the parametric model.

which can be transformed into the finite dimensional optimization problem

$$\min_{c_a, c_b} \frac{1}{n}[y - R_a c_a - R_b c_b]' \, [y - R_a c_a - R_b c_b]$$
$$\text{s.t. } c_a' R_a c_a + c_b' R_b c_b \leq L, \tag{5.2.4}$$

where y is the $n \times 1$ vector of observations on the dependent variable, c_a, c_b are $n \times 1$ vectors of unknowns, and R_a, R_b are (representor) matrices that may be computed directly from $x_{a1}, \ldots, x_{an}$ and $x_{b1}, \ldots, x_{bn}$, respectively. The estimated regression function is of the form $\hat{f}_a(x_a) + \hat{f}_b(x_b) = \sum_1^n \hat{c}_{ai} r_{x_{ai}}(x_a) + \hat{c}_{bi} r_{x_{bi}}(x_b)$. The optimization problem involves a quadratic objective function and a quadratic constraint. (There is also an identifying restriction that may be imposed as a linear function of the c_i, but this does not complicate the problem appreciably.) See Appendix D and Yatchew and Bos (1997).

A similar procedure is available if the model is multiplicatively separable, that is, $f(x_a, x_b) = f_a(x_a) \cdot f_b(x_b)$. Note that this restriction is useful in imposing homotheticity.

5.3 Differencing

5.3.1 *Two Dimensions*

Consider again the pure nonparametric model

$$y = f(x) + \varepsilon, \tag{5.3.1}$$

where x is a vector of dimension 2. Suppose, as in Section 1.2, that we are interested in estimating the residual variance. We would like to ensure that the data $(y_1, x_1) \ldots . (y_n, x_n)$ have been reordered so that the x's are "close".

For illustrative purposes, suppose the x's constitute a uniform grid on the unit square. Each point may be thought of as "occupying" an area of $1/n$, and the distance between adjacent observations is therefore $1/n^{1/2}$.[5] Suppose further that the data have been reordered so that $\|x_i - x_{i-1}\| = n^{-1/2}$, where $\|\cdot\|$ denotes the usual Euclidean distance. If we use the first-order differencing estimator $s_{diff}^2 = \sum_{i=2}^n (y_i - y_{i-1})^2 / 2n$, then

$$\left(s_{diff}^2 - \sigma_\varepsilon^2\right) = \left(\frac{1}{2n}\sum_{i=2}^n (\varepsilon_i - \varepsilon_{i-1})^2 - \sigma_\varepsilon^2\right) + \frac{1}{2n}\sum_{i=2}^n (f(x_i) - f(x_{i-1}))^2$$
$$+ \frac{2}{2n}\sum_{i=2}^n (\varepsilon_i - \varepsilon_{i-1})(f(x_i) - f(x_{i-1})). \tag{5.3.2}$$

[5] If x is a scalar and the data are equally spaced on the unit interval, the distance between adjacent observations is $1/n$, which is much closer.

The first term on the right-hand-side is $O_P(n^{-1/2})$. Assume that f satisfies a Lipschitz constraint $|f(x_a) - f(x_b)| \leq L\|x_a - x_b\|$. Then for the second term we have

$$\frac{1}{2n}\sum_{i=2}^{n}(f(x_i) - f(x_{i-1}))^2 \leq \frac{1}{2n}\sum_{i=2}^{n} L^2\|x_i - x_{i-1}\|^2 = O\left(\frac{1}{n}\right). \tag{5.3.3}$$

Consider now

$$\begin{aligned} Var\left(\frac{2}{2n}\sum_{i=2}^{n}\varepsilon_i(f(x_i) - f(x_{i-1}))\right) &= \frac{\sigma_\varepsilon^2}{n^2}\sum_{i=2}^{n}(f(x_i) - f(x_{i-1}))^2 \\ &\leq \frac{\sigma_\varepsilon^2}{n^2}\sum_{i=2}^{n} L^2\|x_i - x_{i-1}\|^2 = O\left(\frac{1}{n^2}\right), \end{aligned} \tag{5.3.4}$$

from which we can conclude that the third term of (5.3.2) is $O_P(1/n)$.

The point of this exercise is that if x is two-dimensional, differencing removes the nonparametric effect sufficiently quickly, so that

$$\left(s_{diff}^2 - \sigma_\varepsilon^2\right) = \left(\frac{1}{2n}\sum_{i=2}^{n}(\varepsilon_i - \varepsilon_{i-1})^2 - \sigma_\varepsilon^2\right) + O\left(\frac{1}{n}\right) + O_P\left(\frac{1}{n}\right). \tag{5.3.5}$$

Compare this with the one-dimensional case in which the second and third terms are $O(1/n^2)$ and $O_P(1/n^{3/2})$, respectively.

5.3.2 *Higher Dimensions and the Curse of Dimensionality*

With n points distributed on the uniform grid in the unit cube in $\mathbb{R}^q$, each point continues to "occupy" a volume $1/n$, but the distance between adjacent observations is $1/n^{1/q}$ and $\sum(f(x_i) - f(x_{i-1}))^2 = O(n^{1-2/q})$. Thus, (5.3.3) becomes $O(1/n^{2/q})$, and the *variance* of the third term becomes $O(1/n^{1+2/q})$. Hence, with the x's lying in a q-dimensional cube, (5.3.5) becomes

$$\begin{aligned} \left(s_{diff}^2 - \sigma_\varepsilon^2\right) &= \left(\frac{1}{2n}\sum_{i=2}^{n}(\varepsilon_i - \varepsilon_{i-1})^2 - \sigma_\varepsilon^2\right) + O\left(\frac{1}{n^{2/q}}\right) + O_P\left(\frac{1}{n^{1/2+1/q}}\right) \\ &= O_P\left(\frac{1}{n^{1/2}}\right) + O\left(\frac{1}{n^{2/q}}\right) + O_P\left(\frac{1}{n^{1/2+1/q}}\right). \end{aligned} \tag{5.3.6}$$

How does the dimensionality of x affect the differencing estimator? First, s_{diff}^2 remains consistent regardless of the dimension of x. However, the bias term (the second term of (5.3.6)) converges to 0 more slowly as q increases. Second,

s^2_{diff} is $n^{1/2}$-consistent and

$$n^{1/2}\left(s^2_{diff} - \sigma^2_\varepsilon\right) - n^{1/2}\left(\frac{1}{2n}\sum_{i=2}^{n}(\varepsilon_i - \varepsilon_{i-1})^2 - \sigma^2_\varepsilon\right) \xrightarrow{P} 0 \qquad (5.3.7)$$

if q does not exceed 3. This is important because, whenever we have derived the large sample distribution of an estimator or test statistic that uses differencing, we have used the property that the nonparametric effect is being removed sufficiently quickly that it can be ignored. Essentially, this has required that a condition like (5.3.7) hold.

With random x's, similar results hold so long as reasonable ordering rules are used. If x is a scalar, the obvious ordering rule is $x_1 \leq \cdots \leq x_n$. If x is of dimension 2 or 3, we propose the following ordering rule based on the nearest-neighbor algorithm because it is simple to compute. (Other ordering rules for which the conclusion of Proposition 5.3.1 holds can easily be devised.)

Proposition 5.3.1: Suppose x has support the unit cube in $\mathbb{R}^q$ with density bounded away from 0. Select ϵ positive and arbitrarily close to 0. Cover the unit cube with subcubes of volume $1/n^{1-\epsilon}$, each with sides $1/n^{(1-\epsilon)/q}$. Within each subcube, construct a path using the nearest-neighbor algorithm. Following this, knit the paths together by joining endpoints in contiguous subcubes to obtain a reordering of all the data. Then, for any $\epsilon > 0$, $1/n \sum \|x_i - x_{i-1}\|^2 = O_P(n^{-2(1-\epsilon)/q})$.

Because ϵ may be chosen arbitrarily close to 0, we write $1/n \sum \|x_i - x_{i-1}\|^2 \cong O_P(n^{-2/q})$.

We may now assert that propositions in Chapter 4, where we considered only a scalar nonparametric variable, continue to hold so long as q, the number of nonparametric variables, does not exceed 3 and the preceding ordering rule is employed. In particular, the specification test of Section 4.3 and the analysis of the partial linear model of Section 4.5 continue to apply in this more general setting.[6]

However, it is important to keep in mind that, as dimension increases from 1 to 2 to 3, and the x's become progressively more dispersed, bias becomes a much more important issue. From this point of view, using a smoother that efficiently

[6] Additional testing procedures using differencing may be found in Yatchew (1988). Tests of significance, symmetry, and homogeneity are proposed. Although that paper uses sample splitting to obtain the distribution of the test statistic, the device is often unnecessary, and the full data set can be used to calculate the restricted and unrestricted estimators of the residual variance. A test of homotheticity may also be devised. Chapter 6 contains an extensive discussion of hypothesis testing.

removes nonparametric effects becomes more appealing. Nevertheless, there are applications for which differencing may be applied effectively as will be illustrated in Section 5.4.2.

5.4 Empirical Applications

5.4.1 *Hedonic Pricing of Housing Attributes*

Housing prices are very much affected by location, which is an effect that has no natural parametric specification. The price surface may be unimodal, multimodal, or have ridges (for example, prices along subway lines are often higher). Therefore, we include a two-dimensional nonparametric location effect $f(x_1, x_2)$, where x_1, x_2 are location coordinates.

The partial linear model that follows was estimated by Ho (1995) using semi-parametric least squares. The data consist of 92 detached homes in the Ottawa area that sold during 1987. The dependent variable y is *saleprice*; the z variables include lot size (*lotarea*), square footage of housing (*usespc*), number of bedrooms (*nrbed*), average neighborhood income (*avginc*), distance to highway (*dhwy*), presence of garage (*grge*), fireplace (*frplc*), or luxury appointments (*lux*).

Figure 5.1 contains estimates of a pure parametric model in which the location effect is modeled using a linear specification. It also contains estimates of the partial linear model. Having estimated the parametric effects using the double residual method, where *loess* is applied in the first stage, the constructed data $(y_i - z_i\hat{\beta}_{diff}, x_{1i}, x_{2i})$ are then smoothed to estimate the nonparametric effect. For an alternative semiparametric hedonic pricing model in the real estate market, see Anglin and Gencay (1996).

5.4.2 *Household Gasoline Demand in Canada*

We now respecify the model in (4.6.1), allowing *price* and *age* to appear non-parametrically:

$$\begin{aligned} dist = \; & f(price, age) + \beta_1\, income + \beta_2\, drivers + \beta_3\, hhsize \\ & + \beta_4\, youngsingle + \beta_5\, urban + monthly\ dummies + \varepsilon. \end{aligned} \tag{5.4.1}$$

The upper panel of Figure 5.2 illustrates the scatter of data on *price* and *age* and the path we take through the data points to apply differencing. Estimates of the parametric effects are provided using differencing and the double residual method. These do not differ substantially from those in which only *price* is modeled nonparametrically (see Figure 4.3). A test of the joint significance of the nonparametric variables using Proposition 4.3.1 yields a value of 5.96, which is strongly significant. A test of a fully parametric specification where

Estimated models					
$y = \alpha + z\beta + \gamma_1 x_1 + \gamma_2 x_2 + \varepsilon$			$y = z\beta + f(x_1, x_2) + \varepsilon$		
	OLS		Double residual using *loess*		
	Coeff	SE		Coeff	SE
α	74.0	18.0			
frplc	11.7	6.2	*frplc*	12.6	5.8
grge	11.8	5.1	*grge*	12.9	4.9
lux	60.7	10.5	*lux*	57.6	10.6
avginc	.478	.22	*avginc*	.60	.23
dhwy	−15.3	6.7	*dhwy*	1.5	21.4
lotarea	3.2	2.3	*lotarea*	3.1	2.2
nrbed	6.6	4.9	*nrbed*	6.4	4.8
usespc	21.1	11.0	*usespc*	24.7	10.6
γ_1	7.5	2.2			
γ_2	−3.2	2.5			
R^2	.62		R^2	.66	
s^2_{res}	424.3		s^2_{diff}	375.5	

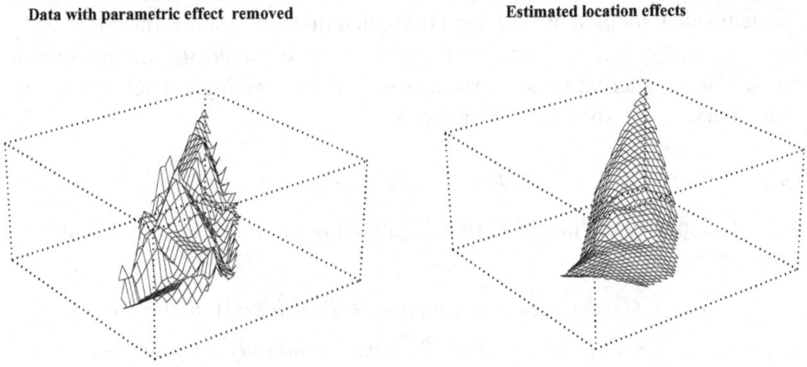

Under the null that location has no effect, (f is constant), $s^2_{res} = 507.4$. For the partial linear model we calculate $R^2 = 1 - s^2_{diff}/s^2_y$. The *loess* function in *S-Plus* is used in applying the double-residual method and to produce the "Estimated location effects" after removal of parametric effects. In the latter case, the dependent variable is $y_i - z_i\hat{\beta}_{diff}$.

Figure 5.1. Hedonic prices of housing attributes.

	Differencing		Double residual	
	Coef	SE	Coef	SE
income	0.287	0.021	0.291	0.021
drivers	0.532	0.035	0.571	0.033
hhsize	0.122	0.029	0.093	0.027
youngssingle	0.198	0.063	0.191	0.061
urban	−0.331	0.020	−0.332	0.020
R^2	.270		.263	
s^2	.496		.501	

Dependent variable is the log of distance traveled. Var(dependent variable) = .679. Order of differencing $m = 10$.

Upper panel right illustrates ordering of data: data are reordered first by age; then for even ages, data are reordered so that price is decreasing, and for odd ages, data are reordered so that price is increasing.

Lower panel right illustrates nonparametric estimate of *age* and *price* effects after removal of estimated parametric effects.

Monthly dummies were included in estimation but are not reported here.

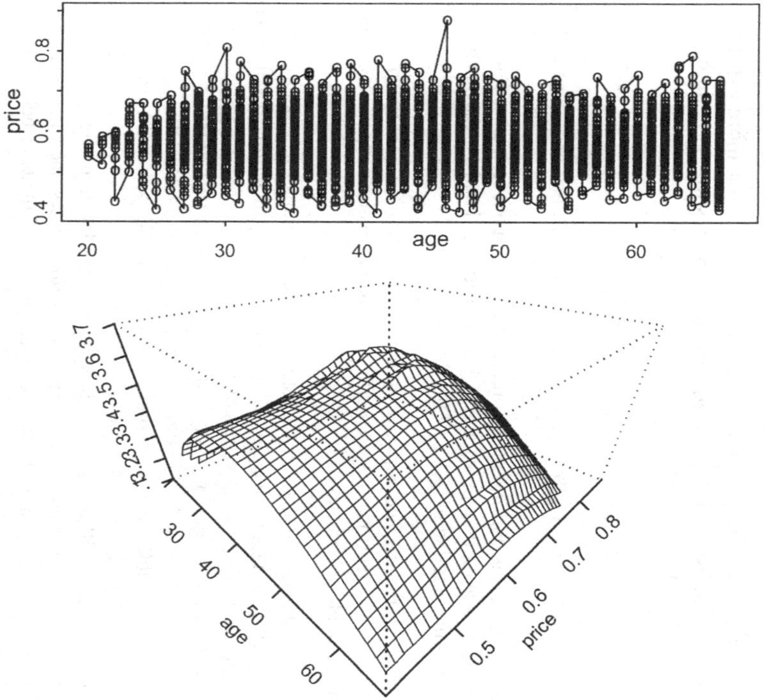

Figure 5.2. Household gasoline demand in Canada.

price and *age* enter log-linearly yields a statistic of 2.16. For more extensive analysis of these data, including the application of other testing procedures, see Yatchew and No (2001).

5.5 Exercises[7]

1. (a) Using a second-order Taylor series expansion for functions of two variables, verify (5.1.1).

(b) Assume that $p(x)$ is uniform on the unit square and that one is using the uniform kernel. Show that the denominator of (5.1.2) converges to 1 and that the numerator reduces to the first line of (5.1.1) if the dimension $d = 2$.

2. *Hedonic Housing Prices*: The objective is to estimate a partial linear specification in which the two-dimensional location effect is modeled using nonparametric and additively separable specifications.

(a) Open the data on housing prices. Estimate a fully parametric model using a linear specification for the location effect. Repeat using a quadratic specification. Calculate the corresponding values of R^2.

(b) Using the double residual method, estimate the partial linear model $y = z\beta + f(x_1, x_2) + \varepsilon$ contained in Figure 5.1. (Use *loess* to estimate the effects of the location variables x_1, x_2 on the dependent variable y and the parametric independent variables z.) Calculate R^2.

(c) Estimate the model allowing an additively separable location effect $y = z\beta + f_1(x_1) + f_2(x_2) + \varepsilon$. (The *gam* function in *S-Plus* allows one to estimate the nonparametric effects using alternative nonparametric estimators such as kernel, spline, or *loess*.) Calculate R^2.

3. *Household Gasoline Consumption*: The objective is to estimate a partial linear specification with a two-dimensional nonparametric effect.

(a) Estimate the gasoline consumption model (5.4.1) using differencing and the ordering procedure pictured in the upper panel of Figure 5.2. Calculate the implied R^2.

(b) Test the significance of the nonparametric effects using the specification test in Proposition 4.3.1.

(c) Reestimate using the double residual method. (You may use *loess* to estimate the first-stage nonparametric regressions.) Compare the estimates of parametric effects, their standard errors, and the corresponding R^2 with the results obtained in Part (a).

(d) Reestimate (5.4.1) using an additively separable specification for the nonparametric variables $f(price, age) = f_1(price) + f_2(age)$ and compare the resulting R^2 fit with those obtained in Parts (a) and (b).

(e) Estimate a fully parametric specification in which *price* and *age* enter log-linearly. Using the results of Part (a) and Proposition 4.3.1, perform a specification test to assess the adequacy of the parametric model.

[7] Data and sample programs for empirical exercises are available on the Web. See the Preface for details.

6 Constrained Estimation and Hypothesis Testing

6.1 The Framework

Economic theory rarely dictates a specific functional form. Instead, it typically specifies a collection of potentially related variables and general functional properties of the relationship. For example, economic theory may imply that the impact of a given variable is positive or negative (monotonicity), that doubling of prices and incomes should not alter consumption patterns (homogeneity of degree zero), that a proportionate increase in all inputs will increase output by the same proportion (constant returns to scale or, equivalently, homogeneity of degree one), that the effect of one variable does not depend on the level of another (additive separability), that the relationship possesses certain curvature properties such as concavity or convexity, or that observed consumption patterns result from optimization of utility subject to a budget constraint (the maximization hypothesis).

Empirical investigation is then required to assess whether one or another variable is significant or whether a particular property holds. In parametric regression modeling, a functional form is selected and properties are tested by imposing restrictions on the parameters. However, rejection of a hypothesis may be a consequence of the specific functional form that has been selected (but not implied by economic theory). Thus, although the translog production function is richer and more flexible than the Cobb–Douglas, it may not capture all the interesting features of the production process and may indeed lead to incorrect rejection of restrictions. Nonparametric procedures, on the other hand, provide both richer families of functions and more robust tests for assessing the implications of economic theory. Within this framework it is also possible to test whether a specific parametric form is adequate.

In the following sections, we therefore focus on the imposition of additional constraints on nonparametric regression estimation and testing of these constraints. However, before proceeding, we provide some standardized notation.

(The ideas are illustrated graphically in Figure 6.1.) Begin with the true model

$$y = f(x) + \varepsilon. \tag{6.1.1}$$

We will maintain that f lies in the set $\Im$, which is a set of smooth functions. The corresponding (unrestricted) estimator is denoted as $\hat{f}_{unr}$ with corresponding estimated residual variance

$$s_{unr}^2 = \frac{1}{n}\sum (y_i - \hat{f}_{unr}(x_i))^2. \tag{6.1.2}$$

We also want to estimate f subject to constraints of the form $f \in \bar{\Im} \subset \Im$, where the set $\bar{\Im}$ combines smoothness with additional functional properties. We denote the restricted estimator as $\hat{f}_{res}$ with corresponding estimated residual variance

$$s_{res}^2 = \frac{1}{n}\sum (y_i - \hat{f}_{res}(x_i))^2. \tag{6.1.3}$$

In some cases, it is a simple matter to ensure that the restricted estimator $\hat{f}_{res}$ satisfies these additional properties everywhere in its domain. In other cases, the estimator may only satisfy the restrictions asymptotically.

Our general null and alternative hypotheses will be of the form

$$\begin{aligned} H_0 &: f \in \bar{\Im} \\ H_1 &: f \in \Im. \end{aligned} \tag{6.1.4}$$

Define $\bar{f}$ to be the "closest" function to f in the restricted set $\bar{\Im}$ in the sense that

$$\bar{f} \textit{ satisfies } \min_{f^* \in \bar{\Im}} \int (f^* - f)^2 \, dx. \tag{6.1.5}$$

When the null hypothesis is true, $\bar{f} = f$ (since $f \in \bar{\Im}$), the integral is equal to zero and the restricted estimator converges to $\bar{f} = f$. If the null hypothesis is not true, we will assume $\hat{f}_{res}$ converges to $\bar{f} \neq f$.

One final important notational convention follows. Because certain tests will depend on the difference between the true regression function and the closest function in $\bar{\Im}$, we will reserve special notation for it. In particular,

$$f_\Delta = f - \bar{f}. \tag{6.1.6}$$

If the null hypothesis is true, $f_\Delta = 0$.

Much of the testing literature for parametric regression models can be embedded in a general and unified theoretical framework. The situation is somewhat less gratifying for nonparametric models, although several approaches show promise. We therefore begin by outlining two generic testing procedures that directly test hypotheses on f – one is analogous to a conventional goodness-of-fit

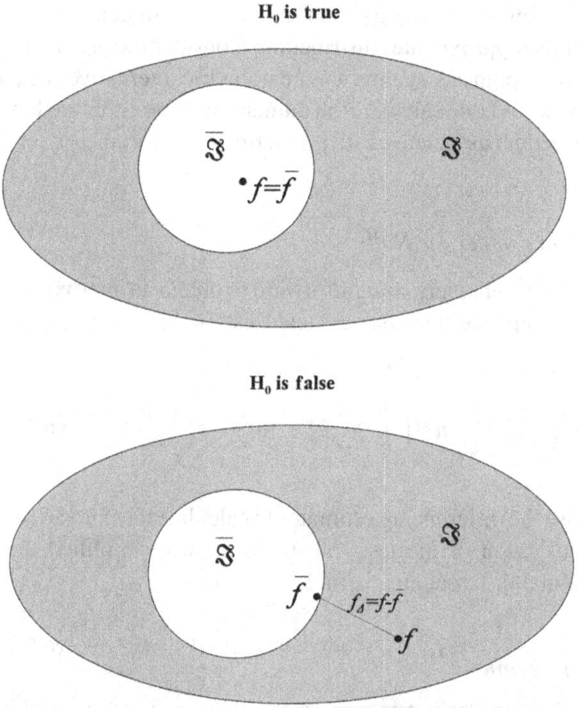

$\Im$ is the "unrestricted" set of functions, $\bar{\Im}$ is the "restricted" set of functions. Let $\bar{f}$ be the closest function in $\bar{\Im}$ to the true regression function f. If H_o is true, then f lies in $\Im$ and $\bar{f} = f$. If H_o is false, then the difference $f_\Delta = f - \bar{f} \neq 0$.

Figure 6.1. Constrained and unconstrained estimation and testing.

test (such as the familiar F or χ^2 tests); the other involves performing a residual regression. (For a third general approach, see Hall and Yatchew 2002.)

6.2 Goodness-of-Fit Tests

6.2.1 Parametric Goodness-of-Fit Tests

A natural basis for testing constraints imposed on the regression function is to compare the restricted estimate of the residual variance with the unrestricted estimate

$$\frac{n^{1/2}\left(s^2_{res} - s^2_{unr}\right)}{s^2_{unr}}. \tag{6.2.1}$$

The reader will recognize that, in the linear regression model with normal residuals, multiplying this statistic by $n^{1/2}/r$, where r is the number of restrictions, yields a statistic very similar to the traditional F-statistic.

The difficulty in applying the usual F-statistic in a nonparametric setting lies in the derivation of its (approximate) distribution. Consider the problem of testing a parametric null hypothesis against a nonparametric alternative (i.e., a specification test). How would one calculate the numerator degrees of freedom, that is, the degrees of freedom associated with restricting a nonparametric form to be parametric?[1]

6.2.2 *Rapid Convergence under the Null*

In some cases, however, it is relatively straightforward to obtain an approximate distribution for (6.2.1). Suppose that the restricted estimator $\hat{f}_{res}$ converges quickly enough so that

$$n^{1/2}\left(s_{res}^2 - \frac{1}{n}\sum_{i=1}^{n}\varepsilon_i^2\right) = n^{1/2}\left(\frac{1}{n}\sum_{i=1}^{n}\hat{\varepsilon}_i^2 - \frac{1}{n}\sum_{i=1}^{n}\varepsilon_i^2\right) \xrightarrow{P} 0. \tag{6.2.2}$$

Furthermore, if we use the differencing estimator to calculate the unrestricted variance, then the distribution of the test statistic is greatly simplified. For example, if we use optimal differencing coefficients, then

$$n^{1/2}\left(s_{diff}^2 - \frac{\varepsilon'\varepsilon}{n} + \frac{1}{mn}\varepsilon'\left(L_1 + L_2 + \cdots + L_m\right)\varepsilon\right) \xrightarrow{P} 0. \tag{6.2.3}$$

Differencing removes the nonparametric regression effect sufficiently quickly so that (6.2.3) holds.[2] If we replace s_{unr}^2 with s_{diff}^2 and combine (6.2.2) and (6.2.3), the numerator of (6.2.1) becomes

$$n^{1/2}\left(s_{res}^2 - s_{diff}^2\right) \cong \frac{1}{mn^{1/2}}\varepsilon'\left(L_1 + L_2 + \cdots + L_m\right)\varepsilon, \tag{6.2.4}$$

and it is easy to show that the right-hand side is approximately $N\left(0, \sigma_\varepsilon^4/m\right)$, in which case

$$V = (mn)^{1/2}\frac{\left(s_{res}^2 - s_{diff}^2\right)}{s_{diff}^2} \xrightarrow{D} N(0,1). \tag{6.2.5}$$

For arbitrary differencing coefficients satisfying (4.1.1), a similar argument yields

$$V = \left(\frac{n}{4\delta}\right)^{1/2}\frac{\left(s_{res}^2 - s_{diff}^2\right)}{s_{diff}^2} \xrightarrow{D} N(0,1), \tag{6.2.6}$$

1 Although, a number of authors have proposed that this be done by calculating the trace of certain "smoother" matrices. See Cleveland (1979), Cleveland and Devlin (1988), and Hastie and Tibshirani (1990, pp. 52–55 and Appendix B).

2 See (4.2.10a) and Lemmas B.2 and B.3 in Appendix B.

where δ is defined in (4.1.6). This is of course precisely the specification test we developed in Section 4.3 except that now the restrictions are not necessarily parametric. They need only be such that the convergence is fast enough to produce (6.2.2).

We have already used this idea to produce a simple test of equality of regression functions in Section 4.4. We can also use it to test other restrictions such as monotonicity, concavity, or additive separability. As in Section 4.3, the test can readily be modified to incorporate heteroskedasticity. Finally, we note that the power of the test can be increased by permitting the order of differencing m to increase with sample size.

6.3 Residual Regression Tests

6.3.1 *Overview*

An alternative approach used by Li (1994), Fan and Li (1996), and Zheng (1996) begins by rewriting the regression model $y = f(x) + \varepsilon$ as

$$y = \bar{f}(x) + [f(x) - \bar{f}(x) + \varepsilon] = \bar{f}(x) + f_{\Delta}(x) + \varepsilon. \qquad (6.3.1)$$

We assume that the restricted regression estimator $\hat{f}_{res}$ estimates $\bar{f}$ consistently and note that if the null hypothesis is true, that is, if $f \in \bar{\Im}$, then $f_{\Delta} = 0$. Thus, if we perform an "auxiliary" regression of the estimated residuals $y_i - \hat{f}_{res}(x_i)$ on x_i to estimate f_{Δ} and perform a significance test, we will have a test of the null hypothesis $f \in \bar{\Im}$.[3]

Equivalently, observe that

$$\begin{aligned} E_{\varepsilon,x}[(y - \bar{f}(x))E_{\varepsilon}[y - \bar{f}(x) \mid x]] &= E_{\varepsilon,x}[(y - \bar{f}(x))f_{\Delta}(x)] \\ &= E_x f_{\Delta}^2(x) \geq 0, \end{aligned} \qquad (6.3.2)$$

where the expression equals zero only if the null hypothesis is true. One way to obtain a sample analogue of the second expression is to calculate

$$\frac{1}{n}\sum (y_i - \hat{f}_{res}(x_i))(\hat{f}_{unr}(x_i) - \hat{f}_{res}(x_i)). \qquad (6.3.3)$$

Note that $\hat{f}_{unr} - \hat{f}_{res}$ is an estimator of $f_{\Delta} = f - \bar{f}$.

A closely related procedure uses the sample analogue

$$\frac{1}{n}\sum (y_i - \hat{f}_{res}(x_i))\hat{f}_{\Delta}(x_i), \qquad (6.3.4)$$

where $\hat{f}_{\Delta}$ is obtained by performing an (unrestricted) nonparametric regression of $y_i - \hat{f}_{res}(x_i)$ on the x_i.

[3] The idea, of course, is not new and has been exploited extensively for specification testing in parametric regression models (see, e.g., MacKinnon 1992).

6.3.2 *U-statistic Test – Scalar x's, Moving Average Smoother*

We begin with the case in which x is a scalar, say, in the unit interval. We assume the data have been reordered so that the x_i are in increasing order. Consider the moving average smoother (Section 3.1) of f_Δ given by

$$\hat{f}_\Delta(x_i) = \frac{1}{k} \sum_{j=\underline{i}, j \neq i}^{\bar{i}} (y_j - \hat{f}_{res}(x_j)), \tag{6.3.5}$$

where this time k is even; $\underline{i} = i - k/2$ and $\bar{i} = i + k/2$ denote the lower and upper limits of summations. We are averaging k values of $(y_j - \hat{f}_{res}(x_j))$ in the neighborhood of x_i. (Momentarily, we will explain why the summation in (6.3.5) excludes the ith observation.) Then (6.3.4) becomes

$$U = \frac{1}{kn} \sum_i \sum_{j=\underline{i}, j \neq i}^{\bar{i}} (y_i - \hat{f}_{res}(x_i))(y_j - \hat{f}_{res}(x_j)). \tag{6.3.6}$$

Using the substitution $y_i - \hat{f}_{res}(x_i) = \varepsilon_i + (f(x_i) - \hat{f}_{res}(x_i))$, we expand U to obtain

$$\begin{aligned} U &\cong U_1 + U_2 + U_3 \\ &= \frac{1}{kn} \sum_i \sum_{j=\underline{i}, j \neq i}^{\bar{i}} \varepsilon_i \varepsilon_j \\ &\quad + \frac{1}{kn} \sum_i \sum_{j=\underline{i}, j \neq i}^{\bar{i}} (f(x_i) - \hat{f}_{res}(x_i))(f(x_j) - \hat{f}_{res}(x_j)) \qquad (6.3.7) \\ &\quad + \frac{2}{kn} \sum_i \sum_{j=\underline{i}, j \neq i}^{\bar{i}} \varepsilon_i (f(x_j) - \hat{f}_{res}(x_j)). \end{aligned}$$

The following results can be demonstrated:

$$U_1 \sim N\left(0, \frac{2\sigma_\varepsilon^4}{kn}\right)$$

$$U_2 = O_P\left(\frac{1}{n} \sum (f(x_i) - \hat{f}_{res}(x_i))^2\right) \tag{6.3.8}$$

$$U_3 = \frac{1}{n^{1/2}} O_P\left(\left(\frac{1}{n} \sum (f(x_i) - \hat{f}_{res}(x_i))^2\right)^{1/2}\right).$$

The random variable U_1 is a U-statistic, and its distribution has been studied extensively.[4] Omission of the ith term avoids terms like ε_i^2 and thus ensures that the mean of U_1 is zero. A modicum of insight into the asymptotic distribution of U_1 may be gleaned by the following reasoning. U_1 is a quadratic form for which the interposing matrix is related to the smoother matrix S for the moving average estimator defined in (3.1.12). It is band diagonal with 0's on the main diagonal, $1/kn$ on the $k/2$ diagonals adjacent to the main diagonal, and 0's everywhere else. Thus, summing each diagonal, we have $U_1 \cong 1/kn \sum_i 2\varepsilon_i\varepsilon_{i-1} + \cdots + 2\varepsilon_i\varepsilon_{i-k/2}$. Note that U_1 is an average of about $kn/2$ distinct objects that are uncorrelated but not independent. Next note that $Var\,(\sum_i 2\varepsilon_i\varepsilon_{i-1} + \cdots + 2\varepsilon_i\varepsilon_{i-k/2}) \cong 4\sigma^4 kn/2$, and thus $Var\,(U_1) \cong 2\sigma^4/kn$. Finally, apply a central limit theorem for dependent processes such as those in McLeish (1974). Keep in mind that the number of terms under the summation sign is growing as k grows.

Suppose now the null hypothesis is true and $\hat{f}_{res} \to f$. If this convergence is sufficiently rapid, the distribution of U is determined by the distribution of U_1, which will form the basis for tests of a variety of null hypotheses.

Put another way, because $k^{1/2}n^{1/2}U_1$ has constant variance, the objective is to select a restricted estimator $\hat{f}_{res}$ that converges to f sufficiently quickly (under the null hypothesis) and a rate of growth for k so that $k^{1/2}n^{1/2}U_2$ and $k^{1/2}n^{1/2}U_3$ both converge to zero. (Note that if the null hypothesis is false, then $k^{1/2}n^{1/2}U$ diverges.)

Let us pause for a moment to consider a special case. If the restricted estimate is a parametric model, then U_2 and U_3 are $O_P(n^{-1})$.[5] Since (for consistency of the estimator) we require $k/n \to 0$, then $k^{1/2}n^{1/2}U_2$ and $k^{1/2}n^{1/2}U_3$ both go to zero. Hence $k^{1/2}n^{1/2}U \sim N(0, 2\sigma_\varepsilon^4)$. This result is a simple variant of the Fan and Li (1996) specification test discussed below.

6.3.3 *U-statistic Test – Vector x's, Kernel Smoother*

We now assume the x_i are random vectors with probability law $p\,(x)$ and $dim\,(x) = d$. We will use a product kernel estimator (see Section 5.1).

[4] The U signifies that such statistics were designed to be unbiased estimators of distribution characteristics. The seminal paper is due to Hoeffding (1948). See Serfling (1980, Chapter 5) for a general introduction as well as Lee (1990). The results on U-statistics most relevant here are contained in Hall (1984) and De Jong (1987).

[5] For example, if we are fitting a mean, then, using (6.3.8), $U_2 = O_P((\bar{y} - \mu)^2) = O_P(n^{-1})$ and $U_3 = n^{-1/2}O_P((\bar{y} - \mu)^2)^{1/2} = n^{-1/2}O_P(n^{-1/2}) = O_P(n^{-1})$.

Consider

$$\frac{1}{\lambda^d n}\sum_{j\neq i}(y_j - \hat{f}_{res}(x_j))\prod_{k=1}^{d} K\left(\frac{x_{jk}-x_{ik}}{\lambda}\right). \tag{6.3.9}$$

In contrast to (6.3.5), this is not a consistent estimator of $f_\Delta(x_i)$ (the denominator of the kernel estimator is missing; see (5.1.2)). However, it is a consistent estimator of $f_\Delta(x_i)p(x_i)$. The conditional moment (replacing 6.3.2)), which motivates the test statistic, is given by

$$E_{\varepsilon,x}[(y-\bar{f}(x))E_\varepsilon[y-\bar{f}(x)\,|\,x]p(x)] = E_x\left[f_\Delta^2(x)p(x)\right] \geq 0, \tag{6.3.10}$$

where equality holds only if the null hypothesis is true. The U statistic becomes

$$U = \frac{1}{\lambda^d n^2}\sum_i\sum_{j\neq i}(y_i - \hat{f}_{res}(x_i))(y_j - \hat{f}_{res}(x_j)) \times \prod_{k=1}^{d} K\left(\frac{x_{jk}-x_{ik}}{\lambda}\right). \tag{6.3.11}$$

Its behavior again depends on the rate at which $\hat{f}_{res}$ converges to f (as in (6.3.8)). We now state the more general result. Suppose

$$\frac{1}{n}\sum(f(x_i) - \hat{f}_{res}(x_i))^2 = O_P(n^{-r}), \tag{6.3.12}$$

and

$$n\lambda^{d/2}n^{-r} = n^{1-r}\lambda^{d/2} \to 0, \tag{6.3.13}$$

then,

$$n\lambda^{d/2}U \sim N\left(0, 2\sigma_\varepsilon^4\int p^2(x)\int K^2(u)\right), \tag{6.3.14}$$

and $\sigma_U^2 = Var(U) = 2\sigma_\varepsilon^4\int p^2(x)\int K^2(u)/\lambda^d n^2$ may be estimated using

$$\hat{\sigma}_U^2 = \frac{2}{n^4\lambda^{2d}}\sum_i\sum_{j\neq i}(y_i - \hat{f}_{res}(x_i))^2(y_j - \hat{f}_{res}(x_j))^2 \times \prod_{k=1}^{d} K^2\left(\frac{x_{jk}-x_{ik}}{\lambda}\right). \tag{6.3.15}$$

We can apply (6.3.11) to (6.3.15) to produce tests of a broad variety of hypotheses, including specification, significance, additive separability, monotonicity, concavity, homotheticity, and demand theory. In each case we need to produce a restricted estimator with a sufficiently rapid rate of convergence.

6.4 Specification Tests[6]

Assume $g(x, \theta)$ is a known function of its arguments, where θ is a finite dimensional parameter vector. In this section we are concerned with tests of

$$H_0 : f \in \bar{\Im} = \{f \in \Im \mid f = g(\cdot, \theta)\ \textit{for some}\ \theta\}. \tag{6.4.1}$$

Let $\hat{\theta}$ be an estimator of the parameter θ, such as nonlinear least squares, which converges at a rate $n^{-1/2}$ to $\bar{\theta}$; $\bar{\theta} = \theta$ if H_0 is true.

6.4.1 *Bierens (1990)*

If the parametric specification under the null hypothesis (6.4.1) is true, then $E_\varepsilon[y - g(x, \bar{\theta}) \mid x] = E_\varepsilon[y - g(x, \theta) \mid x] = E_\varepsilon[\varepsilon \mid x] = 0$ for all x. Suppose that the null hypothesis is false and that the probability that $E_{\varepsilon,x}[y - g(x, \bar{\theta}) \mid x] = 0$ is less than 1. Then, for (almost) any real number τ, the following holds:

$$E_{\varepsilon,x}[e^{\tau x}(y - g(x, \bar{\theta}))] = E_x[e^{\tau x}(f(x) - g(x, \bar{\theta}))] \neq 0. \tag{6.4.2}$$

Bierens proposes a test based on $n^{1/2}$ times the sample analogue of the left expression

$$B(\tau) = n^{1/2}\frac{1}{n}\sum e^{\tau x_i}(y_i - g(x_i, \hat{\theta})). \tag{6.4.3}$$

He then demonstrates that, under the null hypothesis, $B(\tau)$ is asymptotically normal with mean zero and variance given by

$$\sigma^2_{B(\tau)} = E_{\varepsilon,x}\left[(y - g(x, \theta))^2 \cdot \left(e^{\tau x} - b(\tau)' A^{-1}\frac{dg(x, \theta)}{d\theta}\right)^2\right], \tag{6.4.4}$$

where

$$b(\tau) = E_x\left[e^{\tau x}\frac{dg(x, \theta)}{d\theta}\right] \qquad A = E_x\left[\frac{dg(x, \theta)}{d\theta}\right]\left[\frac{dg(x, \theta)}{d\theta}\right]'. \tag{6.4.5}$$

Estimates of $b(\tau)$ and A, say $\hat{b}(\tau)$, $\hat{A}$, are obtained by using sample analogues and replacing θ with $\hat{\theta}$ from a parametric estimation procedure. The variance

[6] There is a huge literature on specification testing. In this section we focus specifically on tests in which the alternative involves a nonparametric component to the regression function. Procedures not discussed here but worthy of note include Azzalini, Bowman, and Härdle (1989); Eubank and Spiegelman (1990); Lee (1991); Eubank and Hart (1992); Wooldridge (1992); Azzalini and Bowman (1993); Gozalo (1993); Whang and Andrews (1993); Horowitz and Härdle (1994); Bierens and Ploeberger (1997); Dette (1999); Ellison and Ellison (2000); Aït-Sahalia, Bickel, and Stoker (2001); Horowitz and Spokoiny (2001); and Stengos and Sun (2001). See also Yatchew (1988, 1992).

Table 6.1. *Bierens (1990) specification test – implementation.*

Test Statistic: Test $H_0 : E(y \mid x) = \theta_1 + \theta_2 x$; under H_0:

$$\frac{B(\tau)}{\hat{\sigma}_{B(\tau)}} = \frac{n^{1/2}}{\hat{\sigma}_{B(\tau)}} \frac{1}{n} \sum e^{\tau x_i} (y_i - \hat{\theta}_1 - \hat{\theta}_2 x_i) \sim N(0,1)$$

$\hat{\theta}_1, \hat{\theta}_2$ are OLS estimators,

$$\hat{\sigma}^2_{B(\tau)} = \frac{1}{n} \sum (y_i - \hat{\theta}_1 - \hat{\theta}_2 x_i)^2 \cdot \left(e^{\tau x_i} - \hat{b}(\tau)' \hat{A}^{-1} \begin{bmatrix} 1 \\ x_i \end{bmatrix} \right)^2$$

$$\hat{b}(\tau) = \begin{bmatrix} \frac{1}{n} \sum e^{\tau x_i} \\ \frac{1}{n} \sum x_i e^{\tau x_i} \end{bmatrix} \qquad \hat{A} = \begin{bmatrix} 1 & \frac{1}{n} \sum x_i \\ \frac{1}{n} \sum x_i & \frac{1}{n} \sum x_i^2 \end{bmatrix}$$

$\sigma^2_{B(\tau)}$ is estimated using

$$\hat{\sigma}^2_{B(\tau)} = \frac{1}{n} \sum (y_i - g(x_i, \hat{\theta}))^2 \cdot \left(e^{\tau x_i} - \hat{b}(\tau)' \hat{A}^{-1} \frac{dg(x_i, \theta)}{d\theta} \right)^2 . \tag{6.4.6}$$

What we have not dealt with so far is how to select τ. Bierens proposes that τ be selected to maximize $B^2(\tau)/\hat{\sigma}^2_{B(\tau)}$. The resulting test procedure is consistent, does not require nonparametric estimation of the regression function, and is applicable if x is a vector (see Table 6.1 for implementation).

6.4.2 *Härdle and Mammen (1993)*

Härdle and Mammen base their specification test on the integrated squared difference $I = \int (\hat{f}_{res}(x) - \hat{f}_{unr}(x))^2 dx$. Here $\hat{f}_{unr}$ is a kernel estimator of f, and $\hat{f}_{res}$ is (for technical reasons a smoothed version of) the parametric estimate $g(x, \hat{\theta})$. Their statistic is given by

$$I = n\lambda^{1/2} \int (\mathrm{K}g(x; \hat{\theta}) - \hat{f}_{unr}(x))^2 \pi(x)\, dx, \tag{6.4.7}$$

where $\pi(x)$ is a weight function selected by the user that permits discrepancies between the nonparametric and parametric estimators to be weighted differently in different parts of the domain, and

$$\mathrm{K}g(x, \hat{\theta}) = \frac{\sum_i K((x - x_i)/\lambda)\, g(x_i, \hat{\theta})}{\sum_i K((x - x_i)/\lambda)}, \tag{6.4.8}$$

where K is the kernel function and $\lambda = O(n^{-1/5})$.[7]

Let $K^{(2)}(\cdot)$ and $K^{(4)}(\cdot)$ be the 2-times and 4-times convolution products of K.[8] Let $p(x)$ be the density of x, which is assumed to have bounded support (e.g., the unit interval), with $p(x)$ bounded away from zero on the support. Then in large samples and under the null hypothesis that the parametric specification is correct,

$$I \sim N\left(\lambda^{-1/2} K^{(2)}(0)\sigma_\varepsilon^2 \int \pi(x)/p(x)\,dx,\right.$$
$$\left. 2K^{(4)}(0)\sigma_\varepsilon^4 \int \pi^2(x)/p^2(x)\,dx\right). \qquad (6.4.9)$$

All elements can be either computed or estimated (see Table 6.2 for implementation). If one sets $\pi(x) = p(x)$, then greater weight is assigned in regions where there are likely to be more observations and, hence, presumably, the discrepancy is being estimated more accurately. In this case, the integrals in (6.4.9) become $\int dx$, and if one uses the uniform kernel the result simplifies to

$$I \sim N\left(1/2\,\lambda^{-1/2}\sigma_\varepsilon^2 \int dx,\quad 2/3\,\sigma_\varepsilon^4 \int dx\right). \qquad (6.4.10)$$

In simulations, Härdle and Mammen found that this normal approximation is substantially inferior to bootstrapping the critical values of the test statistic. They demonstrated that the "wild" bootstrap (see Chapter 8) yields a test procedure that has correct asymptotic size under the null and is consistent under the alternative. (They also demonstrated that conventional bootstrap procedures fail.) Finally, the test can be applied to circumstances under which x is a vector and ε is heteroskedastic.

6.4.3 *Hong and White (1995)*

Hong and White proposed tests based on series expansions, in particular the flexible Fourier form (Gallant 1981). To test a quadratic null, the unrestricted

7 Härdle and Mammen (1993) impose the following conditions: K is symmetric, twice continuously differentiable, integrates to one, and has compact support. The last condition would, strictly speaking, rule out the normal kernel.

8 Recall that $K(\cdot)$ may be viewed as a density. Let u_1, u_2, u_3, u_4 be i.i.d. with density $K(\cdot)$. The convolution products $K^{(2)}(\cdot)$ and $K^{(4)}(\cdot)$ are the densities of $u_1 + u_2$ and $u_1 + u_2 + u_3 + u_4$, respectively. We will need to evaluate these densities at 0. If $K(\cdot)$ is the uniform density on $[-1, 1]$, then $K^{(2)}(0) = 1/2$ and $K^{(4)}(0) = 1/3$. If $K(\cdot)$ is $N(0, 1)$, then $K^{(2)}(0) = 1/(2\sqrt{\pi})$ and $K^{(4)}(0) = 1/(2\sqrt{2\pi})$.

Table 6.2. *Härdle and Mammen (1993) specification test – implementation.*

Test Statistic: Test $H_0 : E(y \mid x) = \theta_0 + \theta_1 x$; using H_o using a uniform kernel:[a]

$$I = n\lambda^{1/2} \int (K(\hat{\theta}_0 + \hat{\theta}_1 x) - \hat{f}_{unr}(x))^2 \hat{p}(x)\, dx$$
$$\sim N\left({}^{1}\!/_{2}\,\lambda^{-1/2}\sigma_\varepsilon^2 \int dx,\ {}^{2}\!/_{3}\,\sigma_\varepsilon^4 \int dx \right).$$

1. Regress y on x to obtain $\hat{\theta}_0 + \hat{\theta}_1 x$.
2. Perform kernel regression using uniform kernel on $(\hat{\theta}_0 + \hat{\theta}_1 x_i, x_i)$ to obtain the smoothed parametric estimate $K(\hat{\theta}_0 + \hat{\theta}_1 x)$.
3. Perform kernel regression using uniform kernel on (y_i, x_i) to obtain $\hat{f}_{unr}(x)$ and s^2_{unr}.
4. Obtain $\hat{p}(x)$ using a kernel density estimation procedure.
5. Calculate $\left(I - {}^{1}\!/_{2}\,\lambda^{-1/2} s^2_{unr} \int dx\right) / \left({}^{2}\!/_{3}\, s^4_{unr} \int dx\right)^{1/2}$ and compare to $N(0, 1)$.

[a] Any symmetric twice-differentiable kernel with compact support may be used, but then the constants in the asymptotic approximation will change.

regression model is given by

$$f(x) = \theta_0 + \theta_1 x + \theta_2 x^2 + \sum_{j=1}^{N^*} Y_{1j} \cos(jx) + Y_{2j} \sin(jx), \qquad (6.4.11)$$

where the number of unknown coefficients $3 + 2N^*$ increases with sample size. The rate at which N^* may be permitted to grow depends on the null hypothesis being tested. Let s^2_{unr} be obtained by estimating model (6.4.11) and s^2_{res} by estimating the parametric regression. Then in large samples

$$\frac{n\left(s^2_{res} - s^2_{unr}\right)}{s^2_{unr}} \sim N(3 + 2N^*, 2(3 + 2N^*)). \qquad (6.4.12)$$

Table 6.3 provides implementation details.

6.4.4 *Li (1994) and Zheng (1996)*

These authors proposed specification tests based on residual regression, which is discussed in a general setting in Section 6.3. If x is a scalar, the test statistic U of (6.3.11) becomes

$$U = \frac{1}{n} \sum_i (y_i - g(x_i, \hat{\theta}))$$
$$\times \left[\frac{1}{\lambda n} \sum_{j \neq 1} (y_j - g(x_j, \hat{\theta})) K\left(\frac{x_i - x_j}{\lambda} \right) \right]. \qquad (6.4.13)$$

Table 6.3. *Hong and White (1995) specification test – implementation.*

Test Statistic: Test $H_0 : E(y \mid x) = \theta_0 + \theta_1 x + \theta_2 x^2$; under the null:[a]

$$\frac{n\left(s_{res}^2 - s_{unr}^2\right)}{s_{unr}^2} \sim N(3 + 2N^*, 2(3 + 2N^*)).$$

1. Rescale the data on x so that $x_i \in [0, 2\pi]$.
2. Estimate $y = \theta_0 + \theta_1 x + \theta_2 x^2 + \varepsilon$ by OLS to obtain s_{res}^2.
3. Determine number of terms in unrestricted model: $N^* = O(n^{.10}\log(n))$.
4. Generate explanatory variables $\cos(jx_i)$, $\sin(jx_i)$, $j = 1, \ldots N^*$.
5. Perform the (unrestricted) regression $y = \theta_o + \theta_1 x + \theta_2 x^2 + \sum_{j=1}^{N^*} \gamma_{1j}\cos(jx) + \gamma_{2j}\sin(jx) + \varepsilon$ to obtain s_{unr}^2.
6. Calculate test statistic and perform a one-tailed test using a critical value from the $N(0, 1)$.

[a] If one is testing the linear model, set $\theta_2 = 0$, $N^* = O(n^{.19}\log(n))$.

Table 6.4. *Li (1994) and Zheng (1996) residual regression test of specification – implementation.*

Test Statistic: Test $H_0 : E(y \mid x) = \theta_0 + \theta_1 x$; under H_o using a uniform kernel:

$$U = \frac{1}{n}\sum_i (y_i - \hat{\theta}_o - \hat{\theta}_1 x_i)\left[\frac{1}{\lambda n}\sum_{j \neq i}(y_j - \hat{\theta}_o - \hat{\theta}_1 x_j)\mathrm{K}_{ij}\right]$$
$$\sim N\left(0, \frac{2\sigma_\varepsilon^4 \int p^2(x) \int K^2}{\lambda n^2}\right),$$

where K_{ij} is defined below.

1. Perform (restricted) regression y on x to obtain $\hat{\theta}_o + \hat{\theta}_1 x_i$.
2. Calculate the kernel matrix K_{ij}, where
   $\mathrm{K}_{ij} = 1/2 \quad if \quad |x_j - x_i| \leq \lambda \quad j \neq i$ (note that diagonal elements $\mathrm{K}_{ii} = 0$)
   $\mathrm{K}_{ij} = 0$ otherwise.
3. Calculate U.
4. Define $\sigma_U^2 = Var(U) = 2\sigma_\varepsilon^4 \int p^2(x) \int K^2/\lambda n^2$ and estimate it using

$$\hat{\sigma}_U^2 = \frac{2}{n^4\lambda^2}\sum_i \sum_{j \neq i}(y_i - \hat{\theta}_o - \hat{\theta}_1 x_i)^2 (y_j - \hat{\theta}_o - \hat{\theta}_1 x_j)^2 \mathrm{K}_{ij}^2.$$

5. Perform a one-sided test comparing $U/\hat{\sigma}_U$ with the critical value from the $N(0, 1)$.

The term in square brackets is a consistent estimator of $f_\Delta(x)p(x) = (f(x) - g(x,\bar{\theta}))p(x)$. Under the null hypothesis this is the zero function, and we have from (6.3.14)

$$n\lambda^{1/2}U \sim N\left(0, 2\sigma_\varepsilon^4 \int p^2(x) \int K^2(u)\right). \tag{6.4.14}$$

Implementation details are contained in Table 6.4. We note that the test is valid under heteroskedasticity.

6.5 Significance Tests

Let us begin by disposing of significance tests where the null hypothesis is of the form $f(x) = \mu$, and μ is a constant. This null model constitutes the simplest possible parametric specification, and so all specification testing methodologies proposed in the previous section immediately yield tests of significance of this kind.[9] If x is a vector, then this null hypothesis corresponds to testing the joint significance of all the explanatory variables.

What is more challenging – and more useful – is the derivation of tests of significance for a subset of the explanatory variables. Consider the following hypotheses:

$$\begin{aligned} H_0 &: f \in \bar{\Im} = \{f \in \Im \mid f(x_1, x_2) \textit{ is smooth and constant wrt } x_2\} \\ H_1 &: f \in \Im = \{f \mid f(x_1, x_2) \textit{ is smooth}\}. \end{aligned} \tag{6.5.1}$$

As before, $\bar{f}$ is the "closest" function to f, the true regression function, in the restricted set $\bar{\Im}$ (Eq. (6.1.5)). If the null hypothesis is true, then $\bar{f}(x) = f(x)$ for all x.

The residual regression tests of Section 6.3 may be used for testing hypotheses of this type. To test hypotheses like the null in (6.5.1), we may apply the results in (6.3.11) through (6.3.15). The restricted estimator under the null $\hat{f}_{res}$ is any one-dimensional nonparametric estimator that converges, say, at the optimal rate. Under the alternative, a two-dimensional kernel estimator is applied. Implementation details are contained in Table 6.5. Additional tests of significance may be found in Racine (1997), Lavergne and Vuong (2000), Aït-Sahalia et al. (2001), and Delgado and Manteiga (2001).

[9] For example, the Bierens (1990) test statistic reduces to

$$\frac{B(\tau)}{\hat{\sigma}_{B(\tau)}} = \frac{n^{1/2}\frac{1}{n}\sum_i e^{\tau x_i}(y_i - \bar{y})}{\left(\frac{1}{n}\sum_i (y_i - \bar{y})^2\left(e^{\tau x_i} - \frac{1}{n}\sum_j e^{\tau x_j}\right)^2\right)^{1/2}} \sim N(0,1),$$

where $\bar{y}$ is the sample mean.

Table 6.5. *Residual regression test of significance – implementation.*[a]

Test Statistic: Test $H_0 : f(x_1, x_2)$ is smooth and constant with respect to x_2, against $H_1 : f(x_1, x_2)$ is smooth; using the uniform kernel, under the null we have

$$U = \frac{1}{n}\sum_i (y_i - \hat{f}_{res}(x_{1i}))\left[\frac{1}{\lambda^2 n}\sum_{j\neq i}(y_j - \hat{f}_{res}(x_{ij}))\mathrm{K}_{ij}\right] \sim N\left(0, \frac{2\sigma^4 \int p^2(x_1, x_2)\int K^2}{\lambda^2 n^2}\right),$$

where K_{ij} is defined below.

1. Perform the restricted regression of y on x_1 to obtain $\hat{f}_{res}(x_1)$.
   The estimator may be a kernel regression, nonparametric least squares, or another estimator that converges at the optimal rate.
2. Calculate the product kernel matrix K_{ij}:
   $\mathrm{K}_{ij} = 1/4 \quad if \quad |x_{1i} - x_{1j}| \leq \lambda \quad and \quad |x_{2i} - x_{2j}| \leq \lambda \quad i \neq j$
   $\mathrm{K}_{ij} = 0$ otherwise.
3. Calculate U.
4. Determine λ. For example, if the $\hat{f}_{res}$ was obtained using an optimal bandwidth, then its rate of convergence is $O_P(n^{-4/5})$, that is, $r = 4/5$. Now using (6.3.13), select λ so that $\lambda n^{1/5} \to 0$, thus $\lambda = O(n^{-1/4})$ suffices.
5. Estimate $\sigma_U^2 = Var(U)$ using
   $$\hat{\sigma}_U^2 = \frac{2}{n^4\lambda^4}\sum_i\sum_{j\neq i}(y_i - \hat{f}_{res}(x_{1i}))^2(y_j - \hat{f}_{res}(x_{1j}))^2\mathrm{K}_{ij}^2.$$
6. Perform a one-sided test comparing $U/\hat{\sigma}_U$ with the critical value from the $N(0, 1)$.

[a] The test described here is similar to those found in Li (1994), Fan and Li (1996), and Zheng (1996).

6.6 Monotonicity, Concavity, and Other Restrictions[10]

6.6.1 *Isotonic Regression*

Suppose we are interested in imposing monotonicity on our estimate of the regression function and in testing this property, that is,

$$\begin{aligned} H_0 &: f \in \bar{\Im} = \{f \in \Im \mid f \textit{ smooth and monotone}\} \\ H_1 &: f \in \Im = \{f \mid f \textit{ smooth}\}. \end{aligned} \tag{6.6.1}$$

[10] There is a substantial literature on estimation and testing subject to constraints such as monotonicity and concavity (convexity). Work on monotonicity and/or concavity includes Wright and Wegman (1980); Schlee (1982); Friedman and Tibshirani (1984); Villalobas and Wahba (1987); Mukarjee (1988); Ramsay (1988); Kelly and Rice (1990); Mammen (1991); Goldman and Ruud (1992); Yatchew (1992); Mukarjee and Stern (1994); Yatchew and Bos (1997); Bowman, Jones, and Gijbels (1998); Diack and Thomas-Agnan (1998); Ramsay (1998); Mammen and Thomas-Agnan (1999); Diack (2000); Gijbels et al. (2000); Hall and Heckman (2000); Hall and Huang (2001); Groeneboom, Jongbloed, and Wellner (2001); Juditsky and Nemirovski (2002); and Hall and Yatchew (2002).

The isotonic regression literature, in the simplest case, considers least-squares regression subject only to monotonicity constraints; that is, given data $(y_1, x_1), \ldots, (y_n, x_n)$ on the model $y_i = f(x_i) + \varepsilon_i$, the optimization problem is given by

$$\min_{\hat{y}_1,\ldots,\hat{y}_n} \frac{1}{n} \sum_i (y_i - \hat{y}_i)^2 \quad \text{s.t. } \hat{y}_j \leq \hat{y}_i \quad \textit{for } x_j \leq x_i, \tag{6.6.2}$$

if f is increasing. The literature goes back several decades (see e.g., Barlow et al. (1972) and Robertson, Wright, and Dykstra (1988)). The estimation problem in (6.6.2) differs from our setup in (6.6.1) in that we impose additional smoothness constraints so that the regression function is estimable under the alternative.

Isotonic regression may be implemented using the function *monreg* in XploRe (see Härdle, Klinke and Turlach 1995) or using GAMS (Brooke et al. 1992).

6.6.2 *Why Monotonicity Does Not Enhance the Rate of Convergence*

If one is willing to impose sufficient smoothness on the estimated regression function and if the true regression function is strictly monotone, then monotonicity constraints will not improve the rate of convergence.

To see why this is the case, consider the following example in a simplified parametric setting. Suppose one is estimating the model $y = \mu + \varepsilon$ subject to the constraint $\mu \leq 2$. The usual (unconstrained) estimator of μ is the sample mean $\bar{y}$. An estimator $\hat{\mu}$ that incorporates the inequality constraint would set $\hat{\mu} = \bar{y}$ if $\bar{y} \leq 2$, and $\hat{\mu} = 2$ if $\bar{y} > 2$. If the true mean is, say, 1.5, then as sample size increases, the probability that the unconstrained estimator equals the constrained estimator goes to 1. Thus, the constraint becomes nonbinding.[11]

In nonparametric regression, an analogous result holds. If the true regression function is strictly monotone (e.g., if the first derivative is bounded away from zero), then with sufficient smoothness assumptions, the monotonicity restrictions become nonbinding as sample size increases. (This happens if the first derivative is estimated consistently, in which case, as sample size increases, the derivative estimate will also be bounded away from zero with probability going to 1.) The constrained estimator then has the same convergence rate as the unconstrained estimator.[12] This negative finding, however, does not imply that monotonicity will be uninformative in small samples (nor does it preclude testing for the presence of this property). Indeed, one could argue that, given the paucity of a priori information present in nonparametric estimation, any additional constraints should be exploited as far as possible particularly

[11] See Wolak (1989) and references therein for tests of inequality constraints in parametric models.

[12] Utreras (1984), Mammen (1991), and Yatchew and Bos (1997) find this result for different estimators.

in moderately sized samples. (Recall Figure 2.4 in which the imposition of monotonicity results in better fit.)

6.6.3 Kernel-Based Algorithms for Estimating Monotone Regression Functions

Mammen (1991) analyzed two estimators that combine smoothing with monotonicity constraints in estimation. The first estimator consists of two steps: smoothing of the data by applying a kernel estimator followed by determination of the closest set of monotonic points to the smoothed points. That is, given data $(y_1, x_1), \ldots., (y_n, x_n)$, let $(\tilde{y}_1, x_1), \ldots., (\tilde{y}_n, x_n)$ be the set of points obtained by applying a kernel estimator; then, solve

$$\min_{\hat{y}_1,\ldots,\hat{y}_n} \frac{1}{n} \sum_i (\tilde{y}_i - \hat{y}_i)^2 \quad \text{s.t. } \hat{y}_i \le \hat{y}_j \quad \textit{if } x_i \le x_j. \tag{6.6.3}$$

The second estimator examined by Mammen reverses the two steps. Mammen demonstrated that, if the true regression function is strictly monotone and if one chooses the optimal bandwidth for twice differentiable functions (i.e., $\lambda = n^{-1/5}$), then both estimators converge at the same rate as a conventional kernel estimator. Hall and Huang (2001) proposed an alternative procedure for producing a monotone estimate from an initial "smooth" estimate.

6.6.4 Nonparametric Least Squares Subject to Monotonicity Constraints

An alternative approach involves augmenting the nonparametric least-squares optimization problem (3.3.3) with monotonicity constraints. Assume the data have been ordered so that $x_1 \le \cdots \le x_n$. For expositional purposes, suppose R is invertible and set Rc in (3.3.3) equal to $\hat{y}$. Consider

$$\begin{aligned} &\min_{\hat{y}} \frac{1}{n}[y - \hat{y}]'[y - \hat{y}] \\ &\qquad \text{s.t.} \quad \hat{y}'R^{-1}\hat{y} \le L \\ &\hat{y}_{i-1} \le \hat{y}_i \quad i = 2, \ldots., n. \end{aligned} \tag{6.6.4a}$$

If f is strictly increasing, the monotonicity constraints are nonbinding in large samples so that the estimator achieves the optimal rate of convergence $n^{-2m/(2m+1)}$, where m is the degree of differentiability. Equation (6.6.4a) illustrates the relative ease with which the nonparametric least-squares estimator can incorporate additional constraints.

Alternatively, let $R^{(1)}$ be the matrix of first derivatives of the representors $r_{x_1}, \ldots, r_{x_n}$ evaluated at the data points $x_1, \ldots, x_n$. Then one may write

$$\min_{c} \frac{1}{n}[y - Rc]'[y - Rc] \quad \text{s.t. } c'Rc \le L \quad R^{(1)}c \ge 0. \tag{6.6.4b}$$

Versions (6.6.4a) and (6.6.4b) are slightly different. Using the mean value theorem, the former ensures that the estimated derivative is positive at some point between each pair of consecutive points. The latter requires the estimated derivative to be positive at the points $x_1, \ldots, x_n$. Neither procedure ensures that the estimated function is monotone everywhere in small samples, but as data accumulate, the smoothness requirement prevents nonmonotonicity.

6.6.5 *Residual Regression and Goodness-of-Fit Tests of Restrictions*

Let $\hat{f}_{res}$ be any of the estimators discussed above that impose smoothness and monotonicity. If f is twice differentiable, they converge at a rate $n^{-4/5}$. Using (6.3.13), if we set $\lambda = o(n^{-2/5})$, then the U-statistic of (6.3.11) with $d = 1$ has the normal distribution specified in (6.3.14) under the null hypothesis of monotonicity.

Suppose we estimate the isotonic regression in (6.6.2), which imposes only monotonicity. Van de Geer (1990) demonstrated that, in this case, $\int(\hat{f} - f)^2 \cong O_P(n^{-2/3})$. Thus, again using (6.3.13), we need $\lambda = o(n^{-2/3})$.

Furthermore, all these estimators converge sufficiently quickly so that (6.2.2) holds and we may apply a goodness-of-fit test. For example, let s^2_{mon} be the estimated residual variance from a smooth monotone or isotonic regression and s^2_{diff} a differencing estimate. Then,

$$(mn)^{1/2}\frac{\left(s^2_{mon} - s^2_{diff}\right)}{s^2_{diff}} \xrightarrow{D} N(0, 1). \qquad (6.6.5)$$

Tests of convexity (concavity) as well as of other restrictions may be implemented in a similar fashion. For example, convexity constraints may be imposed using

$$\begin{aligned} &\min_{\hat{y}_1,\ldots,\hat{y}_n} \frac{1}{n}\sum(y_i - \hat{y}_i)^2 \\ &\text{s.t.} \quad \hat{y}'R^{-1}\hat{y} \leq L \qquad (6.6.6a) \\ &\hat{y}_{i+1} \leq \frac{x_{i+2} - x_{i+1}}{x_{i+2} - x_i}\hat{y}_i + \frac{x_{i+1} - x_i}{x_{i+2} - x_i}\hat{y}_{i+2} \quad \forall i. \end{aligned}$$

Alternatively, let $R^{(2)}$ be the matrix of second derivatives of the representors $r_{x_1}, \ldots, r_{x_n}$ evaluated at the data points $x_1, \ldots, x_n$. Then one may write

$$\min_{\hat{y}} \frac{1}{n}[y - Rc]'[y - Rc] \quad \text{s.t. } c'Rc \leq L \quad R^{(2)}c \geq 0. \qquad (6.6.6b)$$

If sufficient derivatives are bounded and if the function is strictly convex, then the convexity constraints will not enhance the large sample rate of convergence.

The residual regression test may be used to produce tests of separability. The procedure *gam* (generalized linear model) in *S-Plus* estimates such specifications. Additional tests of additively separable models may be found in Barry (1993); Eubank et al. (1995); Sperlich, Tjostheim, and Yang (1999); Dette and Von Lieres und Wilkau (2001); Gozalo and Linton (2001); and Derbort, Dette, and Munk (2002).

Implications of demand theory can also be imposed and tested. See Epstein and Yatchew (1985), Varian (1985, 1990), Matzkin (1994) and references therein, Hausman and Newey (1995), Lewbel (1995), and Yatchew and Bos (1997).

In general, validity of the goodness-of-fit and residual regression tests require first demonstrating that the restricted estimator of the regression function converges sufficiently quickly. If the model is partially linear, then the estimated parametric effect may be first removed (using a $n^{1/2}$-consistent estimator) without altering the asymptotic validity of either the residual regression or the goodness-of-fit tests that are subsequently applied to the nonparametric portion of the model.

6.6.6 *Empirical Application: Estimation of Option Prices*[13]

Option price data have characteristics that are both nonparametric and parametric. The economic theory of option pricing predicts that the price of a call option should be a monotone decreasing convex function of the strike price. It also predicts that the state price density, which is proportional to the second derivative of the call function, should be a valid density function over future values of the underlying asset price and hence should be nonnegative and integrate to 1. Except in a few polar cases, the theory does not prescribe specific functional forms. All this points to a nonparametric approach to estimation.

On the other hand, multiple transactions are typically observed at a finite vector of strike prices. Thus, one could argue that the model for the option price as a function of the strike price is intrinsically parametric. Indeed, given sufficient data, one can obtain a good estimate of the call function by simply taking the mean transactions price at each strike price. Unfortunately, even with large data sets, accurate estimation of the call function at a finite number of points does not ensure good estimates of its first and second derivatives.

In this example we apply the nonparametric least-squares estimator and show how it can incorporate various "shape" constraints such as monotonicity and convexity of the call function.

Suppose we are given data $(x_1, y_1), \ldots, (x_n, y_n)$, where x_i is the strike price and y_i is the option price. Let $X = (X_1, \ldots, X_k)$ be the vector of k distinct strike prices. We will assume that the vector X is in increasing order. As usual,

[13] This application is drawn from Yatchew and Härdle (2001), who apply the techniques to options data on the DAX index. See also Aït-Sahalia and Duarte (2000).

x, y, and X will denote both the variable in question and the vector of observations on that variable. Our model is given by

$$y_i = f(x_i) + \varepsilon_i \quad i = 1, \ldots, n. \tag{6.6.7}$$

We assume the following. The regression function f is four times differentiable, which will ensure consistent and smooth estimates of the function, its first and second derivatives. (Other orders of differentiation can readily be accommodated using the framework that follows.) The vector of distinct strike prices X lies in the interval $[a,b]$. The residuals ε_i are independent but possibly heteroskedastic, and Σ is the diagonal matrix of variances $\sigma_1^2, \ldots, \sigma_n^2$.

We have generated 20 independent transactions prices at each of 25 strike prices. The top panel of Figure 6.2A depicts all 500 observations and the "true" call function. Note that the variance decreases as the option price declines. The second panel depicts the estimated call function obtained by taking the mean transactions price at each of the 25 strike prices. The estimate lies close to the true function. However, under closer examination it may be seen that the estimate is not convex. Although the differences would seem to be *de minimis*, we will soon see that this results in rather poor estimates of derivatives.

Consider the following naive approximations to the first and second derivatives that use first and second divided differences of the point mean estimates $\hat{Y}_1, \ldots, \hat{Y}_k$. In particular, define

$$\frac{\hat{Y}_j - \hat{Y}_{j-1}}{X_j - X_{j-1}} \quad j = 2, \ldots, k \tag{6.6.8}$$

and

$$\frac{\dfrac{\hat{Y}_{j+1} - \hat{Y}_j}{X_{j+1} - X_j} - \dfrac{\hat{Y}_j - \hat{Y}_{j-1}}{X_j - X_{j-1}}}{X_j - X_{j-1}} \quad j = 3, \ldots, k. \tag{6.6.9}$$

By the mean value theorem, these should provide reasonable approximations to the first and second derivatives. The upper panels of Figures 6.2B and 6.2C depict divided difference estimates of the first and second derivatives using point means and (6.6.8) and (6.6.9). The estimates are poor, particularly at low strike prices where the variance of the residual is relatively larger.

Consider now the following nonparametric least-squares problem, which incorporates a smoothness constraint

$$\min_f \frac{1}{n} \sum_i \left[\frac{y_i - f(x_i)}{\sigma_i} \right]^2 \quad \text{s.t. } \|f\|^2_{Sob} \le L. \tag{6.6.10}$$

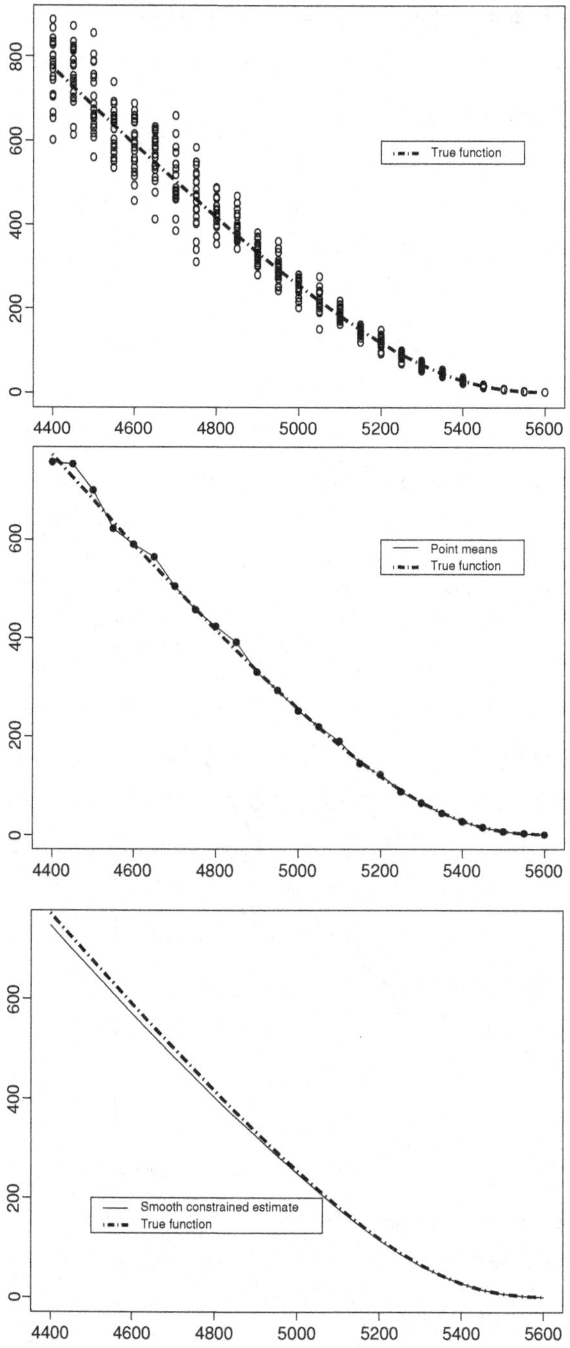

Figure 6.2A. Data and estimated call function.

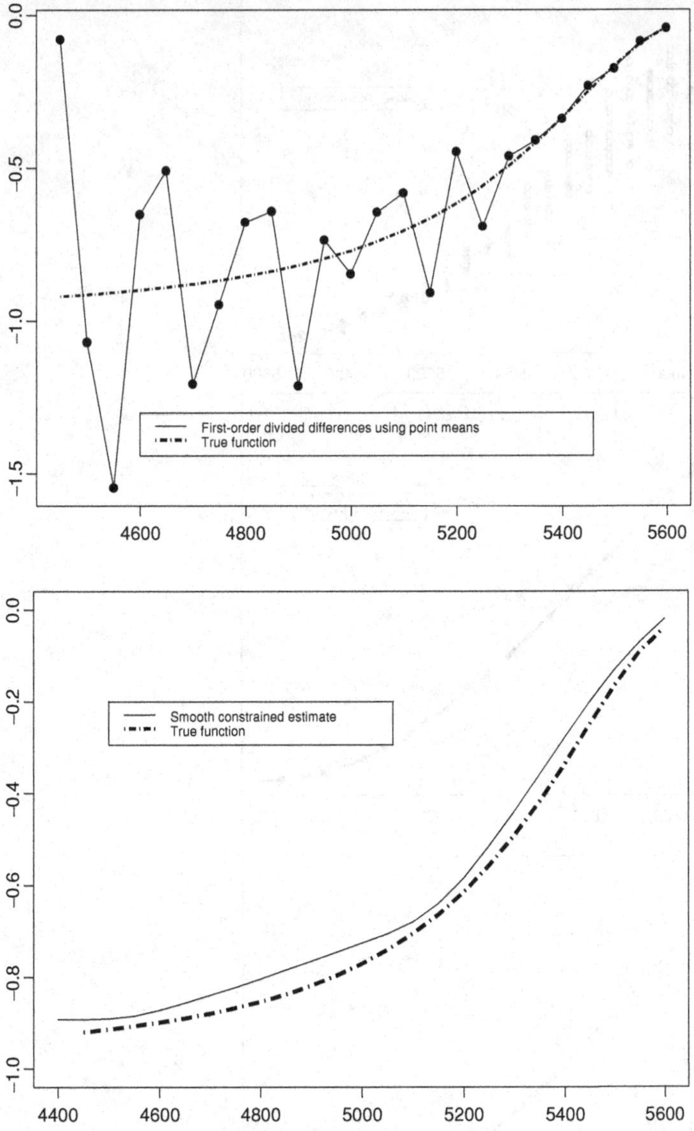

[a] Note the change in vertical scale between the two graphs.

Figure 6.2B. Estimated first derivative.[a]

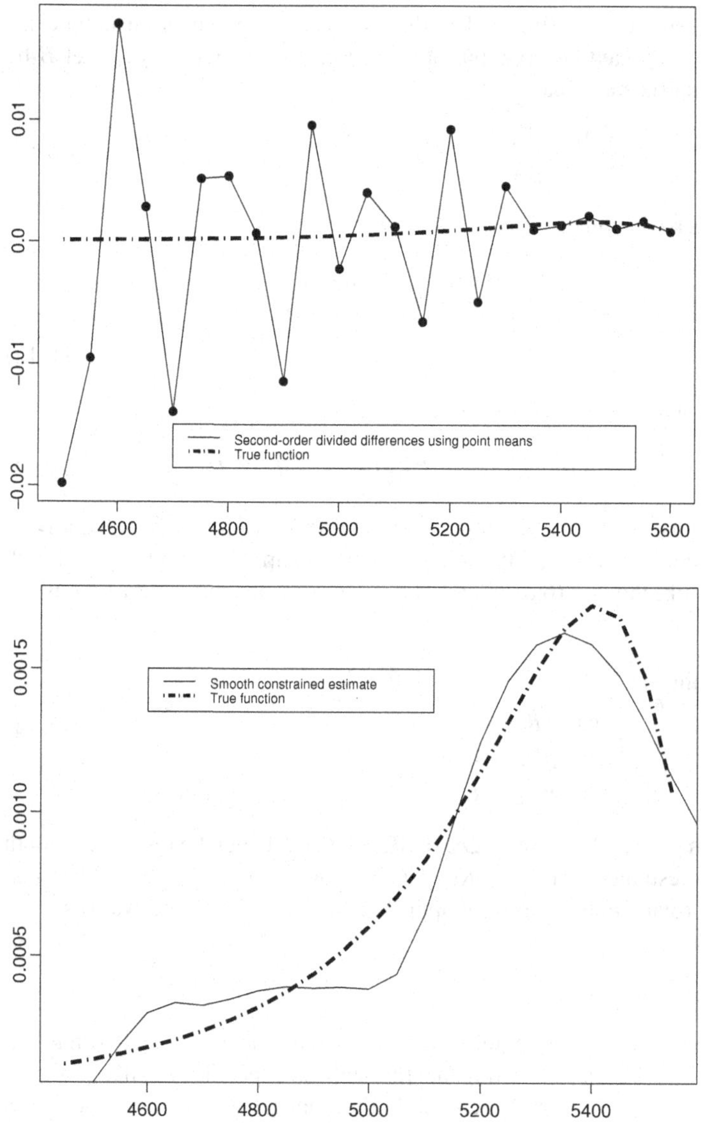

[a] Note the change in vertical scale between the two graphs.

Figure 6.2C. Estimated SPDs.[a]

We will rewrite (6.6.10) to reflect that option pricing data are usually characterized by repeated observations at a fixed vector of strike prices. Let B be the $n \times k$ matrix such that

$$\begin{aligned} B_{ij} &= 1 \quad \textit{if } x_i = X_j \\ &= 0 \quad \textit{otherwise} \end{aligned} \tag{6.6.11}$$

so that (6.6.10) becomes

$$\min_f \frac{1}{n} \Big[\underset{n\times 1}{y} - \underset{n\times k}{B} \underset{k\times 1}{f(X)} \Big]' \underset{n\times n}{\Sigma^{-1}} \Big[\underset{n\times 1}{y} - \underset{n\times k}{B} \underset{k\times 1}{f(X)} \Big] \quad \text{s.t. } \|f\|^2_{Sob} \leq L. \tag{6.6.12}$$

The problem may be solved using

$$\min_c \frac{1}{n}[y - BRc]'\Sigma^{-1}[y - BRc] \quad \text{s.t. } c'Rc \leq L, \tag{6.6.13}$$

where calculation of the $k \times k$ representor matrix R is detailed in Appendix D. One can impose monotonicity and convexity by supplementing (6.6.13) with constraints like those in (6.6.4a) and (6.6.6a), or (6.6.4b) and (6.6.6b). Consider then

$$\begin{aligned} \min_c \frac{1}{n}[y - BRc]' \Sigma^{-1} [y - BRc] & \\ \text{s.t. } c'Rc \leq L & \\ R^{(1)}c \leq 0 & \\ R^{(2)}c \geq 0. & \end{aligned} \tag{6.6.14}$$

The bottom panels of Figures 6.2A, 6.2B, and 6.2C depict the resulting smooth constrained estimates $\hat{f}(X) = R\hat{c}$, $\hat{f}'(X) = R^{(1)}\hat{c}$, and $\hat{f}''(X) = R^{(2)}\hat{c}$ that evidently provide much improved approximations to the true derivatives.

6.7 Conclusions

Because economic theory rarely provides parametric functional forms, exploratory data analysis and testing that rationalizes a specific parametric regression function is particularly beneficial. In this connection, we have described a variety of specification tests.

Even though parametric specification is not its forte, economic theory does play a role in producing other valuable restrictions on the regression function. By specifying which variables are potentially relevant to an equation and excluding myriad others from consideration, rate of convergence is improved. (Exclusion restrictions may come disguised; e.g., as homogeneity of degree zero.) The imposition of exclusion restrictions on either local averaging or minimization estimators is straightforward – one simply reduces the dimensionality of the

Simulated EMSE: $E\left[\frac{1}{n}\sum(\hat{\mu}(x_t)-\mu(x_t))^2\right]$

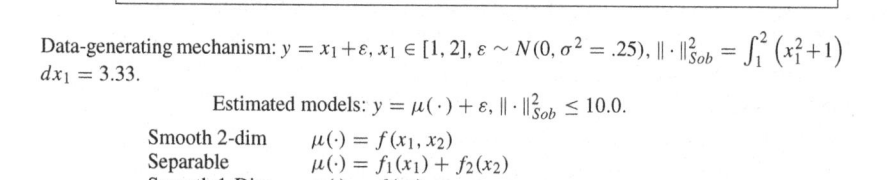

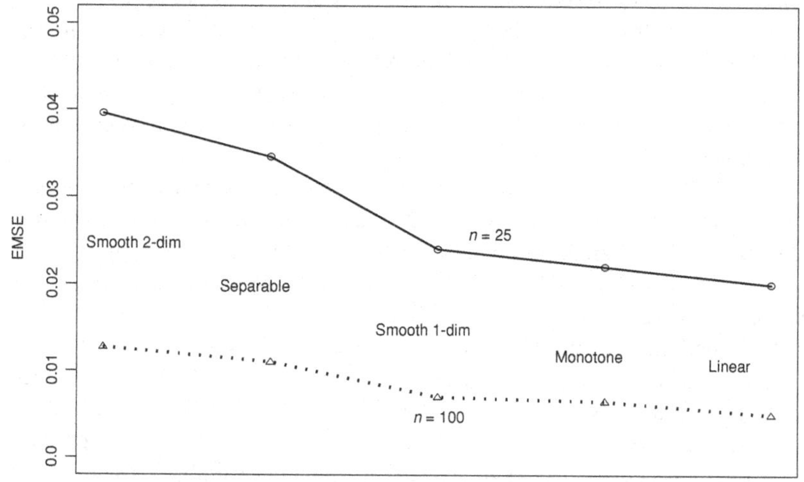

Data-generating mechanism: $y = x_1 + \varepsilon$, $x_1 \in [1, 2]$, $\varepsilon \sim N(0, \sigma^2 = .25)$, $\|\cdot\|^2_{Sob} = \int_1^2 \left(x_1^2 + 1\right) dx_1 = 3.33$.

Estimated models: $y = \mu(\cdot) + \varepsilon$, $\|\cdot\|^2_{Sob} \leq 10.0$.

Smooth 2-dim	$\mu(\cdot) = f(x_1, x_2)$
Separable	$\mu(\cdot) = f_1(x_1) + f_2(x_2)$
Smooth 1-Dim	$\mu(\cdot) = f(x_1)$
Monotone	$\mu(\cdot) = f(x_1)$, $f(x_{1t}) \leq f(x_{1\tau})$, $x_{1t} \leq x_{1\tau}$
Linear	$\mu(\cdot) = \beta_0 + \beta_1 x_1$

Each model is estimated using nonparametric least squares. Sobolev smoothness norms are of fourth order. In each case, 1,000 replications were performed.

Figure 6.3. Constrained estimation – simulated expected mean-squared error.

regression function. Other restrictions that may be driven by considerations of economic theory and that enhance convergence rates are additive separability and semiparametric specifications. Monotonicity and concavity restrictions do not enhance the (large sample) rate of convergence if sufficient smoothness is imposed but are beneficial in small samples. Alternatively, their presence can be used to reduce the dependency on smoothness assumptions.

Figure 6.3 illustrates the consequences of imposing progressively more stringent restrictions on a model that, unbeknown to the investigator, is linear in one variable. The benefits of "learning" that the model is a function of one variable rather than two are evident. The expected mean-squared error (EMSE), given fixed sample size, declines by more than 40 percent as one moves from the smooth two-dimensional to a smooth one-dimensional model. This observation underscores the importance of powerful significance tests for nonparametric models. As expected, separability and linearity can also substantially improve the accuracy of the estimator.

In this chapter we have focused on constrained estimation and hypothesis testing. Because of the curse of dimensionality and the consequences for convergence rates, it is extremely desirable to improve the accuracy of estimates by validating parametric specifications. Accordingly, we have provided implementation details for a variety of specification tests. Reducing the number of explanatory variables or imposing a separable structure also enhances convergence rates.

The discussion of estimation subject to monotonicity and concavity constraints underlines one of the advantages of the nonparametric least-squares estimator: such constraints can be imposed relatively easily. Other implications of economic theory can also be incorporated into the nonparametric least-squares estimation procedure with little difficulty.

As in parametric approaches, a general methodology for testing hypotheses can be based upon an examination of the residuals from the constrained regression. If the null hypothesis is true, these residuals should be unrelated to the explanatory variables. Thus, the procedure involves a nonparametric regression of the constrained residuals on all explanatory variables. The resulting test, which can be applied in a wide variety of circumstances, is based on a U-statistic. An alternative class of procedures that compare restricted and unrestricted estimates of the residual variance is also available.

6.8 Exercises[14]

1. *South African Food Share Engel Curves — Testing Parametric Specifications.* Using data on single individuals, fit linear and quadratic models for *FoodShr* as a function of the *log* of total expenditure *ltexp*. Test these specifications using the following procedures:

(a) Bierens (1990), Table 6.1
(b) Härdle and Mammen (1993), Table 6.2
(c) Hong and White (1995), Table 6.3
(d) Li (1994) and Zheng (1996) residual regression test, Table 6.4

Compare your conclusions to those obtained using the differencing test procedure, Chapter 4, Exercise 9.

2. Repeat Exercise 1 using data on couples with no children and couples with one child.

3. *Option Pricing*: The purpose of this exercise is to estimate a call function and its first and second derivatives using individual point means and a spline estimator.

(a) Using simulated option pricing data and produce a scatterplot of option prices against strike prices. (There are 20 observations at each of 25 strike prices.)

[14] Data and sample programs for empirical exercises are available on the Web. See the Preface for details.

(b) Superimpose the true values $(X_1, f(X_1)), \ldots, (X_{25}, f(X_{25}))$ on the plot in Part (a).
(c) Estimate the call function using individual means at each strike price. Plot the estimates and the true function.
(d) Use the divided difference formulas in (6.6.8) and (6.6.9) to approximate the first and second derivatives of the call function. Plot these against the true first and second derivatives.
(e) Estimate the call function and its first two derivatives using a spline estimator (such as smooth.spline in *S-Plus*). Plot these estimates against the true first and second derivatives. (Note, however, that spline estimators such as smooth.spline, which penalize only the second derivative, as in (3.3.7), do not ensure consistency of the estimates of first and second derivatives.)

4. *Option Pricing*: The purpose of this exercise is to estimate a call function and its first two derivatives using a constrained nonparametric least-squares procedure. Results should be similar to the bottom panels in Figures 6.2A, 6.2B, and 6.2C.[15]

(a) Open the file containing the simulated data and the representor matrices R, $R^{(1)}$, and $R^{(2)}$. Using GAMS (or similar optimization program), solve optimization problem (6.6.14), setting $L = .1$ and Σ equal to the identity matrix.
(b) Calculate the estimates of the call function and its first two derivatives at the vector of observed strike prices: $\hat{f}(X) = R\hat{c}$, $\hat{f}'(X) = R^{(1)}\hat{c}$, and $\hat{f}''(X) = R^{(2)}\hat{c}$. Plot these estimates against the corresponding true functions.
(c) At each strike price calculate the variance of observed option prices. Use these to construct an estimator of Σ, say $\hat{\Sigma}$. Solve (6.6.14) using $\hat{\Sigma}$.

[15] Note that this part will require using a constrained optimization program such as GAMS (Brooke et al. 1992), which stands for General Algebraic Modeling System and is a general package for solving a broad range of linear, nonlinear, integer, and other optimization problems subject to constraints. It should not be confused with the *gam* function in *S-Plus*, which stands for generalized additive models.

7 Index Models and Other Semiparametric Specifications

7.1 Index Models

7.1.1 Introduction

A natural generalization of the conventional linear regression model $y = x\delta + \varepsilon$ is given by the specification

$$y = f(x\delta) + \varepsilon, \tag{7.1.1}$$

where x is a vector of explanatory variables and f is an unknown but smooth function. The regression is a nonparametric function of the linear index $x\delta$ from which the term *index model* arises. The objective is to estimate δ and f.

Such specifications are appealing because they can accommodate multiple explanatory variables (within the linear index) while retaining nonparametric flexibility (through the function f) without succumbing to the curse of dimensionality. The reason is that the nonparametric portion of the model is a function of only one variable, the linear index itself.[1]

7.1.2 Estimation

Suppose one is given independent observations $(y_1, x_1), \ldots, (y_n, x_n)$, where the x_i are, say, p-dimensional row vectors. As usual, y and ε denote both the variable in question and the corresponding column vector of data; X is the $n \times p$ matrix of data on the explanatory variables, and $f(X\delta)$ an n-dimensional column vector. We now rewrite (7.1.1) in matrix notation

$$y = f(X\delta) + \varepsilon. \tag{7.1.2}$$

[1] If the dependent variable y is binary, then (7.1.1) constitutes the semiparametric analogue of probit and logit models. For a foothold into this literature, see Cosslett (1987), Klein and Spady (1993), Cavanagh and Sherman (1998), and Horowitz (1998, Chapter 3) and references therein.

For a fixed δ, one can estimate f using a conventional smoother to obtain $\hat{f}_\delta$. One can then calculate the estimated residual variance using the average residual sum of squares. A basic estimation strategy proposed by Ichimura (1993) and Klein and Spady (1993) consists of searching over different values of δ until the one that minimizes the estimated residual variance is found[2]:

$$s^2 = \min_{\delta} \frac{1}{n}[y - \hat{f}_\delta(X\delta)]'[y - \hat{f}_\delta(X\delta)]. \tag{7.1.3}$$

The estimate $\hat{\delta}$ is the value that satisfies the minimum in (7.1.3), and $\hat{f}_{\hat{\delta}}$ is the corresponding estimate of the unknown regression function f.

Härdle, Hall, and Ichimura (1993) developed a methodology for optimal selection of the smoothing parameter in the estimation of f. Essentially, the grid search in (7.1.3) is embedded in a broader optimization problem in which the smoothing parameter is chosen simultaneously.

7.1.3 *Properties*

Let

$$V = E[f'(x\delta_o)^2(x - E(x\,|\,x\delta_o))'(x - E(x\,|\,x\delta_o))\,|\,x\delta_o], \tag{7.1.4}$$

where δ_o is the true value of δ, and x is a p-dimensional row vector. Then, under general conditions,

$$n^{1/2}(\hat{\delta} - \delta_o) \xrightarrow{D} N(0, \sigma_\varepsilon^2 V^{-1}). \tag{7.1.5}$$

Note that the finite dimensional parameter δ_o is estimated $n^{1/2}$-consistently.

Let S be a smoother that regresses onto the vector $X\hat{\delta}$. Then, $(I - S)X$ regresses the columns of X onto the vector $X\hat{\delta}$ and takes the residuals.

For an arbitrary vector a, let $diag(a)$ be the diagonal matrix with the elements of a on the main diagonal. Next, estimate the derivative of f and evaluate at the vector $X\hat{\delta}$. Call this estimated vector $\hat{f}'(\cdot)$. Then, a consistent estimate of V may be obtained using

$$\frac{1}{n}((I - S)X)'\,diag(\hat{f}'(\cdot)^2)((I - S)X). \tag{7.1.6}$$

Furthermore, σ_ε^2 may be estimated using s^2 in (7.1.3).

[2] For an alternative estimation strategy based on average derivatives, see Härdle and Stoker (1989); Powell, Stock, and Stoker (1989); Härdle and Tsybakov (1993); Horowitz and Härdle (1996); and Hristache, Juditsky, and Spokoiny (2001). See also Stoker (1986, 1991). For a test of a linear null against the linear index model alternative, see Horowitz and Härdle (1994).

7.1.4 Identification

The following conditions are sufficient for identification of δ and f and are likely to be satisfied in many practical applications. First, there is at least one continuous explanatory variable in the vector x. The coefficient of the first continuous variable is set to 1. Such a normalization is required because rescaling of the vector δ by a constant and a similar rescaling of the function f by the inverse of the constant will produce the same regression function.[3] Second, the function f is differentiable and not constant on the support of $x\delta$. Third, the matrix X is of full rank; this is a common assumption that avoids multicollinearity. Finally, varying the discrete components of x does not divide the support of $x\delta$ into disjoint subsets. (For additional details, see Horowitz 1998, pp. 14–20.)

7.1.5 Empirical Application: Engel's Method for Estimation of Equivalence Scales

Earlier, in the context of testing equality of nonparametric Engel curves, we introduced the idea of equivalence scales (Section 4.4.4).[4] Engel's initial observation was that richer households spend a smaller fraction of their income on food. His method for calculating equivalence scales is premised on the assumption that two households of different demographic composition are equally well off if they spend the same share of income on food. Figure 7.1 displays nonparametric estimates of Engel curves for households consisting of single individuals and those consisting of couples with no children. Engel's method amounts to calculating the horizontal difference between the two curves.

Our objective is to *estimate* this horizontal shift and to test whether the two curves are parallel. If they are, then the equivalence scale is said to be "base-independent" because it does not depend on the income levels at which comparisons are made.

To see that this problem can be put in an index model framework, let $\log x$ be the log of household expenditure and let z be a dummy variable that is zero for singles and one for couples. Then, we may write

$$y = f(\log x - z\delta) + \varepsilon. \qquad (7.1.7)$$

We have normalized the coefficient of the continuous variable $\log x$ to 1. Because z is a dummy variable, $z\delta$ simply shifts the Engel curve for couples horizontally by δ. The actual equivalence scale is $\Delta = \exp(\delta)$.

[3] Alternatively, one could set $\|\delta\| = 1$, where the double bars denote the usual Euclidean norm.

[4] Equivalence scale estimation has a long tradition. For an overview, see Deaton (1997), Lewbel (1997), and Van Praag and Warnaar (1997).

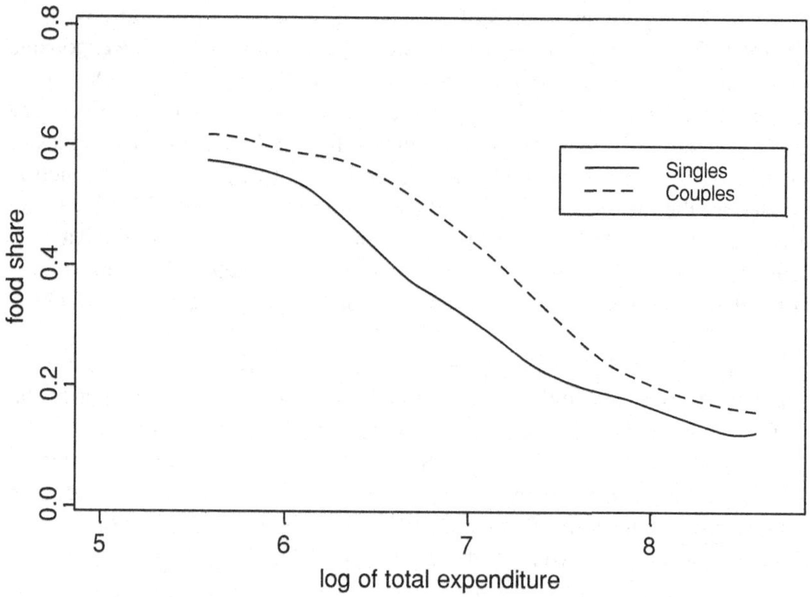

Using the optimal differencing estimator with $m = 25$, we obtain $s^2_{Singles} = .0194$ and $s^2_{Couples} = .0174$. The number of observations is as follows: $n_{Singles} = 1,109$, $n_{Couples} = 890$.

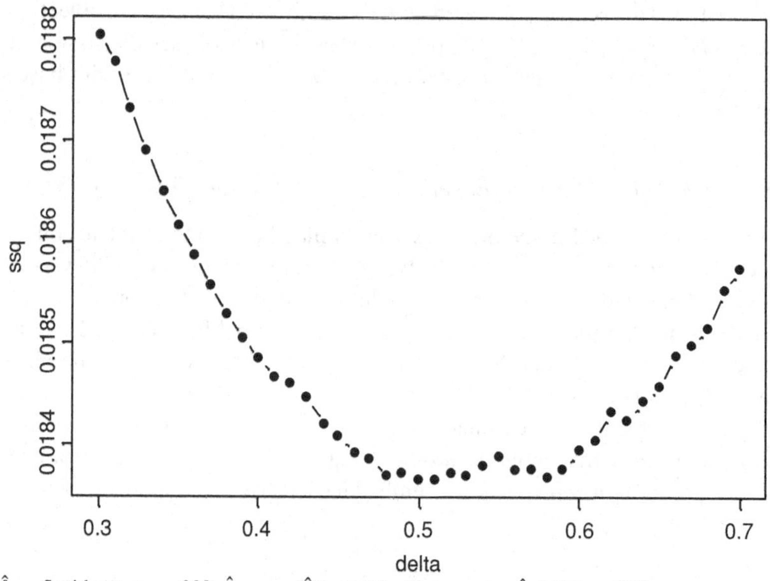

$\hat{\delta} = .5$ with s.e. $s_{\hat{\delta}} = .039$. $\hat{\Delta} = \exp(\hat{\delta}) = 1.65$ with s.e. $s_{\hat{\Delta}} = \hat{\Delta} \cdot 0.039 = .064$

Figure 7.1. Engel's method for estimating equivalence scales.

Figure 7.1 reports the results of applying the estimation procedure we have outlined. The search grid for δ was the interval [.3, .7] that (taking the exponents of the endpoints) maps to equivalence scales for couples versus singles in the range [1.35, 2.01]. In theory one would expect costs for couples not to exceed two times that of singles. The lower panel of Figure 7.1 displays the values of the function being minimized in (7.1.3) for different values of δ. The function is flat over the range .5 to .6. The numerical minimum is about $\hat{\delta} = .5$ with an estimated standard error of .039. To obtain an estimate of the actual equivalence scale we take $\hat{\Delta} = \exp(\hat{\delta}) = 1.65$. Applying the "delta method" (an unfortunate coincidence of nomenclature[5]), we find its standard error to be $s_{\hat{\Delta}} = \hat{\Delta} \cdot 0.039 = .064$.

A simple test of base-independence may now be conducted. It is essentially a test of whether the couples curve overlays the singles curve after a horizontal shift of .5. Even though δ is not known but estimated, because it achieves $n^{1/2}$-convergence, we can use the tests outlined in Section 4.4, treating δ as known.

Using order of differencing $m = 25$, we estimate the residual variances for singles and couples to be .0194 and .0174, respectively. Following (4.4.2), we calculate the weighted average of these using

$$s_w^2 = \frac{n_{Singles}}{n} s_{Singles}^2 + \frac{n_{Couples}}{n} s_{Couples}^2. \tag{7.1.8}$$

This is the "within" or unrestricted estimate of the residual variance. The value is .0183. This is to be compared with the minimized value of the objective function (7.1.3), which is .0184. Applying Proposition 4.3.1 (see discussion in Section 4.4), we obtain a test statistic of 1.27, which is consistent with base-independence.

7.1.6 *Empirical Application: Engel's Method for Multiple Family Types*

The procedure outlined in the previous section may be used to estimate equivalence scales for any *pair* of family types – couples with one child versus singles, couples with one child versus childless couples, and so on. Table 7.1 summarizes the distribution of family types in the South African data. There is considerable variation in family size and composition, and the possible number of pairwise estimates is large.

On the other hand, it is reasonable to assume that families of *similar* composition are informative about each other's equivalence scales. Thus, from an efficiency point of view it is useful to embed these various comparisons within a single model.

[5] See, for example, Greene (2000, p. 118).

Table 7.1. *Distribution of family composition.*

(Number of families)							
Adults \ Children	0	1	2	3	4	5	
1	1109	138	126	85	61	14	1,533
2	890	526	524	309	144	65	2,458
3	373	314	322	233	138	67	1,447
4	222	227	230	160	104	66	1,009
5	105	117	144	116	66	43	591
6	50	44	71	78	45	32	320
	2749	1366	1417	981	558	287	7,358

Yatchew et al. (2003) discuss alternative formulations. We will focus on a parsimonious specification. Suppose the equivalence scale Δ is the following function of the number of adults (A) and the number of children (K)

$$\Delta = \exp(\delta) = (A + \beta_2 K)^{\beta_1}. \tag{7.1.9}$$

Here β_1 reflects scale economies in the household and β_2 measures the effect on the equivalence scale of children relative to adults. Both parameters are restricted to be between 0 and 1.[6] Then we may write the model as

$$y = f(\log x - \beta_1 \log(A + \beta_2 K)) + \varepsilon. \tag{7.1.10}$$

This is a mildly more general specification than the linear index model (7.1.1) because the index is nonlinear. Nevertheless, the estimation strategy that we described earlier remains valid, and we may search over a grid of values of (β_1, β_2), as in (7.1.3). The difference lies in the calculation of the covariance matrix of the estimates. We will replace (7.1.4)–(7.1.6) with their more general counterparts in Section 7.2.

For current purposes it is important to note that the search over (a subset of) a two-dimensional space is substantially more time consuming. As one adds more variables and parameters to the index, the problem becomes progressively more difficult. Figure 7.2 plots the results of the grid search and provides the estimates of the parameters (β_1, β_2). Evidently, the function is quite flat in the direction of β_2. The procedure was performed in *S-Plus*. Much faster searches

[6] See, for example, Citro and Michael (1995, p. 176), who recommend values around .7 for β_1 and β_2.

Objective function – Equation (7.1.3)

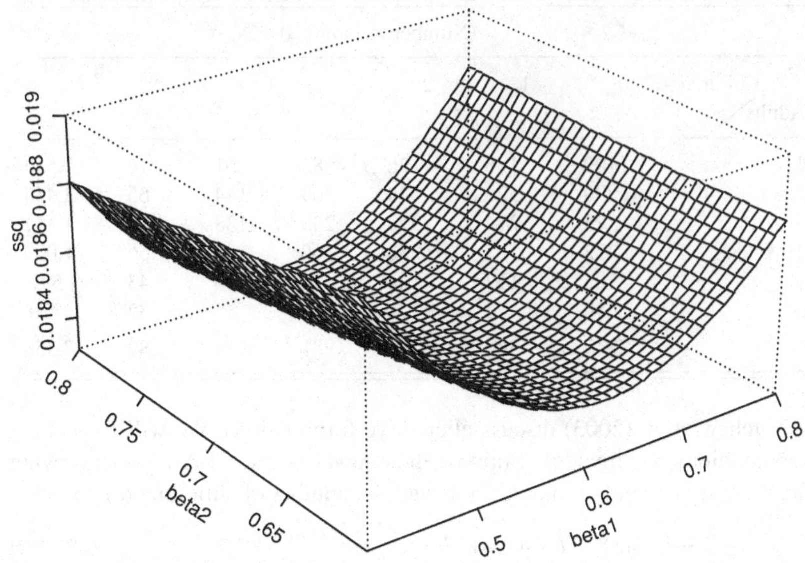

The estimates are $\hat{\beta}_1 = .6$; $\hat{\beta}_2 = .8$; $s_{\hat{\beta}_1} = .0215$; $s_{\hat{\beta}_2} = .0880$.

Figure 7.2. Parsimonious version of Engel's method.

can be conducted using Fortran (we use the matrix version Fortran 90) and other programming languages.

We may now use the "delta method" to estimate the standard errors of the log equivalence scales δ and the actual equivalence scales Δ. For the various family types appearing in Table 7.1, these values are tabulated in Table 7.2. For example, for couples with no children, the estimated equivalence scale is 1.52 relative to a single individual with a standard error of .023, which is much more precise than that obtained using pairwise estimation. (See Figure 7.1, where our pairwise estimate was 1.65 with standard error .064.) Yatchew et al. (2003) found that a parsimonious specification similar to (7.1.10), which incorporates multiple family types, can produce dramatic reductions in standard errors relative to pairwise estimation.

7.2 Partial Linear Index Models

7.2.1 Introduction

We now consider a somewhat more general specification that is a hybrid of the index model and the partial linear model. Suppose we are given data

Table 7.2. *Parsimonious model estimates.*

$\hat{\beta}_1$	$\hat{\beta}_2$				
.6	.8	$corr(\hat{\beta}_1, \hat{\beta}_2)$			
(.0215)	(.0880)	−0.592	$n = 7,358$	$s^2 = .01836$	$R^2 = .509$

Adults	Children	Equivalence scale $\hat{\Delta} = \exp(\hat{\delta})$	se $\hat{\Delta}$	Log equivalence scale $\hat{\delta}$	se $\hat{\delta}$
1	0	1.00	0.000	0.00	0.000
1	1	1.42	0.034	0.35	0.024
1	2	1.77	0.058	0.57	0.033
1	3	2.08	0.078	0.73	0.038
1	4	2.37	0.096	0.86	0.041
1	5	2.63	0.112	0.97	0.043
2	0	1.52	0.023	0.42	0.015
2	1	1.85	0.035	0.62	0.019
2	2	2.16	0.055	0.77	0.026
2	3	2.43	0.075	0.89	0.031
2	4	2.69	0.093	0.99	0.035
2	5	2.93	0.110	1.08	0.038
3	0	1.93	0.046	0.66	0.024
3	1	2.23	0.052	0.80	0.023
3	2	2.50	0.067	0.92	0.027
3	3	2.75	0.083	1.01	0.030
3	4	2.99	0.100	1.09	0.033
3	5	3.21	0.116	1.17	0.036
4	0	2.30	0.068	0.83	0.030
4	1	2.56	0.073	0.94	0.029
4	2	2.81	0.084	1.03	0.030
4	3	3.05	0.098	1.11	0.032
4	4	3.27	0.113	1.18	0.034
4	5	3.48	0.127	1.25	0.037
5	0	2.63	0.091	0.97	0.035
5	1	2.87	0.095	1.05	0.033
5	2	3.10	0.104	1.13	0.034
5	3	3.32	0.116	1.20	0.035
5	4	3.53	0.129	1.26	0.036
5	5	3.74	0.142	1.32	0.038
6	0	2.93	0.113	1.08	0.038
6	1	3.16	0.117	1.15	0.037
6	2	3.38	0.125	1.22	0.037
6	3	3.59	0.135	1.28	0.038
6	4	3.79	0.147	1.33	0.039
6	5	3.98	0.159	1.38	0.040

$(y_1, w_1, z_1), \ldots, (y_n, w_n, z_n)$ on the model $y_i = f(r(w_i, \beta)) + z_i\eta + \varepsilon_i$, where w_i and z_i are finite dimensional vectors of exogenous variables, f is a nonparametric function, r is a known function, β and η are finite dimensional parameter vectors, β_o and η_o are the true parameter values, $r_o = r(w, \beta_o)$, and $\varepsilon_i \mid w_i, z_i$ are i.i.d with mean 0 and variance σ^2. Set up the model in matrix notation, where the ith rows of W and Z are w_i and z_i, respectively:

$$y = f(r(W, \beta)) + Z\eta + \varepsilon. \qquad (7.2.1)$$

The regression function is composed of an index function (with possibly nonlinear index) and a linear component. (We could have made this nonlinear parametric, but the extension will be natural from our discussion below.)

7.2.2 *Estimation*

To estimate this model we need to modify our previous procedures slightly. First, note that if β is known, then (7.2.1) is a partial linear model that may be estimated in a variety of ways. We proceed as follows. For a fixed β, calculate the vector $r(W, \beta)$. Let S be a nonparametric smoother that regresses onto the vector $r(W, \beta)$ and apply the double residual method (Section 3.6):

$$(I - S)y \cong (I - S)f(r(W, \beta_o)) + (I - S)Z\eta_o + (I - S)\varepsilon. \qquad (7.2.2a)$$

If the selected β is close to the true value β_o, then $(I - S)f(r(W, \beta_o)) \cong 0$. Obtain an estimate of η:

$$\hat{\eta}_\beta = [((I - S)Z)'((I - S)Z)]^{-1}((I - S)Z)'(I - S)y. \qquad (7.2.3a)$$

By a grid search over values of β, find

$$s^2 = \min_\beta \frac{1}{n}((I-S)y-(I-S)Z\hat{\eta}_\beta)'((I-S)y-(I-S)Z\hat{\eta}_\beta). \qquad (7.2.4a)$$

Let $\hat{\beta}$ be the value that satisfies (7.2.4). The estimator of η is $\hat{\eta} = \hat{\eta}_{\hat{\beta}}$.

Note that the double residual method requires one to compute a separate nonparametric regression for each column of the matrix Z in (7.2.2), which can be time-consuming. The procedure can be accelerated by using a differencing procedure. For fixed β, let P_β be the permutation matrix that reorders the vector $r(W, \beta)$, so that it is in increasing order, and let D be a differencing matrix. Then

$$DP_\beta y \cong DP_\beta f(r(W, \beta_o)) + DP_\beta Z\eta_o + DP_\beta\varepsilon. \qquad (7.2.2b)$$

Our estimate of η is given by

$$\hat{\eta}_\beta = [(DP_\beta Z)'(DP_\beta Z)]^{-1}(DP_\beta Z)'DP_\beta y, \qquad (7.2.3b)$$

and the optimization problem becomes

$$s^2 = \min_{\beta} \frac{1}{n}(DP_\beta y - DP_\beta Z\hat{\eta}_\beta)'(DP_\beta y - DP_\beta Z\hat{\eta}_\beta). \qquad (7.2.4b)$$

7.2.3 *Covariance Matrix*

Recall that $r_o = r(w, \beta_o)$. To obtain large-sample standard errors, define the following conditional covariance matrices:

$$\Sigma_z = E\left[(z - E(z\,|\,r_o))'(z - E(z\,|\,r_o))\,|\,r_o\right]$$

$$\Sigma_{zf'} = E\left[f'(r_o)\left(\frac{\partial r}{\partial \beta} - E\left(\frac{\partial r}{\partial \beta}\,|\,r_o\right)\right)'(z - E(z\,|\,r_o))\,|\,r_o\right] \qquad (7.2.5)$$

$$\Sigma_{f'} = E\left[f'(r_o)^2\left(\frac{\partial r}{\partial \beta} - E\left(\frac{\partial r}{\partial \beta}\,|\,r_o\right)\right)'\left(\frac{\partial r}{\partial \beta} - E\left(\frac{\partial r}{\partial \beta}\,|\,r_o\right)\right)\,|\,r_o\right].$$

Let

$$V = \begin{bmatrix} \Sigma_z & \Sigma'_{zf'} \\ \Sigma_{zf'} & \Sigma_{f'} \end{bmatrix}; \qquad (7.2.6a)$$

then,

$$n^{1/2}\begin{pmatrix} \hat{\eta} - \eta_o \\ \hat{\beta} - \beta_o \end{pmatrix} \xrightarrow{D} N(0, \sigma^2 V^{-1}). \qquad (7.2.7a)$$

Let $\hat{f}'$ be a consistent estimator of the first derivative of f and define $diag(\hat{f}'(\cdot))$ to be the diagonal matrix with diagonal elements the components of the vector $\hat{f}'(r(W, \hat{\beta}))$. Define R to be the matrix whose ith row is the vector partial derivative $\partial r(w_i, \hat{\beta})/\partial \beta$. Let S be a smoother that regresses onto the vector $r(W, \hat{\beta})$. Then the submatrices of the matrix V in (7.2.6a) may be estimated consistently as follows:

$$\frac{1}{n}((I - S)Z)'((I - S)Z) \xrightarrow{P} \Sigma_z$$

$$\frac{1}{n}((I - S)R)'diag(\hat{f}'(\cdot))((I - S)Z) \xrightarrow{P} \Sigma_{zf'} \qquad (7.2.8a)$$

$$\frac{1}{n}((I - S)R)'diag(\hat{f}'(\cdot)^2)((I - S)R) \xrightarrow{P} \Sigma_{f'}.$$

Proof of the preceding result, which may be found in Yatchew et al. (2003), is a straightforward variation on existing proofs in the literature, particularly Ichimura (1993), Klein and Spady (1993), and Carroll et al. (1997).

For the parsimonious model (7.2.12) below, $\beta = (\beta_1, \beta_2)$, $w = (x, A, K)$, $r(w, \beta) = \log x - \beta_1 \log(A + \beta_2 K)$, and the matrix R has ith row

$$\left(\frac{\partial r(w_i, \beta)}{\partial \beta_1}, \frac{\partial r(w_i, \beta)}{\partial \beta_2}\right)_{\hat{\beta}_1, \hat{\beta}_2} = \left(-\log(A_i + \hat{\beta}_2 K_i), -\frac{\hat{\beta}_1 K_i}{A_i + \hat{\beta}_2 K_i}\right). \tag{7.2.9}$$

Equation (7.2.9) also applies to the parsimonious model (7.1.10). However, in that specification $\eta = 0$, so that (7.2.6a) and (7.2.7b) become

$$V = \Sigma_{f'} \tag{7.2.6b}$$

and

$$n^{1/2}(\hat{\beta} - \beta_o) \xrightarrow{D} N(0, \sigma^2 V^{-1}). \tag{7.2.7b}$$

Furthermore, $V = \Sigma_{f'}$ is estimated using the last equation in (7.2.8a)

$$\frac{1}{n}((I - S)R)' \, diag(\hat{f}'(\cdot)^2)((I - S)R) \xrightarrow{P} \Sigma_{f'}. \tag{7.2.8b}$$

7.2.4 *Base-Independent Equivalence Scales*

To make these ideas more concrete, it is helpful to outline the problem of equivalence scale estimation further. Engel's method, although widely used, is – strictly speaking – not quite correct. The reasons are outlined extensively in Deaton (1997), but the essence of the argument is this: families with children are likely to spend a larger share of income on food than families without children even if they are at the same level of utility. This occurs by virtue of the needs and consumption patterns of children versus adults. The problem can be corrected by a simple modification to Engel's approach: rather than searching for a horizontal shift that superimposes one Engel curve on another, a combined horizontal and vertical shift that achieves the superimposition is sought instead.[7]

Return to the problem of finding the equivalence scale for childless couples versus single individuals, which we considered earlier. Equation (7.1.7) is modified to

$$y = f(\log x - z\delta) + z\eta + \varepsilon, \tag{7.2.10}$$

[7] See Blundell, Duncan, and Pendakur (1998) and Pendakur (1999) for econometric models of this type. For the underlying theoretical arguments, see Lewbel (1989), and Blackorby and Donaldson (1989, 1993, 1994) and references therein.

where, as before, $\log x$ is the log of household expenditure, and z is a dummy variable that is 1 for couples and 0 for singles.[8]

Equation (7.2.10) is a partial linear index model, and it can be generalized easily to accommodate multiple family types. Suppose then that there are $q + 1$ family types and select the first type as the reference to which the other q types will be compared. Let z be a q-dimensional row vector of dummy variables for the q (nonreference) types and store data on these in a matrix Z. Then the model may be written in matrix notation as

$$\underset{n\times 1}{y} = f\Big(\underset{n\times 1}{\log x} - \underset{n\times q}{Z}\ \underset{q\times 1}{\delta}\Big) + \underset{n\times q}{Z}\ \underset{q\times 1}{\eta} + \underset{n\times 1}{\varepsilon}. \tag{7.2.11}$$

If this model is correct, then base-independent equivalence scales exist and are given by the q-dimensional vector $\Delta = \exp(\delta)$.

In our empirical example there are 36 family types (see Table 7.1), and so estimation of (7.2.11) requires search in a 36-dimensional space. As before, a parsimonious version may be specified by making the equivalence scale a function of the number of adults and children in the family (Eq. (7.1.9)). Our model becomes

$$\underset{n\times 1}{y} = f\Big(\underset{n\times 1}{\log x} - \beta_1 \log\Big(\underset{n\times 1}{A} + \beta_2 \underset{n\times 1}{K}\Big)\Big) + \underset{n\times q}{Z}\ \underset{q\times 1}{\eta} + \underset{n\times 1}{\varepsilon}, \tag{7.2.12}$$

where A and K are vectors indicating the number of adults and children in each family. This yields a much simpler estimation problem, for it requires search over a two-dimensional space to estimate (β_1, β_2); the dimension of η affects estimation speed only marginally because it is not estimated by a search.

One of the advantages of semiparametric models of equivalence scales of the form (7.2.12) is that the parametric function inside f may readily be modified to incorporate other demographic variables such as age.

7.2.5 *Testing Base-Independence and Other Hypotheses*

We will want to test base-independence as well as several other hypotheses such as the validity of the parsimonious specification (7.2.12). In each case we will use a goodness-of-fit type statistic (Section 6.2). For convenience, under the alternative hypothesis we will use an optimal differencing estimator to obtain the unrestricted sample variance. Under the null we will use an estimator that

[8] The parameter η has a specific interpretation; it is the elasticity of the equivalence scale with respect to the price of food. For details, see Pendakur (1999) and references therein.

satisfies (6.2.2) and thus our statistics will be of the form

$$(mn)^{1/2}\frac{\left(s_{res}^2 - s_{unr}^2\right)}{s_{unr}^2} \xrightarrow{D} N(0,1). \tag{7.2.13}$$

Consider a test of the base-independent parsimonious specification (7.2.12) against the alternative that Engel curves for the various family types are not similar in shape. That is, under the alternative we have $q + 1$ distinct models,

$$y_j = f_j(\log x_j) + \varepsilon_j \qquad j = 0, 1, \ldots q, \tag{7.2.14}$$

where y_j, $\log x_j$, and ε_j are column vectors of length n_j for the jth family type. In this case we may use the differencing estimator (4.2.4) to estimate $s_{diff,j}^2$, the residual variance for each family type j. We then construct s_{unr}^2 as their weighted combination, where the weights reflect the relative sizes of the subpopulations. That is,

$$s_{unr}^2 = \sum_{j=0}^{q} \frac{n_j}{n} s_{diff,j}^2 = \frac{1}{n}\sum_{j=0}^{q} y_j' D' D y_j. \tag{7.2.15}$$

To complete the test, the restricted estimator s_{res}^2 is obtained directly from (7.2.4a) (or (7.2.4b)), and the test in (7.2.13) may be applied.

Next, consider testing the parsimonious specification (7.2.12) against the more general alternative (7.2.10). Once estimation of the latter is complete (and this may take a while), one may perform the following test procedure. Obtain s_{res}^2 from (7.2.4a). Using $\hat{\delta}$, $\hat{\eta}$ from the unrestricted procedure, construct the set of ordered pairs: $(y_i - z_i\hat{\eta}, \log x_i - z_i\hat{\delta})$ $i = 1, \ldots, n$, where the $\log x_i - z_i\hat{\delta}$ are in increasing order. Define the unrestricted variance s_{unr}^2 to be the differencing estimator (4.2.4) applied to these ordered pairs. Finally, calculate the test statistic (7.2.13).

In selecting the order of differencing m for the unrestricted estimators of the residual variance, the objective is to under smooth estimation of the alternative relative to the null. This ensures that test statistic (7.2.13) admits the simple standard normal approximation under the null. For further details, see Yatchew et al. (2003). Tests of other hypotheses, such as whether adult households and households with children can be embedded in a single model, may also be readily constructed. Finally, tests on η may be constructed using the estimated covariance matrix of $\hat{\eta}$.[9]

[9] Indeed it may be interesting to find a more parsimonious specification for the additively separable portion of the model $z\eta$. After all, one would expect that "similar" family types should have similar values for η as well.

7.3 Exercises[10]

1. *Engel Equivalence Scales for Couples Versus Singles*: The purpose of this exercise is to estimate equivalence scales for pairs of household types using the index model specification (7.1.7). Results should be similar to those in Figure 7.1.

(a) Using the South African data for single individuals, estimate the Engel curve for food share as a function of log expenditure. (Use a smoother such as kernel or *loess*.) Graph your estimate. Repeat using the data on couples with no children.

(b) Set up a grid of values for δ. Let z be a dummy variable that is 0 for singles and 1 for couples. By searching over the grid, find the value $\hat{\delta}$ that satisfies

$$s^2 = \min_{\delta} \frac{1}{n}[y - \hat{f}_\delta(\log x - z\delta)]'\,[y - \hat{f}_\delta(\log x - z\delta)],$$

where y, z, and $\log x$ are n-dimensional vectors.

(c) Estimate the first derivative vector $\hat{f}'(\cdot)$ by applying the perturbation method in (3.7.1) to the ordered pairs $(y_i, \log x_i - z_i\hat{\delta})$. Plot your estimate.

(d) Use a nonparametric smoother, say S, to regress the dummy variable z on the vector $\log x - z\hat{\delta}$. Take the residuals to obtain the vector $(I - S)z$.

(e) Estimate V in (7.1.4) using $((I - S)z)'diag\hat{f}(\cdot)^2((I - S)z)/n$.

(f) Calculate the standard error of $\hat{\delta}$, $s_{\hat{\delta}} = \sqrt{s^2\hat{V}^{-1}/n}$.

(g) Calculate the equivalence scale $\hat{\Delta} = \exp(\hat{\delta})$. Using the delta method, obtain an estimate of the standard error of the equivalence scale $s_{\hat{\Delta}} = \hat{\Delta} \cdot s_{\hat{\delta}}$.

(h) Estimate the residual variance for each of these data sets using a low-order differencing estimator. Use (7.1.8) to calculate the weighted average of the residual variances s_w^2. Are your results consistent with the hypothesis of base-independence?

2. Repeat Exercise 1 for couples with one child versus singles and couples with two children versus singles.

3. *Engel Equivalence Scales for Multiple Family Types*: The purpose of this exercise is to estimate equivalence scales across multiple family types using the index model specification (7.1.10). Results should be similar to those in Figure 7.2 and Table 7.2.

(a) Assemble the data on all family types. Set up a grid of values for $\beta = (\beta_1, \beta_2)$. By searching over the grid, find the value $(\hat{\beta}_1, \hat{\beta}_2)$ that satisfies

$$s^2 = \min_{\beta} \frac{1}{n}[y - \hat{f}_\beta(\log x - \beta_1 \log(A + \beta_2 K))]' \times [y - \hat{f}_\beta(\log x - \beta_1 \log(A + \beta_2 K))].$$

(b) Estimate the first derivative vector $\hat{f}'(\cdot)$ by applying the perturbation method in (3.7.1) to the ordered pairs $(y_i, \log x_i - \hat{\beta}_1 \log(A_i + \hat{\beta}_2 K_i)), i = 1, \ldots, n$. Plot your estimate.

[10] Data and sample programs for empirical exercises are available on the Web. See the Preface for details.

(c) Calculate the matrix R whose ith row is given by

$$\left(-\log(A_i + \hat{\beta}_2 K_i), \; -\frac{\hat{\beta}_1 K_i}{A_i + \hat{\beta}_2 K_i} \right).$$

Use a nonparametric smoother, say S, to regress each column of this matrix on the vector $\log x - \hat{\beta}_1 \log(A + \hat{\beta}_2 K)$ and take the residuals to obtain the matrix $(I - S)R$.

(d) Estimate the covariance matrix of $(\hat{\beta}_1, \hat{\beta}_2)$ using $s^2 \hat{V}^{-1}/n$, where $\hat{V}$ is obtained using (7.2.8b).

(e) Calculate $\hat{\delta} = \hat{\beta}_1 \log(A + \hat{\beta}_2 K)$ and $\hat{\Delta} = \exp(\hat{\delta})$ for the various combinations of adults and children in Table 7.1 and apply the delta method to obtain their standard errors.

4. *General Equivalence Scales for Couples versus Singles*: The purpose of this exercise is to estimate equivalence scales for pairs of household types using the partial linear index model specification (7.2.10). The results should be similar to Yatchew et al. (2003). Note that because you are estimating both δ and η, the precision of your equivalence scales will decline substantially relative to Exercise 1.

(a) Let z be a dummy variable that is 0 for singles and 1 for couples. For fixed δ, let P_δ be the permutation matrix that reorders the vector $\log x - z\delta$ so that it is in increasing order. Let D be a differencing matrix. For example, you may use $D = I - S$, where S is the nearest-neighbor smoothing matrix defined in (3.1.12). Set up a grid of values for δ. Use the method outlined in Section 7.2.2 to obtain estimates $\hat{\delta}$ and $\hat{\eta}$.

(b) Estimate the first derivative vector $\hat{f}'(\cdot)$ by applying the perturbation method in (3.7.1) to the ordered pairs $(y_i - z_i\hat{\eta}, \log x_i - z_i\hat{\delta})$. Plot your estimate.

(c) Use a nonparametric smoother, say S, to regress the dummy variable z on the vector $\log x - z\hat{\delta}$. Take the residuals to obtain the vector $(I - S)z$.

(d) Estimate V in (7.2.6) using (7.2.8), which in this case becomes

$$\frac{1}{n}((I - S)z)'((I - S)z)$$
$$\frac{1}{n}((I - S)z)'\, diag(\hat{f}'(\cdot))((I - S)z)$$
$$\frac{1}{n}((I - S)z)'\, diag(\hat{f}'(\cdot)^2)((I - S)z).$$

(e) Calculate the standard errors of $\hat{\delta}$ and $\hat{\eta}$.

(f) Calculate the equivalence scale $\hat{\Delta} = \exp(\hat{\delta})$. Using the delta method, obtain an estimate of the standard error of the equivalence scale $s_{\hat{\Delta}} = \hat{\Delta} \cdot s_{\hat{\delta}}$.

5. *General Equivalence Scales for Multiple Family Types*: The purpose of this exercise is to estimate equivalence scales for multiple household types using the partial linear index model specification (7.2.12). The results should be similar to those of Yatchew et al. (2003). Note that because you are estimating both β and η, the precision of your equivalence scales will decline substantially relative to Exercise 3.

(a) Assemble the data on all family types. Set up a grid of values for $\beta = (\beta_1, \beta_2)$. Let P_β be the permutation matrix that reorders the vector $\log x - \beta_1 \log(A + \beta_2 K)$ so that it is in increasing order. Let D be a differencing matrix and define $S = I - D$. Use the method outlined in Section 7.2.2 to obtain estimates $\hat{\beta}_1$, $\hat{\beta}_2$, and $\hat{\eta}$.
(b) Estimate the first derivative vector $\hat{f}'(\cdot)$ by applying the perturbation method in (3.7.1) to the ordered pairs $(y_i - z_i\hat{\eta}, \log x_i - \hat{\beta}_1 \log(A_i + \hat{\beta}_2 K_i))$, $i = 1, \ldots, n$. Plot your estimate.
(c) Calculate the R and $(I - S)R$ matrices as in 3(c) above. Calculate $(I - S)Z$.
(d) Estimate V in (7.2.6) using (7.2.8). Calculate the standard errors of $\hat{\beta}$ and $\hat{\eta}$ using $s^2\hat{V}^{-1}/n$.
(e) Calculate $\hat{\delta} = \hat{\beta}_1 \log(A + \hat{\beta}_2 K)$ and $\hat{\Delta} = \exp(\hat{\delta})$ for the various combinations of adults and children in Table 7.1 and apply the delta method to obtain their standard errors.

8 Bootstrap Procedures

8.1 Background

8.1.1 Introduction

Bootstrap procedures, widely attributed to Efron (1979),[1] are simulation-based techniques that provide estimates of variability, confidence intervals, and critical values for tests. The fundamental idea is to create replications by treating the existing data set (say of size n) as a population from which samples (of size n) are obtained. In the bootstrap world, sampling from the original data becomes the data-generating mechanism (DGM). Variation in estimates occurs because, upon selection, each data point is replaced in the population.

In many circumstances, bootstrap procedures are simpler to implement than their asymptotic counterparts. In addition, they are often more accurate. By drawing correctly sized samples from the original data[2] the simulated distribution inherits higher-order moment properties of the true DGM. The conventional asymptotic normal approximation ignores such information.

It is not surprising that major advances in bootstrap techniques and nonparametric procedures have occurred more or less contemporaneously. Both have been driven by the precipitous drop in computing costs. The emergence of automated data collection – which has produced very large data sets – has also contributed indirectly to the development of nonparametric techniques. Furthermore, although the bootstrap requires resampling many times, calculations need not be done serially but can be performed contemporaneously, making the bootstrap particularly suitable for parallel processing.

1 Actually, Monte Carlo inference techniques had been recommended by several authors prior to Efron's work, among them Barnard (1963) and Hartigan (1969, 1971). For additional precursors see Hall (1992, p. 35) and Davison and Hinkley (1997, p. 59).

2 One hopes the data are representative of the underlying population. Prospects for this of course improve as sample size n increases.

We begin with a rudimentary introduction to the bootstrap. (References for further reading in this voluminous literature are provided at the end of this section.) This is followed by a delineation of several bootstrap techniques in nonparametric and semiparametric settings. Throughout this chapter, the superscript B will signify a bootstrap sample, estimate, confidence interval, or test statistic.

At first sight, it might appear that there is a natural, unique way to perform resampling: one should just mimic the methodology used to obtain the original sample. On closer examination, one discovers that there are often several sensible ways to resample the data. In the regression setting, which has been our mainstay throughout this book, we rely principally on taking random samples from estimated residuals, although other approaches are possible.

8.1.2 *Location Scale Models*

As an example, consider the usual location scale model where $y_1, \ldots, y_n$ are i.i.d. with mean μ_y and variance σ_y^2. The distributional family is unknown. The variance of $\bar{y}$ is estimated using $s_{\bar{y}}^2 = s_y^2/n$, where $s_y^2 = \Sigma(y_i - \bar{y})^2/(n-1)$. The central limit theorem, which states that $n^{1/2}(\bar{y} - \mu_y)/s_y \xrightarrow{D} N(0, 1)$, provides the basis for *asymptotic* confidence intervals and test procedures on μ_y.

Bootstrap inference on μ_y proceeds as follows. Take many random samples of size n from the original sample, each time calculating the sample mean $\bar{y}^B$. The bootstrap estimate of the variance of $\bar{y}$ is obtained by calculating the sample variance of the $\bar{y}^B$. Indeed, a bootstrap approximation to the sampling distribution of $\bar{y}$ can be obtained by plotting the histogram of the $\bar{y}^B$. By calculating the .025 and .975 quantiles of this distribution, one can obtain a 95 percent confidence interval for μ_y. The procedure we have just described is an example of the "percentile" method because it works with the percentiles or quantiles of the bootstrap distribution for the parameter estimator of interest, in this case the sample mean.

There is substantial evidence – both theoretical and empirical – that it is usually better to simulate the distribution of a statistic that is a pivot (or at least an asymptotic pivot).[3] In this case, bootstrap inference on the mean would proceed as follows.

[3] Pivots are statistics whose distributions do not depend on any unknown parameters. There are precious few "true pivots". Among them are the following. If the data are i.i.d. normal, then $n^{1/2}(\bar{y} - \mu)/s_y$ is precisely t_{n-1} and $(n-1)s_y^2/\sigma^2$ is precisely χ_{n-1}^2. The Kolmogorov–Smirnov statistic is also a true pivot. On the other hand, there are numerous asymptotic pivots. For example, if the data are i.i.d. with unknown distribution but have a finite mean and variance, then $n^{1/2}(\bar{y} - \mu)/s_y$ converges to a standard normal in large samples and so is an asymptotic pivot.

Take many random samples of size n from the original sample, each time calculating the statistic $t^B = n^{1/2}(\bar{y}^B - \bar{y})/s_y^B$, where $\bar{y}^B$ and s_y^B are the mean and standard deviation of the bootstrapped data. To construct a 95 percent confidence interval for μ_y, obtain the .025 and .975 quantiles of the distribution of t^B, say $c_{.025}, c_{.975}$, and isolate μ_y within the probability statement: $Prob\,[c_{.025} \le n^{1/2}(\bar{y} - \mu_y)/s_y \le c_{.975}] \cong .95$. A two-sided test of the hypothesis H_0: $\mu = \mu_o$ at a 5 percent significance level can be performed by determining whether the resulting confidence interval $[\bar{y} - c_{.975}\, s_y/n^{1/2}, \bar{y} - c_{.025}\, s_y/n^{1/2}]$ contains μ_o. This procedure is an example of the "percentile-t" method because it uses an asymptotic pivot that takes the form of a t-statistic.

An alternative approach to testing H_0: $\mu = \mu_o$, which will be instructive shortly, is to impose the null hypothesis on the bootstrap DGM. In this case, using the original data and sample mean, one calculates the residuals $\hat{\varepsilon}_i = y_i - \bar{y}$. One then takes repeated samples of size n from $\hat{\varepsilon}_1, \ldots, \hat{\varepsilon}_n$, constructs the bootstrap data set $y_i^B = \mu_o + \hat{\varepsilon}_i^B$, $i = 1, \ldots, n$, and calculates $t^B = n^{1/2}(\bar{y}^B - \mu_o)/s_y^B$ each time. (Note that the bootstrap DGM satisfies the null hypothesis.) To obtain critical values $c_{.025}, c_{.975}$ for a two-sided test at a 5 percent significance level, obtain the .025 and .975 quantiles of the (simulated) distribution of t^B. Finally, accept the null hypothesis if the interval contains $t = n^{1/2}(\bar{y} - \mu_o)/s_y$; otherwise, reject it.

8.1.3 *Regression Models*

Suppose we now have data $(y_1, x_1), \ldots, (y_n, x_n)$ on the model $y = f(x) + \varepsilon$, where f may or may not lie in a parametric family. The ε_i are i.i.d. with mean 0, variance σ_ε^2, and are independent of x. A "joint" resampling methodology involves drawing i.i.d. observations with replacement from the original collection of ordered pairs.

Residual resampling, on the other hand, proceeds as follows. First, f is estimated using, say, $\hat{f}$. The estimated residuals $\hat{\varepsilon}_i = y_i - \hat{f}(x_i)$ are assembled and centered so that their mean is zero (just as the true ε_i have a mean of zero). One then samples independently from these to construct a bootstrap data set: $(y_1^B, x_1), \ldots, (y_n^B, x_n)$, where $y_i^B = \hat{f}(x_i) + \hat{\varepsilon}_i^B$. Statistics of interest are then computed from these simulated data.

An alternative residual resampling methodology known as the "wild" or "external" bootstrap is useful particularly in heteroskedastic settings. In this case, for each estimated residual $\hat{\varepsilon}_i = y_i - \hat{f}(x_i)$ one creates a two-point distribution for a random variable, say, ω_i with probabilities as shown in Table 8.1.

The random variable ω_i has the properties $E(\omega_i) = 0$, $E(\omega_i^2) = \hat{\varepsilon}_i^2$, $E(\omega_i^3) = \hat{\varepsilon}_i^3$. One then draws from this distribution to obtain $\hat{\varepsilon}_i^B$. The bootstrap data set $(y_1^B, x_1), \ldots, (y_n^B, x_n)$ is then constructed, where $y_i^B = \hat{f}(x_i) + \hat{\varepsilon}_i^B$, and statistics of interest are calculated. See Wu (1986) and Härdle (1990, pp. 106–108,247).

Table 8.1. *Wild bootstrap.*

ω_i	$Prob(\omega_i)$
$\hat{\varepsilon}_i(1-\sqrt{5})/2$	$(5+\sqrt{5})/10$
$\hat{\varepsilon}_i(1+\sqrt{5})/2$	$(5-\sqrt{5})/10$

8.1.4 *Validity of the Bootstrap*

Suppose that the statistic being used to produce a confidence interval or test statistic has a nondegenerate limiting distribution. To establish that bootstrap-based confidence intervals have correct coverage probabilities in large samples or that bootstrap test procedures have correct asymptotic size, three conditions are typically sufficient (see Beran and Ducharme, 1991, Proposition 1.3, p. 19, and Proposition 4.3, p. 49). The first condition requires that the DGM used for bootstrap simulations of the statistic converges to the true DGM. This is the case if the original estimator is consistent. The second is a continuity condition requiring that small changes in the true DGM will result in small changes to the limiting distribution of the statistic. The third condition – "triangular array convergence" – which is usually the most difficult to verify, requires that, along any path of DGMs converging to the true DGM, the exact sampling distribution of the statistic converges to the limiting distribution under the true DGM. Put another way, if the bootstrap DGM is close to the true DGM and the sample is large, then the distribution of the bootstrap statistic should be close to the limiting distribution of the true statistic.

8.1.5 *Benefits of the Bootstrap*

In the following sections we describe bootstrap techniques in nonparametric and semiparametric regression settings. We advocate their use because they are often more accurate than the asymptotic procedures we have proposed earlier. Moreover, in some cases, there is ambiguity in the implementation of the asymptotic technique with potentially different outcomes.[4] In other cases, no convenient asymptotic approximation is available.

The increased accuracy that can result from bootstrapping has been formally analyzed using Edgeworth expansions. We outline the argument in its simplest form. Let $y_1, \ldots, y_n$ be i.i.d. with mean μ and variance σ^2; $\bar{y}$ and s^2 are the

[4] For example, consider estimation of standard errors for the parameters of the index model that depend on the derivative f' of the nonparametric regression function (see (7.1.4)). The degree of smoothing that one uses to estimate f' can influence the standard errors significantly. As we will see shortly, the bootstrap can be helpful in such situations.

sample mean and variance, respectively. Then $t = n^{1/2}(\bar{y} - \mu)/s$ converges to a standard normal and is therefore an asymptotic pivot. Under quite general regularity conditions, the distribution of t can be expanded as a power series in $n^{1/2}$

$$P[t \le x] = \Phi(x) + \frac{1}{n^{1/2}} q(x)\phi(x) + O\left(\frac{1}{n}\right), \tag{8.1.1}$$

where ϕ and Φ are the standard normal density and distribution functions, respectively, and q is a polynomial whose coefficients depend on moments (or cumulants) of $\bar{y}$. Equation (8.1.1) is an Edgeworth expansion. As n gets large, the right-hand side converges to the standard normal, as one would expect. Furthermore, the error implicit in the normal approximation is $P[t \le x] - \Phi(x) = O(1/n^{1/2})$.

Now, let $t^B = n^{1/2}(\bar{y}^B - \bar{y})/s^B$ be the bootstrap analogue of t. Then it, too, has an expansion similar to (8.1.1),

$$P[t^B \le x] = \Phi(x) + \frac{1}{n^{1/2}} \hat{q}(x)\phi(x) + O_P\left(\frac{1}{n}\right), \tag{8.1.2}$$

where $\hat{q}$ is obtained from q by replacing moments (which appear in the coefficients of q) with corresponding bootstrap estimates. Because moments (and smooth functions of moments) can be estimated $n^{1/2}$-consistently, we have $\hat{q}(x) - q(x) = O_P(1/n^{1/2})$. Thus, subtracting (8.1.2) from (8.1.1), one obtains

$$P[t \le x] - P[t^B \le x] = O_P\left(\frac{1}{n}\right). \tag{8.1.3}$$

That is, the error of approximation of the bootstrap distribution is $O_P(1/n)$ rather than $O(1/n^{1/2})$, which results from using the asymptotic normal.

A similar argument can be advanced in nonparametric regression, which typically entails taking local rather than global averages. Consider the simple moving average smoother of Section 3.1 and suppose that k, the number of neighbors being averaged, increases sufficiently slowly so that the bias term in (3.1.11) disappears quickly. In this case $t = k^{1/2}(\hat{f}(x_o) - f(x_o))/s$ converges to a standard normal, where s^2 estimates the residual variance. Then the statistic admits an Edgeworth expansion (compare with (8.1.1)),

$$P[t \le x] = \Phi(x) + \frac{1}{k^{1/2}} q(x)\phi(x) + o\left(\frac{1}{k^{1/2}}\right). \tag{8.1.4}$$

Let $t^B = k^{1/2}(\hat{f}^B(x_o) - \hat{f}(x_o))/s^B$ be the bootstrap analogue of t. Then it too has an expansion similar to (8.1.4):

$$P[t^B \le x] = \Phi(x) + \frac{1}{k^{1/2}} \hat{q}(x)\phi(x) + o_P\left(\frac{1}{k^{1/2}}\right), \tag{8.1.5}$$

where $\hat{q}(x) - q(x) = o_P(1)$ so that

$$P[t \le x] - P[t^B \le x] = o_P\left(\frac{1}{k^{1/2}}\right). \tag{8.1.6}$$

In summary, (8.1.3) and (8.1.6) indicate that the bootstrap can result in approximations to sampling distributions that are superior to the asymptotic normal. For detailed Edgeworth analysis of an extensive range of bootstrap procedures, see Hall (1992). For an overview, see Horowitz (2001).

8.1.6 Limitations of the Bootstrap

Although the bootstrap works in a broad class of models, there are cases in which it fails or at least requires modification to work properly. A particularly simple example of relevance to econometricians was provided by Andrews (2000). Suppose $y_1, \ldots, y_n$ are drawn from an $N(\mu, 1)$ distribution and one knows that $\mu \ge 0$. The maximum likelihood estimator is then $\hat{\mu} = \max\{\bar{y}, 0\}$. If the true mean is zero, the bootstrap will fail to approximate the distribution of $n^{1/2}(\hat{\mu} - \mu)$ correctly even in large samples. The basic idea extends to much more general models whenever a parameter is inequality constrained and its true value lies on the boundary of the parameter space. Inequality constraints are common; take for example the estimation of equivalence scales that involves a priori constraints on parameters (see discussion following (7.1.9)). In these circumstances, it is possible to modify the bootstrap to regain consistency by taking bootstrap samples of size $m \ll n$.

A second example is the specification test proposed by Härdle and Mammen (1993), which we discussed in Section 6.4.2. In that case, the wild bootstrap succeeds where the conventional bootstrap fails. For various other examples, see Andrews (2000) and Beran (1997) and references therein. In a time series context, bootstrap failures can be spectacular; see Phillips (2001).

8.1.7 Summary of Bootstrap Choices

As we mentioned earlier, a variety of methods are available for implementing the bootstrap. In the regression setting, one chooses first between joint sampling and residual sampling. We will use the latter exclusively. Having done so, one needs to decide whether to assume the residuals are homoskedastic – in which case one can sample them randomly – or whether the residuals are heteroskedastic – in which case a device like the wild bootstrap is required. One must also decide whether to use the "percentile" method or the "percentile-t" method. Although the former will produce confidence intervals and critical values that are asymptotically valid, the latter, which uses a pivot, is typically more accurate. For a detailed discussion of the alternative bootstrap methodologies in a nonparametric setting, their advantages, and disadvantages, see Hall (1992,

Sections 4.4 and 4.5) and Horowitz (2001, Sections 4.2 and 4.3). Finally, one must select the number of bootstrap replications. There is a growing literature on this subject (see, e.g., Andrews and Buchinsky 2000). A practical approach involves increasing the number of bootstrap iterations until there is little change in the resulting critical value or confidence interval.

8.1.8 *Further Reading*

Efron and Tibshirani (1993) provide a readable introduction to the bootstrap. Shao and Tu (1995) provide a more technical survey of various developments. Härdle (1990) discusses applications of the bootstrap in a nonparametric setting. See also Hall (1992, pp. 224–234). Hall (1992) provides extensive Edgeworth analysis explaining why the bootstrap can outperform the traditional asymptotic approach. An abbreviated version of the arguments in Hall (1992) may be found in Hall (1994). LePage and Billard (1992) and Mammen (1992) contain explorations into the limitations of the bootstrap. Beran and Ducharme (1991) provide an approachable treatment of the large sample validity of the bootstrap. Horowitz (1997) offers theory and numerical analysis for a variety of bootstrap methods, whereas Horowitz (2001) provides an extensive review of the bootstrap in econometrics. Davison and Hinkley (1997) contains a practical review of bootstrap methods and their applications with some attention to nonparametric regression.

8.2 Bootstrap Confidence Intervals for Kernel Smoothers

Consider the problem of constructing pointwise confidence intervals for a nonparametric regression function. We have described asymptotic procedures for doing so in Chapter 3. If one uses an optimal bandwidth, these are complicated by the presence of biases (as in (3.2.5)). Indeed, this was the reason that undersmoothing was used to simplify confidence interval construction (see (3.2.7) to (3.2.10)).

Table 8.2 outlines the implementation of several bootstrap procedures. The upper panel delineates construction of percentile confidence intervals. These require only reestimation of the regression function $f(x_o)$ from each bootstrap sample and are therefore the simplest to implement.

The second panel indicates how to construct percentile-t confidence intervals. Because the bootstrap is attempting to mimic the distribution of the asymptotic pivot $t = (\hat{f}(x_o) - f(x_o))/s_{\hat{f}}$, one needs to calculate $\hat{f}^B(x_o)$ and $s_{\hat{f}}^B(x_o)$ from each bootstrap sample. (For the latter, see Section 3.2 and particularly (3.2.8).) The third panel explains how to modify the previous procedures to allow for heteroskedasticity.

In Figure 8.1 we illustrate the application of these techniques to our South African data on food expenditures by single individuals. Note that the

Table 8.2. *Bootstrap confidence intervals at* $f(x_o)$.[a]

Percentile bootstrap confidence interval at $f(x_o)$:

1. Using cross-validation, find the optimal bandwidth $\lambda = O(n^{-1/5})$. Estimate f and call this estimate $\hat{f}_\lambda$.
2. Reestimate f using a wider bandwidth, say $\bar{\lambda} = 1.1\lambda$ (which will result in some oversmoothing) and call this estimate $\hat{f}_{\bar{\lambda}}$.
3. Reestimate f using a narrower bandwidth, say $.9\lambda$ (which will result in some undersmoothing) and calculate the residuals $\hat{\varepsilon}_i$.
4. (a) Center the residuals obtained in Step 3 and sample with replacement to obtain bootstrap residuals $\hat{\varepsilon}_i^B$. Construct a bootstrap data set $y_i^B = \hat{f}_{\bar{\lambda}}(x_i) + \hat{\varepsilon}_i^B, \quad i = 1, \ldots, n$.
   (b) Estimate $f(x_o)$ using the bootstrap data and the original optimal λ to obtain $\hat{f}_\lambda^B(x_o)$.
   (c) Repeat the resampling many times saving the results from (b).
5. To calculate a 95 percent confidence interval for $f(x_o)$, obtain the .025 and .975 quantiles of the distribution of $\hat{f}_\lambda^B(x_o)$.

Percentile-*t* bootstrap confidence interval at $f(x_o)$:
Replace Steps 4 and 5 above with

4. (a) Resample with replacement from the centered residuals to obtain bootstrap residuals $\hat{\varepsilon}_i^B$ and construct a bootstrap data set $y_i^B = \hat{f}_{\bar{\lambda}}(x_i) + \hat{\varepsilon}_i^B, \quad i = 1, \ldots, n$.
   (b) Calculate $\hat{f}_\lambda^B(x_o)$ and $s_{\hat{f}}^B(x_o)$ using (3.2.3) and (3.2.8). Then calculate $t^B = (\hat{f}^B(x_o) - \hat{f}(x_o))/s_{\hat{f}}^B$.
   (c) Repeat the resampling many times saving t^B each time.
5. To calculate a 95 percent confidence interval for $f(x_o)$, obtain $c_{.025}$ and $c_{.975}$, the .025 and .975 quantiles of the empirical distribution of t^B from Step 4(c). A 95 percent confidence interval is given by

$$[\hat{f}(x_o) - c_{.975} \cdot s_{\hat{f}}(x_o), \hat{f}(x_o) - c_{.025} \cdot s_{\hat{f}}(x_o)],$$

   where $\hat{f}(x_o)$ and $s_{\hat{f}}(x_o)$ are calculated using the original data.

Heteroskedasticity:
Replace 4(a) in either of the preceding procedures with

4. (a) Sample using the wild bootstrap (Table 8.1) from the uncentered residuals to obtain bootstrap residuals $\hat{\varepsilon}_i^B$ and construct a bootstrap data set $y_i^B = \hat{f}_{\bar{\lambda}}(x_i) + \hat{\varepsilon}_i^B, \quad i = 1, \ldots, n$.

[a] For definitions of various estimators, see Section 3.2. Note that x_o may be a vector, in which case one is producing a collection of pointwise confidence intervals.
Source: Härdle (1990, pp. 106–107).

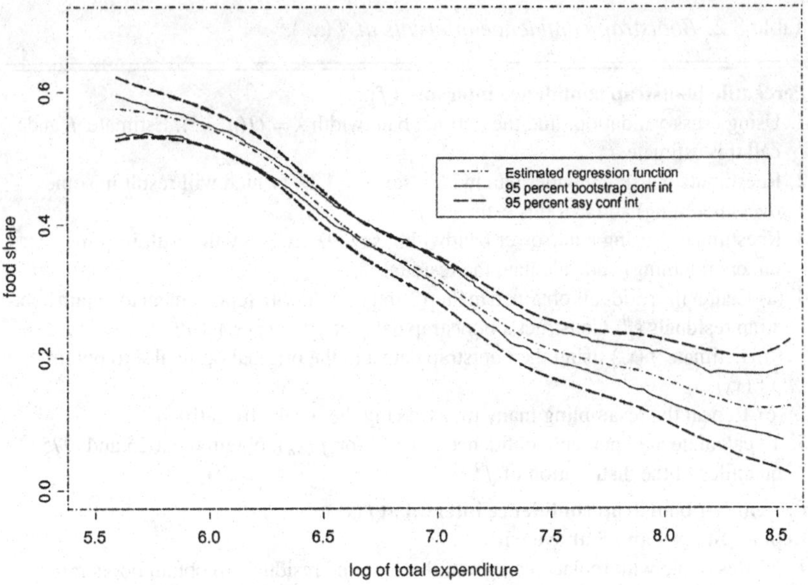

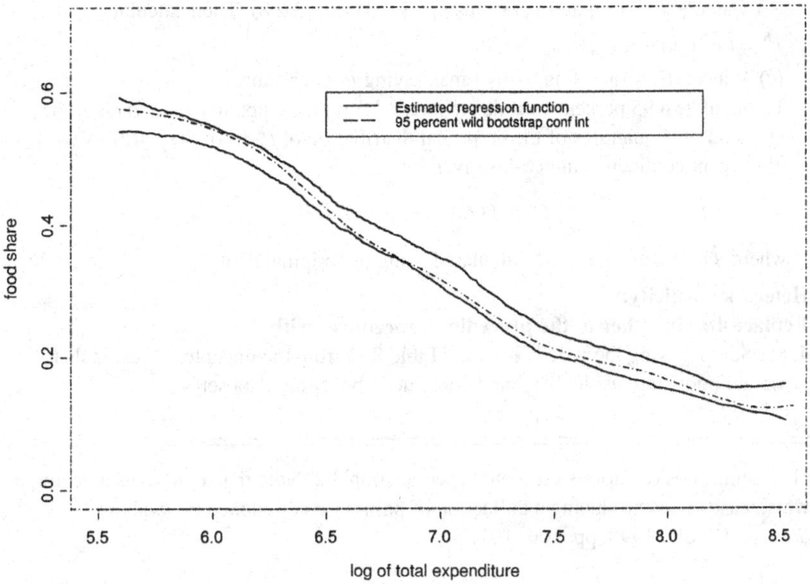

Data: Food share of expenditure by single individuals from South Africa; compare with Figure 3.3.

Figure 8.1. Percentile bootstrap confidence intervals for Engel curves.

heteroskedastic confidence intervals in the lower panel are narrower at high levels of income than their homoskedastic counterparts. This is because there is less variance in food share expenditures at high levels of income, as may be seen from the scatterplot in Figure 3.3.

8.3 Bootstrap Goodness-of-Fit and Residual Regression Tests

8.3.1 Goodness-of-Fit Tests

We have proposed a simple goodness-of-fit statistic for testing various restrictions on the regression function. It involves comparison of the restricted estimate of the residual variance to the differencing estimate. To simplify exposition, we will assume that optimal differencing coefficients are used so that the statistic has the form (see Sections 4.3 and 6.2, and (6.2.5))

$$V = (mn)^{1/2}\frac{\left(s^2_{res} - s^2_{diff}\right)}{s^2_{diff}} \xrightarrow{D} N(0, 1), \qquad (8.3.1)$$

where m is the order of differencing. The essential idea underlying bootstrap critical values is the creation of a DGM that satisfies the null hypothesis. This is done by imposing the restrictions of the null hypothesis on the estimate of the regression function. The resulting restricted estimate of f and the (centered) estimated residuals constitute the bootstrap DGM. Repeated samples are then taken, and the test statistic is recomputed each time. Behavior of the test statistic under the null hypothesis is assessed (and critical values are obtained) by observing the behavior of the bootstrapped test statistic. Table 8.3 contains implementation details. The bootstrap approach requires only the ability to compute the various components of the test statistic and, as such, it is applicable to a variety of hypotheses. Computing time depends on sample size, the number of bootstrap samples that are taken, and the time required to compute the various components of the test statistic.

Goodness-of-fit statistics like (8.3.1) can be obtained in a variety of ways. In calculating the differencing estimator s^2_{diff} one need not use optimal differencing coefficients. For arbitrary coefficients the statistic takes the form (6.2.6). More generally, one can replace s^2_{diff} with other unrestricted estimators of the residual variance such as those obtained by applying a smoother. The key requirement is that one undersmooth when estimating the residual variance under the alternative.

A variety of estimators may also be available under the null, depending on the specific restrictions being imposed. For the null, the key condition is that the difference between the estimated sum of squared residuals and the true sum of squared residuals converge to zero sufficiently quickly (see (6.2.2)).

Table 8.3 *Bootstrap goodness-of-fit tests.*

Hypotheses: $H_o : f \in \bar{\Im}$, $H_1 : f \in \Im$ where $\Im$ is a smooth set of functions and $\bar{\Im}$ is a smooth set of functions with additional constraints.

Test statistic: $V = (mn)^{1/2}(s_{res}^2 - s_{diff}^2)/s_{diff}^2$ where s_{res}^2 is the estimated residual variance from a restricted regression and s_{diff}^2 is an optimal differencing estimator of order m.

Bootstrap test

1. Perform the restricted regression where the constraints of the null hypothesis are imposed. Save the estimates of the regression function $\hat{f}_{res}(x_1), \ldots, \hat{f}_{res}(x_n)$, the residuals $\hat{\varepsilon}_{res,1}, \ldots, \hat{\varepsilon}_{res,n}$, and the estimated residual variance s_{res}^2.
2. Calculate s_{diff}^2.
3. Calculate the value of the test statistic V.
4. (a) Sample with replacement from the centered restricted residuals to obtain $\hat{\varepsilon}_1^B, \ldots, \hat{\varepsilon}_n^B$.
   (b) Construct a bootstrap data set $(y_1^B, x_1), \ldots, (y_n^B, x_n)$, where $y_i^B = \hat{f}_{res}(x_i) + \hat{\varepsilon}_i^B$.
   (c) Using the bootstrap data set, estimate the model under the null and calculate s_{res}^{2B}, s_{diff}^{2B}, and V^B.
   (d) Repeat Steps (a)–(c) multiple times, each time saving the value of the test statistic V^B. Define the bootstrap critical value for a 5 percent significance level test to be the 95th percentile of the V^B.
5. Compare V, the actual value of the statistic, with the bootstrap critical value.

The hypotheses that can be tested using these goodness-of-fit-type statistics include a parametric null, a semiparametric null (such as the partial linear model or index model), equality of regression functions, additive separability, monotonicity, concavity, and base-independence of equivalence scales.

8.3.2 *Residual Regression Tests*

As with goodness-of-fit tests, a wide variety of hypotheses can be tested using residual regression procedures. Recall that the test statistic may be decomposed into three components ($U = U_1 + U_2 + U_3$) as in (6.3.7). The key is to ensure that the estimator of the regression function under the null hypothesis converges sufficiently quickly so that the large sample distribution of U is determined by the first term U_1 (see particularly (6.3.12) and (6.3.13)).

Table 8.4 summarizes a procedure for obtaining bootstrap critical values for the class of residual regression tests we have discussed in Section 6.3 when the residuals are homoskedastic. If the residuals are heteroskedastic, then one replaces random sampling from the centered restricted residuals with sampling using the wild bootstrap.

Table 8.4 *Bootstrap residual regression tests.*

Hypotheses: $H_0 : f \in \bar{\Im}$, $H_1 : f \in \Im$, where $\Im$ is a smooth set of functions and $\bar{\Im}$ is a smooth set of functions with additional constraints.

Test statistic: We implement using the uniform kernel. Let $\mathbf{K}_{ij}$ be the ijth entry of the kernel matrix defined by

$$\mathbf{K}_{ij} = 1/2 \quad \text{if} \quad |x_j - x_i| \le \lambda \quad j \ne i \text{ (note that diagonal elements } \mathbf{K}_{ii} = 0)$$

$$\mathbf{K}_{ij} = 0 \quad \text{otherwise.}$$

Let

$$U = \frac{1}{n}\sum_i (y_i - \hat{f}_{res}(x_i)) \left[\frac{1}{\lambda n} \sum_{j \ne i} (y_j - \hat{f}_{res}(x_j)) \mathbf{K}_{ij} \right] \sim N\left(0, \frac{2\sigma_\varepsilon^4 \int p^2(x) \int K^2}{\lambda n^2}\right).$$

Define $\sigma_U^2 = Var(U) = 2\sigma_\varepsilon^4 \int p^2(x) \int K^2 / \lambda n^2$, which may be estimated using

$$\hat{\sigma}_U^2 = \frac{2}{n^4 \lambda^2} \sum_i \sum_{j \ne i} (y_i - \hat{f}_{res}(x_i))^2 (y_j - \hat{f}_{res}(x_j))^2 \mathbf{K}_{ij}^2.$$

Bootstrap test

1. Perform the restricted regression where the constraints of the null hypothesis are imposed. Save the estimates of the regression function $\hat{f}_{res}(x_1), \ldots, \hat{f}_{res}(x_n)$ and the residuals $\hat{\varepsilon}_{res,1}, \ldots, \hat{\varepsilon}_{res,n}$. Center the residuals so that their mean is zero.
2. Calculate U, $\hat{\sigma}_U$, and $U/\hat{\sigma}_U$.
3. (a) Sample with replacement from the centered restricted residuals to obtain $\hat{\varepsilon}_1^B, \ldots, \hat{\varepsilon}_n^B$ and construct a bootstrap data set $\left(y_1^B, x_1\right), \ldots, \left(y_n^B, x_n\right)$, where $y_i^B = \hat{f}_{res}(x_i) + \hat{\varepsilon}_i^B$.
   (b) Using the bootstrap data set, estimate the model under the null and calculate $\hat{\sigma}_U^B$, U^B, and $U^B/\hat{\sigma}_U^B$.
   (c) Repeat Steps (a) and (b) multiple times, each time saving the value of the standardized test statistic $U^B/\hat{\sigma}_U^B$. Define the bootstrap critical value for a 5 percent significance level test to be the 95th percentile of the $U^B/\hat{\sigma}_U^B$.
4. Compare $U/\hat{\sigma}_U$, the actual value of the statistic, with the bootstrap critical value.

Heteroskedasticity:
Replace 3.(a) with

3. (a) Sample using the wild bootstrap (Table 8.1) from $\hat{\varepsilon}_{res,1}, \ldots, \hat{\varepsilon}_{res,n}$ to obtain $\hat{\varepsilon}_1^B, \ldots, \hat{\varepsilon}_n^B$.

Li and Wang (1998) found that the bootstrap approximation to the distribution of residual regression tests is superior to the asymptotic approximation. Yatchew and Sun (2001) found similar results for goodness-of-fit tests. A principal reason is that the bootstrap corrects for the nonzero mean in the finite sample distributions of these test statistics.

8.4 Bootstrap Inference in Partial Linear and Index Models

8.4.1 Partial Linear Models

Let us return to the partial linear model $y = z\beta + f(x) + \varepsilon$, which we have discussed in Sections 1.3, 3.6, and 4.5. Table 8.5 summarizes how to construct bootstrap confidence intervals for the components of β using the double residual estimation procedure. Under homoskedasticity, we use random sampling from centered residuals. Under heteroskedasticity, we use the wild bootstrap. Validity of bootstrap procedures in the partial linear model has been confirmed (see, e.g., Mammen and Van de Geer 1997 and Yatchew and Bos 1997). Linton (1995b) studied higher-order approximations to the distributions of estimators of the partial linear model. See also Härdle, Liang, and Gao (2000).

We illustrate two of the preceding bootstrap procedures by applying them to our data on electricity distribution costs (see Sections 1.6 and 4.6.2). With wages and capital prices entering in a Cobb–Douglas format, the specification is given by

$$\begin{aligned} tc = \; & f(cust) + \beta_1\, wage + \beta_2\, pcap + \beta_3\, PUC + \beta_4\, kwh \\ & + \beta_5\, life + \beta_6\, lf + \beta_7\, kmwire + \varepsilon. \end{aligned} \tag{8.4.1}$$

We reestimate this model using the double residual method and apply the bootstrap procedure outlined in Table 8.5 to obtain percentile-t confidence intervals for the components of β. The process is repeated using the wild bootstrap. The results are summarized in Table 8.6 in which asymptotic confidence intervals are also reported.

8.4.2 Index Models

Let us return to the index model

$$y = f(x\delta) + \varepsilon, \tag{8.4.2}$$

which we have studied in Chapter 7. To estimate the standard error of $\hat{\delta}$ one needs to estimate the derivative f' (see (7.1.4)–(7.1.6)). The result can be quite sensitive to the smoothing parameter used to estimate f'. Unfortunately, cross-validation does not provide good guidance for smoothing parameter selection if one is interested in the *derivative* of a function.

The bootstrap provides an alternative mechanism for calibrating standard errors or, more importantly, for directly obtaining confidence intervals for δ. However, the estimator $\hat{\delta}$ requires a grid search and thus the bootstrap can be time-consuming. This limitation continues to diminish as computing speeds increase and search algorithms become more intelligent. In the examples and

Table 8.5 *Percentile-t bootstrap confidence intervals for β in the partial linear model.*[a]

Let $y = f(x) + z\beta + \varepsilon$, where z is a p-dimensional vector. To construct bootstrap confidence intervals for the components of β using the double residual estimation procedure, proceed as follows:

1. (a) Estimate $h(x) = E(y \mid x)$ and $g(x) = E(z \mid x)$ to obtain the vector $\hat{h}(x)$ and the $n \times p$ matrix $\hat{g}(x)$.
   (b) Estimate β using the double residual estimator $\hat{\beta} = ((Z - \hat{g}(x))'(Z - \hat{g}(x)))^{-1}(Z - \hat{g}(x))'(y - \hat{h}(x))$.
   (c) Estimate the residual variance $s^2 = (y - \hat{h}(x) - (Z - \hat{g}(x))\hat{\beta})'(y - \hat{h}(x) - (Z - \hat{g}(x))\hat{\beta})/n$.
   (d) Estimate the covariance matrix of $\hat{\beta}$ using $\hat{\Sigma}_{\hat{\beta}} = s^2((Z - \hat{g}(x))'(Z - \hat{g}(x)))^{-1}$.
   (e) Perform a kernel regression of $y - Z\hat{\beta}$ on x to obtain $\hat{f}$.

The DGM for the regression function is the vector $Z\hat{\beta} + \hat{f}(x)$. The estimated residuals $\hat{\varepsilon} = y - Z\hat{\beta} - \hat{f}(x)$ will provide the DGM for the residuals.

2. (a) Sample with replacement from the centered residuals to obtain $\hat{\varepsilon}_1^B, \ldots, \hat{\varepsilon}_n^B$.
   (b) Construct a bootstrap data set $(y_1^B, x_1, z_1), \ldots, (y_n^B, x_n, z_n)$, where $y_i^B = \hat{f}(x_i) + z_i\hat{\beta} + \hat{\varepsilon}_i^B$.
   (c) Perform a kernel regression of y^B on x to obtain $\hat{h}^B(x)$.
   (d) Calculate the bootstrap estimate $\hat{\beta}^B = ((Z - \hat{g}(x))'(Z - \hat{g}(x)))^{-1}(Z - \hat{g}(x))'(y^B - \hat{h}^B(x))$.
   (e) Calculate the bootstrap residual variance $s^{2^B} = (y^B - \hat{h}^B(x) - (Z - \hat{g}(x))\hat{\beta}^B)'(y^B - \hat{h}^B(x) - (Z - \hat{g}(x))\hat{\beta}^B)/n$.
   (f) Calculate the estimated covariance matrix of $\hat{\beta}^B$ using $\hat{\Sigma}_{\hat{\beta}}^B = s^{2^B}((Z - \hat{g}(x))'(Z - \hat{g}(x)))^{-1}$.
   (g) For each component of β, calculate the bootstrap t-statistic $t_j^B = \left(\hat{\beta}_j^B - \hat{\beta}_j\right) / \left[\hat{\Sigma}_{\hat{\beta}}^B\right]_{jj}^{1/2}, \quad j = 1, \ldots, p$.
   (h) Repeat Steps (a)–(g) multiple times saving the results from Step (g).
3. To calculate a 95 percent confidence interval for, say, β_j, proceed as follows. Let $c_{.025}$ and $c_{.975}$ be the .025 and .975 quantiles of the empirical distribution of t_j^B from Step 2 (g). A 95 percent confidence interval is given by

$$\left[\hat{\beta}_j - c_{.975} \cdot \left[\hat{\Sigma}_{\hat{\beta}}\right]_{jj}^{1/2}, \quad \hat{\beta}_j - c_{.025} \cdot \left[\hat{\Sigma}_{\hat{\beta}}\right]_{jj}^{1/2}\right].$$

Heteroskedasticity:
Replace 2(a) with

2. (a) Sample using the wild bootstrap (Table 8.1) from the uncentered residuals $\hat{\varepsilon}_1, \ldots, \hat{\varepsilon}_n$ to obtain $\hat{\varepsilon}_1^B, \ldots, \hat{\varepsilon}_n^B$.

---

[a] See, in particular, Section 3.6.3 for definitions of terms and notation.

Table 8.6 *Asymptotic versus bootstrap confidence intervals: Scale economies in electricity distribution.*

	Partial linear model[a]			
			95 percent Confidence intervals Asymptotic *Percentile-t Bootstrap* *Wild Bootstrap*	
Variable	Coef	Asy SE		
wage	0.692	0.279	0.146	1.238
			0.031	*1.326*
			0.079	*1.351*
pcap	0.504	0.066	0.374	0.634
			0.358	*0.659*
			0.354	*0.651*
PUC	−0.067	0.035	−0.136	0.003
			−0.144	*0.019*
			−0.134	*−0.004*
kwh	0.015	0.080	−0.142	0.172
			−0.156	*0.194*
			−0.155	*0.202*
life	−0.500	0.111	−0.716	−0.281
			−0.747	*−0.240*
			−0.734	*−0.283*
lf	1.279	0.398	0.499	2.057
			0.387	*2.120*
			0.510	*2.064*
kmwire	0.356	0.081	0.197	0.516
			0.200	*0.538*
			0.196	*0.524*
s^2	.017			
R^2	.692			

[a] Model estimated using kernel double residual method. Number of bootstrap replications = 1,000.

exercises to follow, we use *S-Plus.* Much faster results can be obtained if one uses Fortran or other programming languages.

A further advantage of the bootstrap is that it incorporates nonnormality, which can emerge if the sample is of moderate size and the ex ante bounds on δ are tight. For example, suppose one is estimating an equivalence scale by searching over values of δ in the interval $[a, b]$. The bootstrap can often

Table 8.7 *Confidence intervals for δ in the index model: Percentile method.*

Let $y = f(x\delta) + \varepsilon$. To construct bootstrap confidence intervals for the components of δ, proceed as follows:

1. Using a grid search, find $\hat{\delta}$ the value that minimizes (7.1.3). Perform a nonparametric regression on the ordered pairs $(y_i, x_i\hat{\delta})$ to obtain $\hat{f}(x_i\hat{\delta}), i = 1, \ldots, n$. Calculate the residuals $\hat{\varepsilon}_i = y_i - \hat{f}(x_i\hat{\delta})$.
2. (a) Sample with replacement from the centered residuals to obtain $\hat{\varepsilon}_i^B, i = 1, \ldots, n$.
   (b) Construct the bootstrap data set $(y_1^B, x_1), \ldots\ldots, (y_n^B, x_n)$ where $y_i^B = \hat{f}(x_i\hat{\delta}) + \hat{\varepsilon}_i^B$.
   (c) Using the bootstrap data, obtain $\hat{\delta}^B$ by minimizing (7.1.3).
3. Repeat Step 2 multiple times to obtain the bootstrap distribution of $\hat{\delta}^B$. For a 95 percent confidence interval for a component of δ, extract the corresponding .025 and .975 quantiles.

Heteroskedasticity:
Replace 2 (a) with
2. (a) Sample using the wild bootstrap (Table 8.1) from $\hat{\varepsilon}_i$ to obtain $\hat{\varepsilon}_i^B$ for $i = 1, \ldots, n$.

outperform the normal approximation to the sampling distribution of $\hat{\delta}$, particularly if estimates of δ are frequently at or near the boundary (although as we have indicated above, the bootstrap fails if the true value of δ is actually on the boundary). Table 8.7 outlines a procedure for constructing bootstrap confidence intervals for δ. We describe the percentile method because of its simplicity and because no estimate of f' is required.

The discussion thus far has been of index models, but all the points that have been made apply also to the partial linear index models discussed in Section 7.2. The bootstrap procedure described in Table 8.7 can readily be extended to this case.

Figure 8.2 illustrates the application of the procedure to estimation of the equivalence scale for couples versus singles using the South African data set. If Engel's method is used, then the index model becomes $y = f(\log x - z\delta) + \varepsilon$, where x is household expenditure, z is a dummy variable distinguishing couples from singles, and δ is the log equivalence scale.[5] The resulting estimate is $\hat{\Delta} = \exp(\hat{\delta}) = 1.65$ with asymptotic standard error .064 (see Figure 7.1). The 95 percent asymptotic confidence interval is given by [1.52, 1.78]. The bootstrap confidence interval is very similar at [1.55,1.80].

[5] See Gozalo (1997) for an alternative analysis of equivalence scale estimation using the bootstrap.

	Engel equivalence scale	General equivalence scale
Asymptotic confidence interval:	[1.52,1.78]	[1.17, 2.13]
Bootstrap confidence interval:	[1.55,1.80]	[1.43, 1.89]

Bootstrap sampling distribution of $\hat{\Delta}$

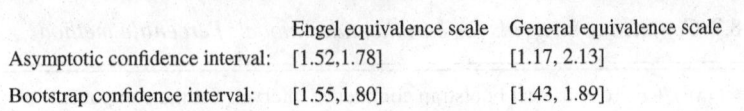

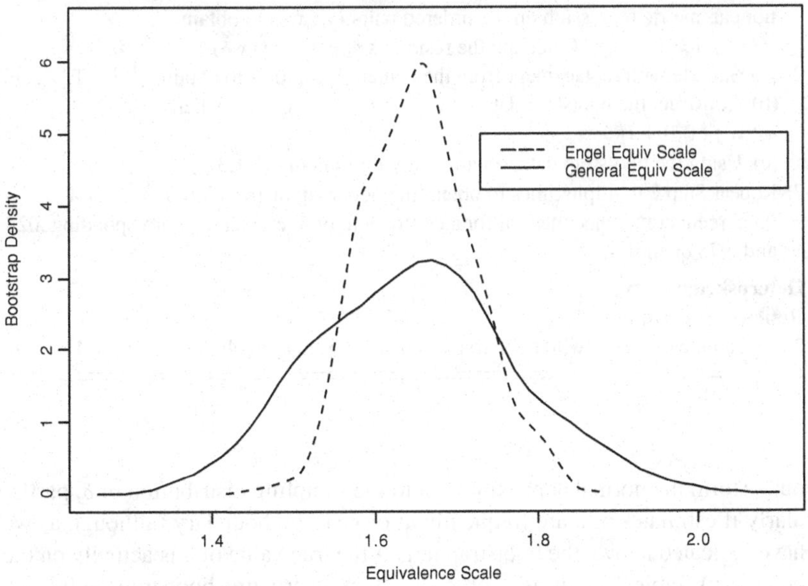

Figure 8.2. Equivalence scale estimation for singles versus couples: Asymptotic versus bootstrap methods.

Next we use the theoretically more valid approach to constructing equivalence scales embodied in the model

$$y = f(\log x - z\delta) + z\eta + \varepsilon. \tag{8.4.3}$$

In this case we need to estimate both δ and a vertical shift parameter η (see Section 7.2 for further discussion). The estimate $\hat{\Delta}$ remains at 1.65, but its standard error increases substantially to .24 (Chapter 7, Exercise 4). The asymptotic confidence interval is [1.17,2.13]. Note that the asymptotic approach does not preclude confidence intervals extending beyond the domain of search. By comparison, the bootstrap interval is much tighter at [1.43,1.89].

Figure 8.2 summarizes these results and plots the bootstrap distributions of the estimated equivalence scale using Engel's method and the more general approach using the partial linear index model.

8.5 Exercises[6]

1. *South African Food Share Data*: For single individuals in this data set, perform the following:

    (a) Construct pointwise confidence intervals for food share as a function of log of total expenditure. Use the bootstrap procedure outlined in Table 8.2. (You may use either the percentile or the percentile-t method.)
    (b) Repeat using the wild bootstrap.
    (c) Test the log-linearity of the preceding Engel curve by constructing critical values using:

        (i) the goodness-of-fit test procedure outlined in Table 8.3 with order of differencing $m = 10$,
        (ii) the residual regression test procedure outlined in Table 8.4.

    (d) Repeat the residual regression test using the wild bootstrap to allow for the possibility of heteroskedasticity.
    (e) Repeat Parts (c) and (d) but this time testing whether food share is quadratic in the log of total expenditure.

2. *South African Food Share Data*: Repeat Exercise 1 for childless couples and for couples with one child.

3. *Scale Economies in Electricity Distribution*:

    (a) Using the percentile-t bootstrap procedure outlined in Table 8.5, construct 95 percent two-sided confidence intervals for the seven parameters in the parametric portion of the "Semiparametric Cobb–Douglas" specification in Table 8.6 (see also Figure 4.5).
    (b) Repeat Part (a) using the wild bootstrap.
    (c) Outline a bootstrap procedure for performing tests of the general linear hypothesis $R\beta = r$ in the partial linear model. (For the asymptotic test, see Section 3.6.) Test the "Semiparametric Translog" specification in Figure 4.5 against the "Semiparametric Cobb–Douglas."
    (d) Remove the estimated parametric effects and test a quadratic specification for the scale effect against the "Semiparametric Cobb–Douglas" by using the bootstrap procedures outlined in Tables 8.3 and 8.4.
    (e) Following the procedure outlined in Table 8.2, design a methodology for constructing confidence intervals for the nonparametric portion of a partial linear model. Why is your procedure valid? Use the procedure to construct a 95 percent confidence interval for the scale effect in the Semiparametric Cobb–Douglas specification.

4. *Equivalence Scales for Singles Versus Couples*: This exercise applies bootstrap procedures to produce confidence intervals for equivalence scales using the food share data for South African singles and couples.

[6] Data and sample programs for empirical exercises are available on the Web. See the Preface for details.

(a) Simulate the sampling distribution of the estimated Engel equivalence scale using the method in Table 8.7. Plot your results and calculate a 95 percent confidence interval. Compare your results to the asymptotic confidence interval (see Chapter 7, Exercise 1).
(b) Adapt the bootstrap procedure in Table 8.7 so that it applies to the partial linear index model in (8.4.3) (refer to Section 7.2). Simulate the sampling distribution of the estimated general equivalence scale. Plot your results and calculate a 95 percent confidence interval. Compare your results to the asymptotic confidence interval (see Chapter 7, Exercise 4.).

5. *Equivalence Scales for Childless Couples Versus Couples with Children*:
   (a) Repeat Exercise 4 for childless couples versus couples with one child.
   (b) Repeat Exercise 4 for childless couples versus couples with two children.

Appendix A – Mathematical Preliminaries

Suppose $a_n, n = 1, \ldots, \infty$ is a sequence of numbers. Then the sequence a_n is of smaller order than the sequence n^{-r}, written $a_n = o(n^{-r})$ if $n^r a_n$ converges to zero. For example, if $a_n = n^{-1/4}$, then $a_n = o(n^{-1/5})$ because $n^{1/5} \cdot n^{-1/4} \to 0$. A sequence is $o(1)$ if it converges to 0.

The sequence a_n is the same order as the sequence n^{-r}, written $a_n = O(n^{-r})$ if $n^r a_n$ is a bounded sequence. For example, the sequence $a_n = 7n^{-1/4} + 3n^{-1/5} = O(n^{-1/5})$ because $n^{1/5} a_n$ converges to 3 and hence is a bounded sequence. A sequence is $O(1)$ if it is bounded.

Now suppose $a_n, n = 1, \ldots, \infty$ is a sequence of random variables. Then, $a_n = o_P(n^{-r})$ if $n^r a_n$ converges in probability to zero. For example, let $a_n = \bar{\varepsilon}_n = 1/n \sum_{i=1}^{n} \varepsilon_i$, where ε_i are i.i.d. with mean zero and variance σ_ε^2. Then $E(\bar{\varepsilon}_n) = 0$, $Var(\bar{\varepsilon}_n) = \sigma_\varepsilon^2/n$. Because the mean is 0 and the variance converges to 0, the sequence $\bar{\varepsilon}_n$ converges in probability to 0 and is $o_P(1)$. Furthermore, for any $r < 1/2$, $\bar{\varepsilon}_n = o_P(n^{-r})$ since $Var(n^r \bar{\varepsilon}_n) = \sigma_\varepsilon^2 / n^{1-2r}$ converges to 0.

A sequence of random variables $b_n, n = 1, \ldots, \infty$ is bounded in probability if, for any $\delta > 0$, no matter how small, there exists a constant B_δ and a point in the sequence n_δ such that for all $n > n_\delta$, $Prob\,[|b_n| > B_\delta] < \delta$.

Write $a_n = O_P(1)$ if a_n is bounded in probability and $a_n = O_P(n^{-r})$ if $n^r a_n$ is bounded in probability. For example, suppose $n^r a_n$ converges to a random variable with finite mean and variance, then $a_n = O_P(n^{-r})$. Thus, using the central limit theorem we find that $n^{1/2}\,\bar{\varepsilon}_n$ converges to an $N(0, \sigma_\varepsilon^2)$, in which case $\bar{\varepsilon}_n = O_P(n^{-1/2})$ and $n^{1/2}\,\bar{\varepsilon}_n = O_P(1)$.

Suppose $y_i = \mu_y + \varepsilon_i$, where μ_y is a constant, and define the sample mean $\bar{y}_n$ based on n observations. Then

$$\bar{y}_n = O_P(\mu_y + \bar{\varepsilon}_n) = \mu_y + O_P(\bar{\varepsilon}_n) = O(1) + O_P\left(n^{-1/2}\right) \text{ and}$$
$$n^{1/2}(\bar{y}_n - \mu_y) = n^{1/2}\bar{\varepsilon}_n = O_P(1).$$

Let λ_n be a sequence of real numbers converging to zero. In the main text, λ has usually been used to represent the shrinking bandwidth in kernel regression (although we have suppressed the n subscript). Typically, we consider sequences of the form $\lambda_n = n^{-r}$, where $0 < r < 1$. Let $a_n = 1/(\lambda_n n) \sum_{i=1}^{\lambda_n n} \varepsilon_i$ be the average of the first $\lambda_n n = n^{1-r}$ values of ε_i. For example, if $n = 100$, $r = 1/5$, then we are averaging the first $39.8 \cong 40$ observations. Then,

$$E[a_n] = 0 \quad \text{and} \quad Var[a_n] = \sigma_\varepsilon^2/\lambda_n n = \sigma_\varepsilon^2/n^{1-r}.$$

Hence,

$$a_n = O_P\left((\lambda_n n)^{-1/2}\right) = O_P\left(n^{-1/2(1-r)}\right).$$

Suppose now that we draw n observations from the uniform distribution on [0,1]. Assume again that $0 < r < 1$, in which case $0 < \lambda_n = n^{-r} < 1$. Then the proportion of observations falling in an interval of width $2\lambda_n$ will be approximately $2\lambda_n$ and the number of observations in the same interval will be about $2n\lambda_n$.

If we draw n observations from the uniform distribution on the unit square $[0,1]^2$ then the proportion of observations falling in a square of dimension $2\lambda_n \cdot 2\lambda_n$ will be approximately $4\lambda_n^2$, and the number of observations in the same square will be about $4n\lambda_n^2$.

Appendix B – Proofs

Notation: If A, B are matrices of identical dimension, define $[A \odot B]_{ij} = A_{ij}B_{ij}$.

Lemma B.1: (a) Suppose the components of $\vartheta = (\vartheta_1, \ldots, \vartheta_\xi)'$ are i.i.d. with $E\vartheta_i = 0$, $Var(\vartheta_i) = \sigma_\vartheta^2$, $E\vartheta_i^4 = \eta_\vartheta$, and covariance matrix $\sigma_\vartheta^2 I_\xi$. If A is a symmetric matrix, then $E(\vartheta' A\vartheta) = \sigma_\vartheta^2 trA$ and $Var(\vartheta' A\vartheta) = (\eta_\vartheta - 3\sigma_\vartheta^4)trA \odot A + \sigma_\vartheta^4 2trAA$.

(b) Consider the heteroskedastic case in which $Var(\vartheta_i) = \sigma_i^2$, $E\vartheta_i^4 = \eta_i$, ϑ has the diagonal covariance matrix Ω, and η is the diagonal matrix with entries η_i. Then $E(\vartheta' A\vartheta) = trA\Omega$ and $Var(\vartheta' A\vartheta) = tr(\eta \odot A \odot A - 3\Omega^2 \odot A \odot A) + 2tr(\Omega A \Omega A)$. For results of this type see, for example, Schott (1997, p. 391, Theorem 9.18), or they may be proved directly.

Lemma B.2: Suppose x has support the unit interval with density bounded away from 0. Given n observations on x, reorder them so that they are in increasing order: $x_1 \leq \cdots \leq x_n$. Then for any ϵ positive and arbitrarily close to 0, $1/n \sum (x_i - x_{i-1})^2 = O_P(n^{-2(1-\epsilon)})$.

Proof: Partition the unit interval into $n^{1-\epsilon}$ subintervals and note that the probability of an empty subinterval goes to zero as n increases. The maximum distance between observations in adjacent subintervals is $2/n^{1-\epsilon}$, and the maximum distance between observations within a subinterval is $1/n^{1-\epsilon}$, from which the result follows immediately. ■

Comment on Lemma B.2: Because ϵ may be chosen arbitrarily close to zero, we write $1/n \sum (x_i - x_{i-1})^2 \cong O_P(n^{-2})$. Note also that for fixed j, $1/n \sum (x_i - x_{i-j})^2 \cong O_P(n^{-2})$. For an *arbitrary* collection of points in the unit interval, the maximum value that $1/n \sum (x_i - x_{i-1})^2$ can take is $1/n$, which occurs when all observations are at one of the two endpoints of the interval.

Lemma B.3: Suppose $(x_i, \varepsilon_i), i = 1, \ldots, n$ are i.i.d. The x_i have density bounded away from zero on the unit interval, and $\varepsilon_i \,|\, x_i \sim (0, \sigma_\varepsilon^2)$. Assume data have been reordered so that $x_1 \leq \cdots \leq x_n$. Define $f(x) = (f(x_1), \ldots, f(x_n))'$, where the function f has a bounded first derivative. Let D be a differencing matrix of say order m. Then $f(x)'D'Df(x) = O_P(n^{-1+\epsilon})$ and $Var(f(x)'D'D\varepsilon) = O_P(n^{-1+\epsilon})$, where ϵ is positive and arbitrarily close to 0.

Proof: The result follows immediately from Yatchew (1997, Appendix, Equations (A.2) and (A.3)). ■

Lemma B.4: Suppose $(y_i, x_i, z_i, w_i), i = 1, \ldots, n$ are i.i.d., where y and x are scalars and z and w are p- and q-dimensional row vectors, respectively. Suppose the data have been reordered so that $x_1 \leq \cdots \leq x_n$. Let Z be the $n \times p$ matrix of observations on z and W the $n \times q$ matrix of observations on w. Suppose $E(z \,|\, x)$ and $E(w \,|\, x)$ are smooth vector functions of x having first derivatives bounded. Let $\Sigma_{z|x} = E_x Var(z \,|\, x)$, $\Sigma_{w|x} = E_x Var(w \,|\, x)$, and $\Sigma_{zw|x} = E_x Cov(z, w \,|\, x)$, where $Cov(z, w \,|\, x)$ is the $p \times q$ matrix of covariances between the z and w variables conditional on x. Let $d_0, d_1, \ldots, d_m$ be differencing weights satisfying constraints (4.1.1), define δ using (4.1.6), and let D be the corresponding differencing matrix as in (4.1.2). Then

$$\frac{Z'D'DZ}{n} \xrightarrow{P} \Sigma_{z|x} \qquad \frac{Z'D'DD'DZ}{n} \xrightarrow{P} (1+2\delta)\Sigma_{z|x}$$

$$\frac{W'D'DW}{n} \xrightarrow{P} \Sigma_{w|x} \qquad \frac{W'D'DD'DW}{n} \xrightarrow{P} (1+2\delta)\Sigma_{w|x}$$

$$\frac{Z'D'DW}{n} \xrightarrow{P} \Sigma_{zw|x} \qquad \frac{Z'D'DD'DW}{n} \xrightarrow{P} (1+2\delta)\Sigma_{zw|x}.$$

Proof: Because z has a smooth regression function on x, write $z_i = g(x_i) + u_i$, where g is a vector function with first derivatives bounded, $E(u_i \,|\, x_i) = 0$, and $E(Var(z_i \,|\, x_i)) = \Sigma_{z|x}$. Let $g(x)$ be the $n \times p$ matrix with ith row $g(x_i)$. Let U be the $n \times p$ matrix with ith row u_i. Then

$$\frac{Z'D'DZ}{n} = \frac{U'D'DU}{n} + \frac{g(x)'D'Dg(x)}{n} + \frac{g(x)'D'DU}{n} + \frac{U'D'Dg(x)}{n}$$
$$\cong \frac{U'D'DU}{n} + O_P\left(\frac{1}{n^{3/2}}\right).$$

The second line uses Lemma B.3. Using (4.1.4), write

$$\frac{U'D'DU}{n} \doteq \frac{U'L_0U}{n} + \sum_{j=0}^{m-1} d_j d_{j+1} \frac{U'(L_1 + L_1')U}{n} + \cdots + d_0 d_m \frac{U'(L_m + L_m')U}{n}$$

and note that all terms but the first on the right-hand side converge to zero matrices. Thus, $U'DD'U/n \xrightarrow{P} \Sigma_{z|x}$ and $Z'DD'Z/n \xrightarrow{P} \Sigma_{z|x}$. Because the diagonal entries of $D'DD'D$ are $1+2\delta$, we may use similar arguments to show that $U'D'DD'DU/n \xrightarrow{P} (1+2\delta)\Sigma_{z|x}$ and that $Z'D'DD'DZ/n \xrightarrow{P} (1+2\delta)\Sigma_{z|x}$. Convergence of other quantities in the statement of the lemma may be proved by analogous reasoning. ■

Comments on Lemma B.4: More generally, suppose $(y_i, x_i, h(z_i))$, $i = 1, \ldots, n$ are i.i.d., where h is a p-dimensional vector function such that $E(h(z) \mid x)$ has the first derivative bounded. Define $\Sigma_{h(z)|x}$ to be the $p \times p$ conditional covariance matrix of $h(z)$ given x. Let $h(Z)$ be the $n \times p$ matrix whose ith row is $h(z_i)$. Then

$$\frac{h(Z)'D'Dh(Z)}{n} \xrightarrow{P} \Sigma_{h(z)|x} \qquad \frac{h(Z)'D'DD'Dh(Z)}{n} \xrightarrow{P} (1+2\delta)\Sigma_{h(z)|x}.$$

Proof of Proposition 4.2.1: For the mean and variance use (4.2.6) and (4.2.7). From (4.1.4) note that s^2_{diff} has a band structure and thus a finitely dependent central limit theorem may be applied (see e.g., Serfling 1980). ■

Proof of Proposition 4.2.2: Use (4.2.13) to conclude that

$$\frac{1}{n}\sum_{i=1}^{n-m}(d_0 y_i + \cdots + d_m y_{i+m})^4 \xrightarrow{P} \eta_\varepsilon\left(\sum_{i=0}^{m} d_i^4\right) + 6\sigma_\varepsilon^4\left(\sum_{i=0}^{m-1} d_i^2 \sum_{j=i+1}^{m} d_j^2\right),$$

from which the result follows immediately. ■

Proof of Proposition 4.3.1: If optimal differencing coefficients are used, then in large samples,

$$n^{1/2}\left(s^2_{res} - s^2_{diff}\right)$$
$$\cong n^{1/2}\left(\frac{1}{n}\sum \varepsilon_i^2 - \frac{1}{n}\sum (d_0\varepsilon_i + d_1\varepsilon_{i+1} + \cdots + d_m\varepsilon_{i+m})^2\right)$$

$$\doteq -n^{1/2}\left(\left(\sum_{j=0}^{m-1} d_j d_{j+1}\right)\frac{2}{n}\sum \varepsilon_i\varepsilon_{i+1} + \left(\sum_{j=0}^{m-2} d_j d_{j+2}\right)\right.$$

$$\left.\times \frac{2}{n}\sum \varepsilon_i\varepsilon_{i+2} + \cdots + d_0 d_m \frac{2}{n}\sum \varepsilon_i\varepsilon_{i+m}\right)$$

$$= +\frac{n^{1/2}}{m}\left(\frac{1}{n}\sum \varepsilon_i\varepsilon_{i+1} + \frac{1}{n}\sum \varepsilon_i\varepsilon_{i+2} + \cdots + \frac{1}{n}\sum \varepsilon_i\varepsilon_{i+m}\right),$$

which is asymptotically $N(0, \sigma_\varepsilon^4/m)$. To obtain the third line, use the condition $\sum_0^m d_j^2 = 1$. To obtain the fourth, use $\sum_j d_j d_{j+k} = -1/2m, k = 1, \ldots, m$. For arbitrary differencing coefficients, use (4.1.6). ■

Proof of Propositions 4.4.1 and 4.4.2: See Yatchew (1999). ■

Proof of Proposition 4.5.1: Define $g(x)$ and U as in the proof of Lemma B.4. Using Lemma B.3, note that differencing removes both $f(x)$, the direct effect of x, and $g(x)$, the indirect effect of x, sufficiently quickly that we have the following approximation:

$$n^{1/2}(\hat\beta - \beta) \cong \left(\frac{Z'D'DZ}{n}\right)^{-1}\frac{Z'D'D\varepsilon}{n^{1/2}}$$

$$\cong \left(\frac{U'D'DU}{n}\right)^{-1}\left(\frac{U'D'D\varepsilon}{n^{1/2}}\right). \qquad \text{(B4.5.1)}$$

Using Lemma B.4 and $\delta = 1/4m$ (see (4.2.8) and Appendix C), note that with optimal differencing coefficients

$$Var\left(\frac{U'D'D\varepsilon}{n^{1/2}}\right) = \sigma_\varepsilon^2 E\left[\frac{U'D'DD'DU}{n}\right] \xrightarrow{P} \sigma_\varepsilon^2\left(1 + \frac{1}{2m}\right)\Sigma_{z|x}$$

and $(U'DD'U/n)^{-1} \xrightarrow{P} \Sigma_{z|x}^{-1}$. Thus,

$$Var\left(n^{1/2}(\hat\beta - \beta)\right) \xrightarrow{P} \sigma_\varepsilon^2\left(1 + \frac{1}{2m}\right)\Sigma_{z|x}^{-1}.$$

Use (4.2.9) to write

$$\frac{U'D'D\varepsilon}{n^{1/2}} \doteq \frac{U'L_0\varepsilon}{n^{1/2}} - \frac{1}{2m}\left(\frac{U'(L_1 + L_1')\varepsilon}{n^{1/2}} + \cdots\cdots + \frac{U'(L_m + L_m')\varepsilon}{n^{1/2}}\right),$$

and conclude asymptotic normality.
For arbitrary differencing coefficients, use (4.1.6). ■

Proof of Proposition 4.5.2: Using Proposition 4.5.1, we have under the null hypothesis

$$n^{1/2}(R\hat{\beta}_{diff} - r) \overset{A}{\sim} N\left(0, (1+2\delta)\sigma_\varepsilon^2 R \sum\nolimits_{z|x}^{-1} R'\right),$$

from which (4.5.7) follows immediately.
To derive (4.5.7a) we will rely on the analogous analysis for conventional linear models. Thus, rewrite (4.5.2) to be approximately $y^* = Z^*\beta + \varepsilon^*$. Define $\hat{\beta}_{unr}$ to be the OLS estimator applied to this model (this is just the usual differencing estimator in (4.5.3)). Define $\hat{\beta}_{res}$ to be the restricted OLS estimator. Then

$$\hat{\beta}_{res} - \hat{\beta}_{unr} = -(Z^{*'}Z^*)^{-1}R'[R(Z^{*'}Z^*)^{-1}R']^{-1}(R\hat{\beta}_{unr} - r).$$

Next write the difference of the residual sums of squares from these two regressions as

$$\hat{\varepsilon}^{*'}_{res}\hat{\varepsilon}^{*}_{res} - \hat{\varepsilon}^{*'}_{unr}\hat{\varepsilon}^{*}_{unr} = (\hat{\beta}_{res} - \hat{\beta}_{unr})'(Z^{*'}Z^*)(\hat{\beta}_{res} - \hat{\beta}_{unr}).$$

See for example, Greene (2000, pp. 281–3). Combining these two results yields

$$\hat{\varepsilon}^{*'}_{res}\hat{\varepsilon}^{*}_{res} - \hat{\varepsilon}^{*'}_{unr}\hat{\varepsilon}^{*}_{unr} = (R\hat{\beta}_{unr} - r)'[R(Z^{*'}Z^*)^{-1}R']^{-1}(R\hat{\beta}_{unr} - r).$$

Divide both sides by $s^2_{unr}(1+2\delta) = s^2_{diff}(1+2\delta)$ to obtain

$$\frac{n\left(s^2_{res} - s^2_{diff}\right)}{s^2_{diff}(1+2\delta)} = (R\hat{\beta} - r)'\left(R\hat{\sum}_{\beta}R'\right)^{-1}(R\hat{\beta} - r)$$

and recall that s^2_{res} is the restricted differencing estimator. ■

Proof of Proposition 4.7.1: Consistency and asymptotic normality may be shown using standard proofs for nonlinear least squares. To derive the large sample covariance matrix, proceed as follows. Take the first-order conditions for β

$$\frac{1}{n}\frac{\partial r(Z,\hat{\beta})}{\partial \beta}D'D(y - r(Z,\hat{\beta})) = 0;$$

then, expand in a first-order Taylor series. Note that terms involving the second derivatives of $r(\cdot)$ converge to zero. Thus one obtains

$$\frac{1}{n}\frac{\partial r(Z,\beta)}{\partial \beta}D'D\varepsilon - \frac{1}{n}\frac{\partial r(Z,\beta)}{\partial \beta}D'D\frac{\partial r(Z,\beta)}{\partial \beta'}(\hat{\beta}_{diffnls} - \beta) \cong 0.$$

Refer to Comments on Lemma B.4 and set $h(z) = \partial r(z, \beta)/\partial \beta$ to conclude

$$\frac{1}{n}\frac{\partial r(Z,\beta)}{\partial \beta} D'D \frac{\partial r(Z,\beta)}{\partial \beta'} \xrightarrow{P} \Sigma_{\frac{\partial r}{\partial \beta}|x}$$

$$\frac{1}{n}\frac{\partial r(Z,\beta)}{\partial \beta} D'DD'D \frac{\partial r(Z,\beta)}{\partial \beta'} \xrightarrow{P} (1+2\delta)\Sigma_{\frac{\partial r}{\partial \beta}|x}.$$

The convergence is retained if we replace β with $\hat{\beta}_{diffnls}$. Thus, we may write

$$n^{1/2}\left(\hat{\beta}_{diffnls} - \beta\right) \cong \Sigma^{-1}_{\frac{\partial r}{\partial \beta}|x} \cdot \frac{\partial r(Z,\beta)}{\partial \beta}\frac{D'D\varepsilon}{n^{1/2}}.$$

Next, note that

$$Var\left(\frac{\partial r(Z,\beta)}{\partial \beta}\frac{D'D\varepsilon}{n^{1/2}}\right) = \sigma_\varepsilon^2 E\left[\frac{1}{n}\frac{\partial r(Z,\beta)}{\partial \beta} D'DD'D \frac{\partial r(Z,\beta)}{\partial \beta'}\right] \xrightarrow{P} (1+2\delta)\Sigma_{\frac{\partial r}{\partial \beta}|x},$$

and thus

$$Var\left(n^{1/2}\left(\hat{\beta}_{nls} - \beta\right)\right) \xrightarrow{P} (1+2\delta)\Sigma^{-1}_{\frac{\partial r}{\partial \beta}|x}.$$

Asymptotic normality follows straightforwardly. ■

Proof of Theorem 4.8.1: Define $g(x)$ and U as in the proof of Lemma B.4 above. Because w, the vector of instruments, has a smooth regression function on x, write $w_i = h(x_i) + v_i$, where h is a vector function with first derivatives bounded, $E(v_i \mid x_i) = 0$, and $E(Var(w_i \mid x_i)) = \Sigma_{w|x}$. Let W be the $n \times q$ matrix with ith row w_i. Let $h(x)$ be the $n \times q$ matrix with ith row $h(x_i)$. Let V be the $n \times q$ matrix with ith row v_i. Using Lemma B.3, note that differencing removes $f(x)$, $g(x)$, and $h(x)$ sufficiently quickly that we have the following approximation:

$$\begin{aligned} n^{1/2}(\hat{\beta}_{diff2sls} - \beta) &\cong \left(\frac{Z'D'DW}{n}\left(\frac{W'D'DW}{n}\right)^{-1}\frac{W'D'DZ}{n}\right)^{-1} \\ &\quad \times \frac{Z'D'DW}{n}\left(\frac{W'D'DW}{n}\right)^{-1}\frac{W'D'D\varepsilon}{n^{1/2}} \\ &\cong \left(\frac{U'D'DV}{n}\left(\frac{V'D'DV}{n}\right)^{-1}\frac{V'D'DU}{n}\right)^{-1} \\ &\quad \times \frac{U'D'DV}{n}\left(\frac{V'D'DV}{n}\right)^{-1}\frac{V'D'D\varepsilon}{n^{1/2}}. \end{aligned} \tag{B4.8.1}$$

Using Lemma B.4

$$Var\left(\frac{V'D'D\varepsilon}{n^{1/2}}\right) = \sigma_\varepsilon^2 E\left[\frac{V'D'DD'DV}{n}\right] \xrightarrow{P} \sigma_\varepsilon^2(1+2\delta)\Sigma_{w|x}$$

$$V'D'DV/n \xrightarrow{P} \Sigma_{w|x}$$
$$U'D'DV/n \xrightarrow{P} \Sigma_{zw|x}.$$

Thus, after simplification,

$$Var\left(n^{1/2}(\hat{\beta}_{diff2sls} - \beta)\right) \xrightarrow{P} \sigma_\varepsilon^2(1+2\delta)\left[\Sigma_{zw|x}\Sigma_{w|x}^{-1}\Sigma'_{zw|x}\right]^{-1}.$$

Finally, expand $\frac{V'D'D\varepsilon}{n^{1/2}}$ and conclude asymptotic normality. ■

Proof of Proposition 4.8.2: Note that

$$Var\left(n^{1/2}\left(\hat{\beta}_{diff} - \hat{\beta}_{diff2sls}\right)\right)$$
$$= nVar\left(\hat{\beta}_{diff}\right) + nVar\left(\hat{\beta}_{diff2sls}\right) - 2nCov\left(\hat{\beta}_{diff}, \hat{\beta}_{diff2sls}\right).$$

Using Propositions 4.5.1 and 4.8.1, we know that the first term converges to $\sigma_\varepsilon^2(1+2\delta)\Sigma_{z|x}^{-1}$ and the second to $\sigma_\varepsilon^2(1+2\delta)[\Sigma_{zw|x}\Sigma_{w|x}^{-1}\Sigma'_{zw|x}]^{-1}$. We need to establish the limit of the third term. Using (B4.5.1) and (B4.8.1) and Lemma B.4, we have

$$nCov(\hat{\beta}_{diff}, \hat{\beta}_{diff2sls}) \cong E\left[n^{1/2}(\hat{\beta}_{diff} - \beta)n^{1/2}(\hat{\beta}_{diff2sls} - \beta)'\right]$$

$$\cong E\left[\left(\frac{Z'D'DZ}{n}\right)^{-1}\frac{Z'D'D\varepsilon}{n^{1/2}}\frac{\varepsilon'D'DW}{n^{1/2}}\left(\frac{W'D'DW}{n}\right)^{-1}\right.$$
$$\left.\times\frac{W'D'DZ}{n}\left(\frac{Z'D'DW}{n}\left(\frac{W'D'DW}{n}\right)^{-1}\frac{W'D'DZ}{n}\right)^{-1}\right]$$

$$= \sigma_\varepsilon^2 E\left[\left(\frac{Z'D'DZ}{n}\right)^{-1}\frac{Z'D'D'D'DW}{n}\left(\frac{W'D'DW}{n}\right)^{-1}\right.$$
$$\left.\times\frac{W'D'DZ}{n}\left(\frac{Z'D'DW}{n}\left(\frac{W'D'DW}{n}\right)^{-1}\frac{W'D'DZ}{n}\right)^{-1}\right]$$

$$\xrightarrow{P} \sigma_\varepsilon^2(1+2\delta)\Sigma_{z|x}^{-1}\left[\Sigma_{zw|x}\Sigma_{w|x}^{-1}\Sigma'_{zw|x}\right]\left[\Sigma_{zw|x}\Sigma_{w|x}^{-1}\Sigma'_{zw|x}\right]^{-1}$$
$$= \sigma_\varepsilon^2(1+2\delta)\Sigma_{z|x}^{-1}.$$

Hence,

$$Var\left(n^{1/2}(\hat{\beta}_{diff} - \hat{\beta}_{diff2sls})\right) \xrightarrow{P} \sigma_\varepsilon^2(1+2\delta)\left(\left[\Sigma_{zw|x}\Sigma_{w|x}^{-1}\Sigma'_{zw|x}\right]^{-1} - \Sigma_{z|x}^{-1}\right),$$

and the result follows immediately. ■

Proof of Proposition 5.3.1: There are $n^{1-\epsilon}$ subcubes, and note that the probability of an empty subcube goes to zero as n increases. The maximum segment within each q-dimensional subcube is proportional to $1/n^{(1-\epsilon)/q}$ as is the maximum segment between points in contiguous subcubes from which the result follows immediately. ■

Appendix C – Optimal Differencing Weights

Proposition C1: Define δ as in Equation (4.1.6) and consider the optimization problem

$$\min_{d_0,d_1,\ldots,d_m} \delta = \sum_{k=1}^{m}\left(\sum_{j=0}^{m-k} d_j d_{j+k}\right)^2 \quad \text{s.t.} \sum_{j=0}^{m} d_j = 0 \quad \sum_{j=0}^{m} d_j^2 = 1; \tag{C1.1}$$

then,

$$\sum_{j=0}^{m-k} d_j d_{j+k} = -\frac{1}{2m} \qquad k = 1,\ldots,m, \tag{C1.2}$$

in which case $\delta = 1/4m$. Furthermore, $d_0, d_1, \ldots, d_m$ may be chosen so that the roots of

$$d_0 z^m + d_1 z^{m-1} + \cdots + d_{m-1} z^1 + d_m = 0 \tag{C1.3}$$

lie on or outside the unit circle.

Proof of Proposition C1: For purposes of interpretation it will be convenient to think of differencing of residuals as a moving average process. Define

$$\varepsilon_i^* = d_0 \varepsilon_i + \cdots + d_m \varepsilon_{i+m}$$

and

$$\rho_k = \sum_{j=0}^{m-k} d_j d_{j+k} \qquad k = 0,\ldots,m.$$

Note that $\rho_k = corr(\varepsilon_i^*, \varepsilon_{i+k}^*)$. For $k = 0$, we have $\rho_0 = \sum_{j=0}^m d_j^2 = 1$. Next we have

$$0 = \left(\sum_{j=0}^m d_j\right)^2 = \sum_{j=0}^m d_j^2 + 2\sum_{k=1}^m \left(\sum_{j=0}^{m-k} d_j d_{j+k}\right) = 1 + 2\sum_{k=1}^m \rho_k,$$

which implies $\sum_{k=1}^m \rho_k = -\,{}^1\!/_2$. Thus (C1.1) may be written as

$$\min_{\rho_1,\ldots,\rho_m} \sum_{k=1}^m \rho_k^2 \quad \text{s.t.} \sum_{k=1}^m \rho_k = -\,{}^1\!/_2,$$

which is minimized when the ρ_k are equal to each other, in which case $\rho_k = -1/2m$, $k = 1, \ldots, m$. Thus we have proved (C1.2).

As Hall et al. (1990) point out, the objective is to select moving average weights that reproduce the covariance structure

$$\begin{aligned} &cov\,(d_0\varepsilon_i + \cdots + d_m\varepsilon_{i+m}, d_0\varepsilon_{i+k} + \cdots + d_m\varepsilon_{i+m+k}) \\ &\quad = -\frac{1}{2m}\sigma_\varepsilon^2 \qquad k = 1, \ldots, m \\ &\quad = 0 \qquad\qquad\;\; k > m \end{aligned} \tag{C1.4}$$

$$var\,(d_0\varepsilon_i + \cdots + d_m\varepsilon_{i+m}) = \sigma_\varepsilon^2.$$

This can be achieved by solving

$$R(z) = -\frac{1}{2m}[z^{2m} + z^{2m-1} + \cdots + z^{m+1} - 2mz^m + z^{m-1} + \cdots + z + 1] = 0.$$

It is easy to show that "1" is a root of $R(z)$ with multiplicity 2. Furthermore, the polynomial is "self-reciprocal" (see, e.g., Anderson 1971, p. 224, and Barbeau 1995, pp. 22–23, 152) so that if $r = (a + b\imath)$ is a root, then so is $1/r = (a - b\imath)/(a^2 + b^2)$, where $\imath$ denotes $\sqrt{-1}$.

Thus, the set of all roots is given by $\Re = \{1, r_2, \ldots, r_m, 1, 1/r_2, \ldots, 1/r_m\}$, where $|r_j| = |a_j + b_j\imath| = (a_j^2 + b_j^2)^{1/2} > 1$, $j = 2, \ldots, m$. A self-reciprocal polynomial may be rewritten in the form $R(z) = z^m M(z) M(1/z)$, where M is a polynomial with real coefficients. There are, however, multiple ways to construct M. In particular, obtain any partition of the roots $\Re = S \cup S^c$ satisfying the following conditions: if $s \in S$, then $1/s \in S^c$; if in addition s is complex and $s \in S$, then $\bar{s} \in S$. Compose M using the roots in S and normalize the coefficients of M so that their sum of squares equals 1. Then, by construction, the coefficients reproduce the covariance structure in (C1.4) and are therefore optimal differencing weights. Valid partitioning requires only that reciprocal pairs be separated (so that $z^m M(z) M(1/z) = R(z)$) and that conjugate pairs be kept together (to ensure that M has real coefficients). Of course, there is only one partition that separates the two unit roots and those that are respectively inside and outside the unit circle. ■

Comment: For example, if $m = 4$, then the roots of $R(z)$ are given by

$$\mathfrak{R} = \{1, r_2 = -.2137 - 1.7979\imath, r_3 = -.2137 + 1.7976\imath, \\ r_4 = -1.9219, 1, 1/r_2, 1/r_3, 1/r_4\}.$$

Note that r_2, r_3, r_4 lie outside the unit circle. If one takes $S = \{1, r_2, r_3, r_4\}$, then the differencing weights are (0.8873, −0.3099, −0.2464, −0.1901, −0.1409). Table 4.1 in Chapter 4 tabulates differencing weights up to order 10, where S consists of the root "1" and all roots outside the unit circle. Note that the "spike" occurs at d_0 whether m is even or odd. The remaining weights $d_1, \ldots, d_m$ are negative and monotonically increasing to 0. (Order or sign reversal preserves optimality of a sequence.) The pattern persists for all values of m.

In contrast, if one takes $S = \{1, 1/r_2, 1/r_3, r_4\}$ then the differencing weights become (0.2708, −0.0142, 0.6909, −0.4858, −0.4617), which are those obtained by Hall et al. (1990, p. 523, Table 1).

Differencing Coefficients: $m = 25$

```
0.97873,-0.06128,-0.05915,-0.05705,-0.05500,-0.05298,-0.05100,
-0.04906,-0.04715,-0.04528,-0.04345,-0.04166,-0.03990,-0.03818,
-0.03650,-0.03486,-0.03325,-0.03168,-0.03015,-0.02865,-0.02719,
-0.02577,-0.02438,-0.02303,-0.02171,-0.02043
```

Differencing Coefficients: $m = 50$

```
0.98918,-0.03132,-0.03077,-0.03023,-0.02969,-0.02916,-0.02863,
-0.02811,-0.02759,-0.02708,-0.02657,-0.02606,-0.02556,-0.02507,
-0.02458,-0.02409,-0.02361,-0.02314,-0.02266,-0.02220,-0.02174,
-0.02128,-0.02083,-0.02038,-0.01994,-0.01950,-0.01907,-0.01864,
-0.01822,-0.01780,-0.01739,-0.01698,-0.01658,-0.01618,-0.01578,
-0.01539,-0.01501,-0.01463,-0.01425,-0.01388,-0.01352,-0.01316,
-0.01280,-0.01245,-0.01210,-0.01176,-0.01142,-0.01108,-0.01075,
-0.01043,-0.01011
```

Differencing Coefficients: $m = 100$

```
0.99454083,-0.01583636,-0.01569757,-0.01555936,-0.01542178,
-0.01528478,-0.01514841,-0.01501262,-0.01487745,-0.01474289,
-0.01460892,-0.01447556,-0.01434282,-0.01421067,-0.01407914,
```

```
-0.01394819,-0.01381786,-0.01368816,-0.01355903,-0.01343053,
-0.01330264,-0.01317535,-0.01304868,-0.01292260,-0.01279714,
-0.01267228,-0.01254803,-0.01242439,-0.01230136,-0.01217894,
-0.01205713,-0.01193592,-0.01181533,-0.01169534,-0.01157596,
-0.01145719,-0.01133903,-0.01122148,-0.01110453,-0.01098819,
-0.01087247,-0.01075735,-0.01064283,-0.01052892,-0.01041563,
-0.01030293,-0.01019085,-0.01007937,-0.00996850,-0.00985823,
-0.00974857,-0.00963952,-0.00953107,-0.00942322,-0.00931598,
-0.00920935,-0.00910332,-0.00899789,-0.00889306,-0.00878884,
-0.00868522,-0.00858220,-0.00847978,-0.00837797,-0.00827675,
-0.00817614,-0.00807612,-0.00797670,-0.00787788,-0.00777966,
-0.00768203,-0.00758500,-0.00748857,-0.00739273,-0.00729749,
-0.00720284,-0.00710878,-0.00701532,-0.00692245,-0.00683017,
-0.00673848,-0.00664738,-0.00655687,-0.00646694,-0.00637761,
-0.00628886,-0.00620070,-0.00611312,-0.00602612,-0.00593971,
-0.00585389,-0.00576864,-0.00568397,-0.00559989,-0.00551638,
-0.00543345,-0.00535110,-0.00526933,-0.00518813,-0.00510750,
-0.00502745
```

Appendix D – Nonparametric Least Squares

The results in this appendix are widely used in the spline function literature. See particularly Wahba (1990). A collection of proofs may be found in Yatchew and Bos (1997).

1. Sobolev Space Results

Let $\mathbb{N}$ be the nonnegative natural numbers. Let $Q^q \subset \mathbb{R}^q$ be the unit cube, which will be the domain of the nonparametric regression models below. (The estimators remain valid if the domain is a rectangular cube.) Suppose $\alpha = (\alpha_1, \ldots, \alpha_q) \in \mathbb{N}^q$, define $|\alpha|_\infty = \max|\alpha_i|$, and let $x = (x_1, \ldots, x_q) \in \mathbb{R}^q$. We use the following conventional derivative notation $D^\alpha f(x) = \partial^{\alpha_1 + \cdots + \alpha_q} f(x) / \partial x_1^{\alpha_1} \cdots \partial x_q^{\alpha_q}$.

Let C^m be the space of m-times continuously differentiable scalar functions, that is, $C^m = \{f : Q^q \to \mathbb{R}^1 | D^\alpha f \in C^0, |\alpha|_\infty \leq m\}$ and $C^0 = \{f : Q^q \to \mathbb{R}^1 | f \textit{ continuous on } Q^q\}$. On the space C^m, define the norm, $\|f\|_{\infty,m} = \sum_{|\alpha|_\infty \leq m} \max_{x \in Q^q} |D^\alpha f(x)|$, in which case C^m is a complete, normed, linear space, that is, a Banach space. Consider the following inner product of scalar functions and the induced norm

$$\langle f, g \rangle_{Sob} = \sum_{|\alpha|_\infty \leq m} \int_{Q^q} D^\alpha f D^\alpha g$$

$$\|f\|_{Sob} = \left[\sum_{|\alpha|_\infty \leq m} \int_{Q^q} [D^\alpha f]^2 \right]^{1/2}$$

and define the Sobolev space $\mathcal{H}^m$ as the completion of $\{f \in C^m\}$ with respect to $\|f\|_{Sob}$. The following results on the Sobolev space $\mathcal{H}^m$ are particularly useful.

Proposition D.1: $\mathcal{H}^m$ is a Hilbert space.

The Hilbert space property allows one to take projections and to express $\mathcal{H}^m$ as a direct sum of subspaces that are orthogonal to one another.

Proposition D.2: Given $a \in Q^q$ and $b \in \mathbb{N}^q$, $|b|_\infty \leq m - 1$, there exists a function $r_a^b \in \mathcal{H}^m$ called a *representor* s.t. $\langle r_a^b, f\rangle_{Sob} = D^b f(a)$ for all $f \in \mathcal{H}^m$. Furthermore, $r_a^b(x) = \prod_{i=1}^q r_{a_i}^{b_i}(x_i)$ for all $x \in Q^q$, where $r_{a_i}^{b_i}(.)$ is the representor in the Sobolev space of functions of one variable on Q^1 with inner product $\langle f, g\rangle_{Sob} = \sum_{\alpha=0}^m \int_{Q^1} \frac{d^\alpha f}{dx^\alpha}\frac{d^\alpha g}{dx^\alpha}$.

If b equals the zero vector, then we have representors of function evaluation, which we have denoted in the text as $r_a = r_a^0$. Proposition D.2 further assures us of the existence of representors for derivative evaluation (of order $|b|_\infty \leq m - 1$). The problem of solving for representors is well known (see Wahba 1990). For the inner product above, representors of function evaluation consist of two functions spliced together, each of which is a linear combination of trigonometric functions. Formulas may be derived using elementary methods, in particular integration by parts and the solution of a linear differential equation. Details may be found in Section 3 in this appendix. Finally, Proposition D.2 states that representors in spaces of functions of several variables may be written as products of representors in spaces of functions of one variable. This particularly facilitates their implementation, for one simply calculates one-dimensional representors and then multiplies them together.

Proposition D.3: The embedding $\mathcal{H}^m \to C^{m-1}$ is compact.

Compactness of the embedding means that, given a ball of functions in $\mathcal{H}^m$ (with respect to $\|f\|_{Sob}$), its closure is compact in C^{m-1} (with respect to $\|f\|_{\infty,m}$). This result ensures that functions in a bounded ball in $\mathcal{H}^m$ have all lower-order derivatives bounded in supnorm.

Proposition D.4: Divide x into two subsets $x = (x_a, x_b)$. If $f(x_a, x_b)$ is of the form $f_a(x_a) + f_b(x_b)$ and either $\int f_a = 0$ or $\int f_b = 0$, then $\|f\|_{Sob}^2 = \|f_a\|_{Sob}^2 + \|f_b\|_{Sob}^2$.

This result is useful for analyzing additively separable models.

2. Nonparametric Least Squares

Computation of Estimator

Given data $(y_1, x_1), \ldots, (y_n, x_n)$ on a nonparametric regression model $y = f(x) + \upsilon$ (x can be a vector). Let $r_{x_1}, \ldots, r_{x_n}$ be the representors of function evaluation at $x_1, \ldots, x_n$, respectively, that is, $\langle r_{x_i}, f\rangle_{Sob} = f(x_i)$ for all

$f \in \mathcal{H}^m$. Let R be the $n \times n$ representor matrix whose columns (and rows) equal the representors evaluated at $x_1, \ldots, x_n$; that is, $R_{ij} = \langle r_{x_i}, r_{x_j} \rangle_{Sob} = r_{x_i}(x_j) = r_{x_j}(x_i)$.

Proposition D.5: Let $y = (y_1, \ldots, y_n)'$ and define

$$\hat{\sigma}^2 = \min_f \frac{1}{n} \sum_i [y_i - f(x_i)]^2 \quad \text{s.t. } \|f\|^2_{Sob} \le L$$

$$s^2 = \min_c \frac{1}{n} [y - Rc]'[y - Rc] \quad \text{s.t. } c'Rc \le L,$$

where c is an $n \times 1$ vector. Then $\hat{\sigma}^2 = s^2$. Furthermore, there exists a solution to the infinite dimensional problem of the form $\hat{f} = \sum_1^n \hat{c}_i r_{x_i}$, where $\hat{c} = (\hat{c}_1, \ldots, \hat{c}_n)'$ solves the finite dimensional problem.

This result ensures the computability of the estimator; $\hat{f}$ can be expressed as a linear combination of the representors with the number of terms equal to the number of observations. Perfect fit is precluded, except by extraordinary coincidence, since the coefficients must satisfy the quadratic smoothness constraint.

Additive Separability

Partition $x = (x_a, x_b)$ with dimensions q_a, q_b, respectively, and $x \in Q^{q_a+q_b} = [0, 1]^{q_a+q_b}$. Define

$$\bar{\Im} = \Big\{ f(x_a, x_b) \in \mathcal{H}^m \colon f(x_a, x_b) = f_a(x_a) + f_b(x_b),\ \|f_a + f_b\|^2_{Sob} \le L,\ \int f_b = 0 \Big\},$$

where the integral constraint is an identification condition.

Proposition D.6: Given data $(y_1, x_{a1}, x_{b1}), \ldots, (y_n, x_{an}, x_{bn})$, let $y = (y_1, \ldots, y_n)'$ and define

$$\hat{\sigma}^2 = \min_{f_a, f_b} \frac{1}{n} \sum_t [y_i - f_a(x_{ai}) - f_b(x_{bi})]^2 \quad \text{s.t. } \|f_a + f_b\|^2_{Sob} \le L, \quad \int f_b = 0$$

$$s^2 = \min_{c_a, c_b} \frac{1}{n} [y - R_a c_a - R_b c_b]' [y - R_a c_a - R_b c_b] \quad \text{s.t. } c_a' R_a c_a + c_b' R_b c_b \le L, \quad \sum_i c_{bi} = 0,$$

where c_a, c_b are $n \times 1$ vectors and R_a, R_b are the representor matrices on $[0,1]^{q_a}$ at $x_{a1}, \ldots, x_{an}$ and on $[0,1]^{q_b}$ at $x_{b1}, \ldots, x_{bn}$, respectively. Then

$\hat{\sigma}^2 = s^2$. Furthermore, there exists a solution to the infinite dimensional problem of the form $\hat{f}_a(x_a) + \hat{f}_b(x_b) = \sum_1^n \hat{c}_{ai} r_{x_{ai}}(x_a) + \hat{c}_{bi} r_{x_{bi}}(x_b)$, where $\hat{c}_a = (\hat{c}_{a1}, \ldots, \hat{c}_{an})'$, $\hat{c}_b = (\hat{c}_{b1}, \ldots, \hat{c}_{bn})'$ solve the finite dimensional problem.

The sets of functions $\{f_a(x_a)\}$ and $\{f_b(x_b) | \int f_b = 0\}$ are orthogonal in the Sobolev space $\mathcal{H}^m$ on $Q^{q_a+q_b}$. Thus, using the Hilbert space property of $\mathcal{H}^m$ (Proposition D.1), it can be shown that a function $f_a + f_b$ satisfying the infinite dimensional optimization problem has a unique representation as a sum of functions from the two subspaces.

For extensions to multiplicative separability and homothetic demand, see Yatchew and Bos (1997).

3. Calculation of Representors

Let $\langle f,g \rangle_{Sob} = \int_0^1 \sum_{k=0}^m f^{(k)}(x) g^{(k)}(x) dx$, where bracketed superscripts denote derivatives. We construct a function $r_a \in \mathcal{H}^m[0,1]$ such that $\langle f,r_a \rangle_{Sob} = f(a)$ for all $f \in \mathcal{H}^m[0,1]$. This representor of function evaluation r_a will be of the form

$$r_a(x) = \begin{cases} L_a(x) & 0 \le x \le a \\ R_a(x) & a \le x \le 1 \end{cases},$$

where L_a and R_a are both analytic functions. For r_a of this form to be an element of $\mathcal{H}^m[0,1]$, it suffices that $L_a^{(k)}(a) = R_a^{(k)}(a)$, $0 \le k \le m-1$. Now write

$$\begin{aligned} f(a) &= \langle r_a, f \rangle_{Sob} \\ &= \int_0^a \sum_{k=0}^m L_a^{(k)}(x) f^{(k)}(x) dx + \int_a^1 \sum_{k=0}^m R_a^{(k)}(x) f^{(k)}(x) dx. \end{aligned}$$

We ask that this be true for all $f \in \mathcal{H}^m[0,1]$, but by density it suffices to demonstrate the result for all $f \in C^\infty[0,1]$. Hence, assume that $f \in C^\infty[0,1]$. Thus, integrating by parts, we have

$$\begin{aligned} \sum_{k=0}^m \int_0^a L_a^{(k)}(x) f^{(k)}(x) dx &= \sum_{k=0}^m \left\{ \sum_{j=0}^{k-1} (-1)^j L_a^{(k+j)}(x) f^{(k-j-1)}(x) \Big|_0^a \right. \\ &\qquad \left. + (-1)^k \int_0^a L_a^{(2k)}(x) f(x) dx \right\} \\ &= \sum_{k=0}^m \sum_{j=0}^{k-1} (-1)^j L_a^{(k+j)}(x) f^{(k-j-1)}(x) \Big|_0^a \\ &\qquad + \int_0^a \left\{ \sum_{k=0}^m (-1)^k L_a^{(2k)}(x) \right\} f(x) dx. \end{aligned}$$

If we let $i = k - j - 1$ in the first sum, this may be written as

$$\begin{aligned}
\sum_{k=0}^{m} \int_0^a L_a^{(k)}(x) f^{(k)}(x)dx &= \sum_{k=1}^{m}\sum_{i=0}^{k-1}(-1)^{k-i-1} L_a^{(2k-1-i)}(x) f^{(i)}(x)\Big|_0^a \\
&\quad + \int_0^a \left\{\sum_{k=0}^{m}(-1)^k L_a^{(2k)}(x)\right\} f(x)dx \\
&= \sum_{i=0}^{m-1}\sum_{k=i+1}^{m}(-1)^{k-i-1} L_a^{(2k-1-i)}(x) f^{(i)}(x)\Big|_0^a \\
&\quad + \int_0^a \left\{\sum_{k=0}^{m}(-1)^k L_a^{(2k)}(x)\right\} f(x)dx \\
&= \sum_{i=0}^{m-1} f^{(i)}(a)\left\{\sum_{k=i+1}^{m}(-1)^{k-i-1} L_a^{(2k-1-i)}(a)\right\} \\
&\quad - \sum_{i=0}^{m-1} f^{(i)}(0)\left\{\sum_{k=i+1}^{m}(-1)^{k-i-1} L_a^{(2k-1-i)}(0)\right\} \\
&\quad + \int_0^a \left\{\sum_{k=0}^{m}(-1)^k L_a^{(2k)}(x)\right\} f(x)dx.
\end{aligned}$$

Similarly, $\int_a^1 \sum_{k=0}^{m} R_a^{(k)}(x) f^{(k)}(x)\, dx$ may be written as

$$\begin{aligned}
&- \sum_{i=0}^{m-1} f^{(i)}(a)\left\{\sum_{k=i+1}^{m}(-1)^{k-i-1} R_a^{(2k-1-i)}(a)\right\} \\
&+ \sum_{i=0}^{m-1} f^{(i)}(1)\left\{\sum_{k=i+1}^{m}(-1)^{k-i-1} R_a^{(2k-1-i)}(1)\right\} \\
&+ \int_a^1 \left\{\sum_{k=0}^{m}(-1)^k R_a^{(2k)}(x)\right\} f(x)dx.
\end{aligned}$$

Thus, since $f(x)$ is arbitrary, we require both L_a and R_a to be solutions of the constant coefficient differential equation

$$\sum_{k=0}^{m}(-1)^k u^{(2k)}(x) = 0.$$

Boundary conditions are obtained by setting the coefficients of $f^{(i)}(a)$, $1 \leq i \leq m-1$, $f^{(i)}(0)$, $0 \leq i \leq m-1$ and $f^{(i)}(1)$, $0 \leq i \leq m-1$ to zero and the coefficient of $f(a)$ to 1. That is,

$$\sum_{k=i+1}^{m} (-1)^{k-i-1} \left\{ L_a^{(2k-1-i)}(a) - R_a^{(2k-1-i)}(a) \right\} = 0 \quad 1 \leq i \leq m-1$$

$$\sum_{k=i+1}^{m} (-1)^{k-i-1} L_a^{(2k-1-i)}(0) = 0 \qquad 0 \leq i \leq m-1$$

$$\sum_{k=i+1}^{m} (-1)^{k-i-1} R_a^{(2k-1-i)}(1) = 0 \qquad 0 \leq i \leq m-1$$

$$\sum_{k=1}^{m} (-1)^{k-1} \left\{ L_a^{(2k-1)}(a) - R_a^{(2k-1)}(a) \right\} = 1.$$

Furthermore, for $r_a \in \mathcal{H}^m[0,1]$, we require, $L_a^{(k)}(a) = R_a^{(k)}(a)$, $0 \leq k \leq m-1$. This results in $(m-1) + m + m + 1 + m = 4m$ boundary conditions. The general solution of the preceding differential equation is obtained by finding the roots of its characteristic polynomial $P_m(\lambda) = \sum_{k=0}^{m} (-1)^k \lambda^{2k}$. This is easily done by noting that $(1+\lambda^2)P_m(\lambda) = 1 + (-1)^m \lambda^{2m+2}$, and thus the characteristic roots are given by $\lambda_k = e^{i\theta_k}$, $\lambda_k \neq \pm i$, where

$$\theta_k = \begin{cases} \dfrac{(2k+1)\pi}{2m+2} & m \text{ even} \\[2ex] \dfrac{2k\pi}{2m+2} & m \text{ odd} \end{cases}.$$

The general solution is given by the linear combination $\sum_k a_k \, e^{(Re(\lambda_k))x} \sin(Im(\lambda_k))x$, where the sum is taken over $2m$ linearly independent real solutions of the differential equation above.

Let $L_a(x) = \sum_{k=1}^{2m} a_k u_k(x)$ and $R_a(x) = \sum_{k=1}^{2m} b_k u_k(x)$, where the u_k, $1 \leq k \leq 2m$ are $2m$ basis functions of the solution space of the differential equation. To show that r_a exists and is unique, we need only demonstrate that the boundary conditions uniquely determine the a_k and b_k. Because we have $4k$ unknowns ($2m$ a_k's and $2m$ b_k's) and $4m$ boundary conditions, the boundary conditions constitute a square $4m \times 4m$ linear system in the a_k's and b_k's. Thus, it suffices to show that the only solution of the associated homogenous system is the zero vector. Now suppose that $L_a^h(x)$ and $R_a^h(x)$ are the functions corresponding to solutions of the homogeneous system (i.e., with the coefficient of $f(a)$ in the boundary conditions set to 0 instead of 1). Then, by exactly the same integration by parts, it follows that $\langle r_a^h, f \rangle_{Sob} = 0$ for all $f \in C^\infty[0,1]$. Hence, r_a^h, $L_a^h(x)$, and $R_a^h(x)$ are all identically zero and thus, by the linear independence of the $u_k(x)$, so are the a_k's and b_k's.

Appendix E – Variable Definitions

Engel Curves and Equivalence Scale Estimation

Source: Living Standards Measurement Survey, http://www.worldbank.org/lsms/

ltexp	log(total monthly household expenditure)
FoodShr	share of total expenditure on food
A	number of adults in the household
K	number of children in the household

Scale Economies in Electricity Distribution

Source: Ontario municipal distributors. See Yatchew (2000).

tc	log(total cost per customer)
cust	log (number of customers)
wage	log(wage of lineman)
pcap	log(accumulated gross investment/kilometers of distribution wire)
PUC	public utility commission dummy
kwh	log(kilowatt hour sales per customer)
life	log(remaining lifetime of fixed assets)
lf	log(load factor)
kmwire	log(kilometers of distribution wire per customer)

Household Gasoline Consumption

Source: National Private Vehicle Use Survey, Statistics Canada. See Yatchew and No (2001).

dist	log (distance traveled per month)
price	log (price of liter of gasoline)
income	log (annual household income)
drivers	log (number of licensed drivers in household)
hhsize	log (number of members of household)

youngsingle	dummy for singles up to age 35
age	log(age)
retire	dummy for households where head is over 65
urban	dummy for urban dwellers

Weather and Electricity Demand

Source: Ontario Hydro Corporation, 1997

elec	log of monthly electricity sales
temp	heating and cooling degree days relative to 68 °F
relprice	log of ratio of price of electricity to the price of natural gas
gdp	log of Ontario gross GDP

Housing Prices

Source: Ph.D. Thesis, Michael Ho (1995)

saleprice	sale price of house
frplc	dummy for fireplace(s)
grge	dummy for garage
lux	dummy for luxury appointments
avginc	average neighborhood income
dwhy	distance to highway
ltarea	area of lot
nrbed	number of bedrooms
usespc	usable space
x_1, x_2	location coordinates

Option Prices and State Price Densities

Source: Simulated data. See Yatchew and Härdle (2001)

x	strike price
y	option price
X	vector of distinct strike prices

References

Aït-Sahalia, Y. and J. Duarte (2000), "Nonparametric Option Pricing Under Shape Restrictions," manuscript, Princeton University.

Aït-Sahalia, Y., P. Bickel, and T. Stoker (2001), "Goodness-of-Fit Tests for Regression Using Kernel Methods," *Journal of Econometrics*, **105**, 363–412.

Anderson, T. W. (1971), *The Statistical Analysis of Time Series*, New York: Wiley.

Andrews, D. W. K. (1994a), "Empirical Process Methods in Econometrics," in R. Engle and D. McFadden (eds.), *The Handbook of Econometrics,* Vol. IV, Amsterdam: North Holland, 2247–2294.

Andrews, D. W. K. (1994b), "Asymptotics for Semiparametric Econometric Models via Stochastic Equicontinuity," *Econometrica*, **62**, 43–72.

Andrews, D. (2000), "Inconsistency of the Bootstrap When a Parameter is on the Boundary of the Parameter Space," *Econometrica*, **68**, 399–405.

Andrews, D. W. K. and M. Buchinsky (2000), "A Three-Step Method for Choosing the Number of Bootstrap Repetitions," *Econometrica*, **68**, 23–51.

Anglin, P. and R. Gencay (1996), "Semiparametric Estimation of a Hedonic Price Function," *Journal of Applied Econometrics*, **11**, 633–648.

Azzalini, A. and A. Bowman (1993), "On the Use of Nonparametric Regression for Checking Linear Relationships," *Journal of the Royal Statistical Society, B*, **55**, 549–557.

Azzalini A., A. Bowman, and W. Härdle (1989), "On the Use of Nonparametric Regression for Model Checking," *Biometrika*, **76**, 1–11.

Baltagi, B., J. Hidalgo, and Q. Li (1996), "A Nonparametric Test for Poolability Using Panel Data," *Journal of Econometrics*, **75**, 345–367.

Barbeau E. (1995), *Polynomials*, New York: Springer-Verlag.

Barlow, R. E., D. J. Bartholomew, J. M. Bremner, and H. D. Brunk (1972), *Statistical Inference Under Order Restrictions*, New York: Wiley.

Barnard, G. A. (1963), Discussion of "The Spectral Analysis of Point Processes," by M. S. Bartlett, *Journal of the Royal Statistical Society, B*, **25**, 294.

Barry, D. (1993), "Testing for Additivity of a Regression Function," *Annals of Statistics*, **21**, 235–254.

Beran, R. (1997), "Diagnosing Bootstrap Success," *Annals of the Institute of Statistical Mathematics*, **49**, 1–24.

Beran, R. and G. Ducharme (1991), *Asymptotic Theory for Bootstrap Methods in Statistics*, Centre de Recherches Mathématiques, Univerisité de Montréal.

Bierens, H. (1990), "A Consistent Conditional Moment Test of Functional Form," *Econometrica*, **58**, 1443–1458.

Bierens, H. and Ploberger, W. (1997), "Asymptotic Theory of Integrated Conditional Moments," *Econometrica*, **65**, 1129–1151.

Bickel, P., C. Klaasen, Y. Ritov and J. Wellner (1993), Efficient and Adaptive Estimation for Semiparametric Models, Baltimore: John Hopkins University Press.

Bickel, P. and J. Kwon (2001), "Inference for Semiparametric Models: Some Questions and an Answer," *Statistica Sinica*, **11**, 863–960 (with discussion).

Blackorby, C. and D. Donaldson (1989), "Adult Equivalence Scales, Interpersonal Comparisons of Well-Being and Applied Welfare Economics," Department of Economics Discussion Paper 89-24, University of British Columbia.

Blackorby, C. and D. Donaldson (1993), "Adult Equivalence Scales and the Economic Implementation of Interpersonal Comparisons of Well-Being," *Social Choice and Applied Welfare*, **10**, 335–361.

Blackorby, C. and D. Donaldson (1994), "Measuring the Costs of Children: A Theoretical Framework," in R. Blundell, I. Preston, and I. Walker (eds.), *The Economics of Household Behavior*, Cambridge: Cambridge University Press, 51–69.

Blundell, R. and A. Duncan (1998), "Kernel Regression in Empirical Microeconomics," *Journal of Human Resources*, **33**, 62–87.

Blundell, R., A. Duncan, and K. Pendakur (1998), "Semiparametric Estimation and Consumer Demand," *Journal of Applied Econometrics*, **13**, 435–461.

Bowman, A. W., M. C. Jones, and I. Gijbels (1998), "Testing Monotonicity of Regression," *Journal of Computational and Graphical Statistics*, **7**, 489–500.

Brooke, A., D. Kendrick, and A. Meeraus (1992), *GAMS*, Redwood City, CA: Scientific Press.

Buja, A., T. Hastie, and R. Tibshirani (1989), "Linear Smoothers and Additive Models," *Annals of Statistics*, **17**, 453–555 (with discussion).

Carroll, R. J., J. Fan, I. Gijbels, and M. P. Wand (1997), "Generalized Partially Linear Single Index Models," *Journal of the American Statistical Association*, **92**, 477–489.

Cavanagh, C. and R. Sherman (1998), "Rank Estimator for Monotonic Index Models," *Journal of Econometrics*, **84**, 351–381.

Chambers, J. M. and T. Hastie (1993), *Statistical Models in S*, New York: Chapman and Hall.

Chen, H. (1988), "Convergence Rates for Parametric Components in a Partly Linear Model," *Annals of Statistics*, **16**, 136–146.

Citro, C. and R. T. Michael (eds.) (1995), *Measuring Poverty – A New Approach*, Washington, DC: National Academy Press.

Clark, R. (1975), "A Calibration Curve for Radiocarbon Dates," *Antiquity*, **49**, 251–266.

Cleveland, W. (1979), "Robust Locally Weighted Regression and Smoothing Scatterplots," *Journal of the American Statistical Association*, **74**, 829–836.

Cleveland, W. and S. Devlin (1988), "Locally Weighted Regression: An Approach to Regression Analysis by Local Fitting," *Journal of the American Statistical Association*, **83**, 596–610.

Cosslett, S. (1987), "Efficiency Bounds for Distribution-Free Estimators of the Binary Choice and Censored Regression Models," *Econometrica*, **55**, 559–586.

Davison, A. and D. Hinkley (1997), *Bootstrap Methods and Their Applications*, Cambridge: Cambridge University Press.

Deaton, A. (1997), *The Analysis of Household Surveys: A Microeconomic Approach to Development Policy*, Baltimore: Johns Hopkins University Press for the World Bank.

DeJong, P. (1987), "A Central Limit Theorem for Generalized Quadratic Forms," *Probability Theory and Related Fields*, **75**, 261–277.

Delgado, M. (1993), "Testing the Equality of Nonparametric Regression Curves," *Statistics and Probability Letters*, **17**, 199–204.

Delgado, M. and W. G. Manteiga (2001), "Significance Testing in Nonparametric Regression Based on the Bootstrap," *Annals of Statistics*, **29**, 1469–1507.

Delgado, M. and P. M. Robinson (1992), "Nonparametric and Semiparametric Methods for Economic Research," *Journal of Economic Surveys*, **6**, 201–250.

Derbort, S., H. Dette, and A. Munk (2002), "A Test for Additivity in Nonparametric Regression," *Annals of the Institute of Statistical Mathematics*, **54**, 60–82.

Dette, H. (1999), "A Consistent Test for the Functional Form of a Regression Based on a Difference of Variance Estimators," *Annals of Statistics*, **27**, 1012–1040.

Dette, H. and C. Von Lieres und Wilkau (2001), "Testing Additivity by Kernel-Based Methods – What Is a Reasonable Test?" *Bernoulli*, **7**, 669–697.

Diack, C. (2000), "Sur la Convergence des Tests de Schlee et de Yatchew," *Canadian Journal of Statistics*, **28**, 653–668.

Diack, C. and C. Thomas-Agnan (1998), "A Nonparametric Test of the Non-Convexity of Regression," *Nonparametric Statistics*, **9**, 335–362.

DiNardo, J. and J. Tobias (2001), "Nonparametric Density and Regression Estimation," *Journal of Economic Perspectives*, **15**, 11–28.

Dudley, R. M. (1984), "A Course on Empirical Processes," *Lecture Notes in Mathematics*, Ecole d'Été de Probabilités de Saint-Flour XII-1982, New York: Springer-Verlag.

Efron, B. (1979), "Bootstrap Methods: Another Look at the Jackknife," *Annals of Statistics*, **7**, 1–26.

Efron, B. and R. J. Tibshirani (1993), *An Introduction to the Bootstrap*, New York: Chapman and Hall.

Ellison, G. and S. Ellison (2000), "A Simple Framework for Nonparametric Specification Testing," *Journal of Econometrics*, **96**, 1–23.

Engle, R., C. Granger, J. Rice, and A. Weiss (1986), "Semiparametric Estimates of the Relation Between Weather and Electricity Sales," *Journal of the American Statistical Association*, **81**, 310–320.

Epstein, L. and A. Yatchew (1985), "Nonparametric Hypothesis Testing Procedures and Applications to Demand Analysis," *Journal of Econometrics*, **30**, 150–169.

Eubank, R. (1988), *Spline Smoothing and Nonparametric Regression*, New York: Marcel Dekker.

Eubank, R. and J. Hart (1992), "Testing Goodness-of-Fit in Regression via Order Selection Criteria," *Annals of Statistics*, **20**, 1412–1425.

Eubank, R. and P. Speckman (1993), "Confidence Bands in Nonparametric Regression," *Journal of the American Statistical Association*, **88**, 1287–1301.

Eubank, R. and C. H. Spiegelman (1990), "Testing the Goodness of Fit of a Linear Model via Nonparametric Regression Techniques," *Journal of the American Statistical Association*, **85**, 387–392.

Eubank, R., J. Hart, D. Simpson, and L. Stefanski (1995), "Testing for Additivity in Nonparametric Regression," *Annals of Statistics*, **23**, 1896–1920.

Fan, J. and I. Gijbels (1996), *Local Polynomial Modelling and Its Applications*, New York: Chapman and Hall.

Fan, J. and L. Huang (2001), "Goodness-of-Fit Tests for Parametric Regression Models," *Journal of the American Statistical Association*, **96**, 640–652.

Fan, J. Q. and S. K. Lin (1998), "Test of Significance When Data Are Curves," *Journal of the American Statistical Association*, **93**, 1007–1021.

Fan, Y. and Q. Li (1996), "Consistent Model Specification Tests: Omitted Variables and Semiparametric Functional Forms," *Econometrica*, **64**, 865–890.

Friedman, J. and R. Tibshirani (1984), "The Monotone Smoothing of Scatterplots," *Technometrics*, **26**, 243–250.

Gallant, R. (1981), "Unbiased Determination of Production Technologies," *Journal of Econometrics*, **20**, 285–323.

Gijbels, I., P. Hall, M. C. Jones, and I. Koch (2000), "Tests for Monotonicity of a Regression Mean with Guaranteed Level," *Biometrika*, **87**, 663–673.

Goldman, S. and P. Ruud (1992), "Nonparametric Multivariate Regression Subject to Monotonicity and Convexity Constraints," manuscript, University of California, Berkeley.

Golub, G. and C. Van Loan (1989), *Matrix Computations*, Baltimore: Johns Hopkins.

Gozalo, P. (1993), "A Consistent Specification Test for Nonparametric Estimation of Regression Function Models," *Econometric Theory*, **9**, 451–477.

Gozalo, P. (1997), "Nonparametric Bootstrap Analysis with Applications to Demographic Effects in Demand Functions," *Journal of Econometrics*, **81**, 357–393.

Gozalo, P. and O. Linton (2001), "Testing Additivity in Generalized Nonparametric Regression Models," *Journal of Econometrics*, **104**, 1–48.

Green, P. and B. Silverman (1994), *Nonparametric Regression and Generalized Linear Models*, London: Chapman and Hall.

Greene, W. (2000), *Econometric Analysis*, 4th ed, Englewood Cliffs, NJ: Prentice Hall.

Groeneboom, P., G. Jongbloed, and J. A. Wellner (2001), "Estimation of a Convex Function: Characterizations and Asymptotic Theory," *Annals of Statistics*, **29**, 1653–1698.

Hall, P. (1984), "Central Limit Theorem for Integrated Square Error of Multivariate Nonparametric Density Estimators," *Journal of Multivariate Analysis*, **14**, 1–16.

Hall, P. (1992), *The Bootstrap and Edgeworth Expansion*, New York: Springer-Verlag.

Hall, P. (1994), "Methodology and Theory for the Bootstrap," in R. Engle and D. McFadden (eds.), *The Handbook of Econometrics*, Vol. IV, Amsterdam: North Holland, 2342–2381.

Hall, P. and J. D. Hart (1990), "Bootstrap Test for Difference Between Means in Nonparametric Regression," *Journal of the American Statistical Association*, **85**, 1039–1049.

Hall, P. and N. Heckman (2000), "Testing for Monotonicity of a Regression Mean by Calibrating for Linear Functions," *Annals of Statistics*, **28**, 20–39.

Hall, P. and L. Huang (2001), "Nonparametric Kernel Regression Subject to Monotonicity Constraints," *Annals of Statistics*, **29**, 624–647.

Hall, P. and A. Yatchew (2002), "Unified Approach to Testing Functional Hypotheses in Semiparametric Contexts" unpublished manuscript, Australian National University, School of Mathematical Sciences.

Hall, P., J. Kay, and D. Titterington (1990), "Asymptotically Optimal Difference-Based Estimation of Variance in Nonparametric Regression," *Biometrika*, **77**, 521–528.

Härdle, W. (1990), *Applied Nonparametric Regression*, Econometric Society Monograph Series, 19, Cambridge University Press.

Härdle, W. and O. Linton (1994), "Applied Nonparametric Methods," in R. Engle and D. McFadden (eds.), *The Handbook of Econometrics*, Vol. IV, Amsterdam: North Holland, 2297–2334.

Härdle, W. and E. Mammen (1993), "Comparing Nonparametric versus Parametric Regression Fits," *Annals of Statistics*, **21**, 1926–1947.

Härdle, W. and J. Marron (1985), "Optimal Bandwidth Selection in Nonparametric Regression Estimation," *Annals of Statistics*, **13**, 1465–1481.

Härdle, W. and J. Marron (1990), "Semiparametric Comparison of Regression Curves," *Annals of Statistics*, **18**, 63–89.

Härdle, W. and T. Stoker (1989), "Investigating Smooth Multiple Regression by the Method of Average Derivatives," *Journal of the American Statistical Association*, **84**, 986–995.

Härdle, W. and A. Tsybakov (1993), "How Sensitive Are Average Derivatives?" *Journal of Econometrics*, **58**, 31–48.

Härdle, W., P. Hall, and J. Marron (1988), "How Far Are Automatically Chosen Regression Smoothing Parameters from Their Optimum?" *Journal of the American Statistical Association*, **83**, 86–99 (with discussion).

Härdle, W., P. Hall, and H. Ichimura (1993), "Optimal Smoothing in Single Index Models," *Annals of Statistics*, **21**, 157–178.

Härdle, W., S. Klinke, and B. Turlach (1995), *XploRe: An Interactive Statistical Computing Environment*, New York: Springer-Verlag.

Härdle, W., H. Liang, and J. Gao (2000), *Partially Linear Models*, Heidelberg: Physica-Verlag.

Hart, J. (1997), *Nonparametric Smoothing and Lack-of-Fit Tests*, New York: Springer-Verlag.

Hartigan, J. A. (1969), "Using Subsample Values as Typical Values," *Journal of the American Statistical Association*, **64**, 1303–1317.

Hartigan, J. A. (1971), "Error Analysis by Replaced Samples," *Journal of the Royal Statistical Society, B*, **33**, 98–110.

Hastie, T. and R. Tibshirani (1987), "Generalized Additive Models: Some Applications," *Journal of the American Statistical Association*, **82**, 371–386.

Hastie, T. and R. Tibshirani (1990), *Generalized Additive Models*, London: Chapman and Hall.

Hausman, J. (1978), "Specification Tests in Econometrics," *Econometrica*, **46**, 1251–1271.

Hausman, J. and W. Newey (1995), "Nonparametric Estimation of Exact Consumer Surplus and Deadweight Loss," *Econometrica*, **63**, 1445–1476.

Ho, M. (1995), *Essays on the Housing Market*, unpublished Ph.D. dissertation, University of Toronto.

Hoeffding, W. (1948), "A Class of Statistics with Asymptotically Normal Distribution," *Annals of Mathematical Statistics*, **19**, 293–325.

Holly, A. and D. Sargan (1982), "Testing for Endogeneity in a Limited Information Framework," *Cahiers de Recherches Economiques*, No. 8204, Universite de Lausanne.

Hong, Y. and H. White (1995), "Consistent Specification Testing via Nonparametric Series Regression," *Econometrica*, **63**, 1133–1160.

Horowitz, J. (1997), "Bootstrap Methods in Econometrics: Theory and Numerical Performance," in D. M. Kreps and K. F. Wallis (eds.), *Advances in Economics and Econometrics: Theory and Applications*, Seventh World Congress, Vol. 3, Ch. 7, Cambridge University Press, V.

Horowitz, J. (1998), *Semiparametric Methods in Econometrics*, Berlin: Springer-Verlag.

Horowitz, J. (2001), "The Bootstrap," in J. Heckman and E. Leamer (eds.), *Handbook of Econometrics*, Vol. 5, Ch. 52, 3159–3228.

Horowitz, J. and W. Härdle (1994), "Testing a Parametric Model Against a Semiparametric Alternative," *Econometric Theory*, **10**, 821–848.

Horowitz, J. and W. Härdle (1996), "Direct Semiparametric Estimation of Single-Index Models with Discrete Covariates," *Journal of the American Statistical Association*, **91**, 1632–1640.

Horowitz, J. and V. Spokoiny (2001), "An Adaptive, Rate-Optimal Test of a Parametric Mean-Regression Model Against a Nonparametric Alternative," *Econometrica*, **69**, 599–631.

Hristache, M., A. Juditsky, and V. Spokoiny (2001), "Direct Estimation of the Index Coefficient in a Single Index Model," *Annals of Statistics*, **29**, 595–623.

Ichimura, H. (1993), "Semiparametric Least Squares (SLS) and Weighted SLS Estimation of Single-Index Models," *Journal of Econometrics*, **58**, 71–120.

Juditsky, A. and A. Nemirovski (2002), "On Nonparametric Tests of Positivity/ Monotonicity/ Convexity," *Annals of Statistics*, **30**, 498–527.

Kelly, C. and J. Rice (1990), "Monotone Smoothing with Application to Dose-Response Curves and the Assessment of Synergism," *Biometrics*, **46**, 1071–1085.

King, E., J. D. Hart, and T. E. Wehrly (1991), "Testing the Equality of Regression Curves Using Linear Smoothers," *Statistics and Probability Letters*, **12**, 239–247.

Klein, R. and R. Spady (1993), "An Efficient Semiparametric Estimator for Binary Response Models," *Econometrica*, **61**, 387–422.

Koul, H. L. and A. Schick (1997), "Testing for the Equality of Two Nonparametric Regression Curves," *Journal of Statistical Planning and Inference*, **65**, 293–314.

Krause, A. and M. Olson (1997), *The Basic of S and S-Plus*, New York: Springer-Verlag.

Kulasekera, K. B. (1995), "Comparison of Regression Curves Using Quasi-Residuals," *Journal of the American Statistical Association*, **90**, 1085–1093.

Kulasekera, K. B. and J. Wang (1997), "Smoothing Parameter Selection for Power Optimality in Testing of Regression Curves," *Journal of the American Statistical Association*, **92**, 500–511.

Lavergne, P. (2001), "An Equality Test Across Nonparametric Regressions," *Journal of Econometrics*, **103**, 307–344.

Lavergne, P. and Q. Vuong (2000), "Nonparametric Significance Testing," *Econometric Theory*, **16**, 576–601.

Lee, A. J. (1990), *U-Statistics: Theory and Practice*, New York: Marcel Dekker.

Lee, B. J. (1991), "A Model Specification Test Against the Nonparametric Alternative," manuscript, Department of Economics, University of Colorado.

LePage, R. and L. Billard (1992), *Exploring the Limits of the Bootstrap*, New York: Wiley.

Lewbel, A. (1989), "Household Equivalence Scales and Welfare Comparisons," *Journal of Public Economics*, **39**, 377–391.

Lewbel, A. (1995), "Consistent Nonparametric Hypothesis Tests with an Application to Slutsky Symmetry," *Journal of Econometrics*, **67**, 379–401.

Lewbel, A. (1997), "Consumer Demand Systems and Household Equivalence Scales," in M. H. Pesaran and P. Schmidt (eds.), *Handbook of Applied Econometrics, Volume II: Microeconomics*, Oxford: Blackwell Handbooks in Economics, 166–201.

Lewbel, A. (2000), "Semiparametric Qualitative Response Model Estimation with Unknown Hereoscedasticity or Instrumental Variables," *Journal of Econometrics*, **97**, 145–177.

Li, K. (1986), "Asymptotic Optimality of C_L and Generalized Cross-Validation in Ridge Regression with Application to Spline Smoothing," *Annals of Statistics*, **14**, 1101–1112.

Li, K. (1987), "Asymptotic Optimality for C_P, C_L, Cross-Validation and Generalized Cross-Validation: Discrete Index Set," *Annals of Statistics*, **15**, 958–975.

Li, Q. (1994), "Some Simple Consistent Tests for a Parametric Regression Function versus Semiparametric or Nonparametric Alternatives," manuscript, Department of Economics, University of Guelph.

Li, Q. and S. Wang (1998), "A Simple Consistent Bootstrap Test for a Parametric Regression Function," *Journal of Econometrics*, **87**, 145–165.

Linton, O. (1995a), "Estimation in Semiparametric Models: A Review," in G. S. Maddala, P. C. B. Phillips, and T. N. Srinivasan (eds.), *Advances in Econometrics and Quantitative Economics, Essays in Honor of Professor C. R. Rao*, Oxford: Blackwell, 146–171.

Linton, O. (1995b), "Second-Order Approximation in the Partially Linear Regression Model," *Econometrica*, **63**, 1079–1112.

Linton, O. (1997), "Efficient Estimation of Additive Nonparametric Regression Models," *Biometrika*, **84**, 469–474.

Linton, O. (2000), "Efficient Estimation of Generalized Additive Nonparametric Regression Models," *Econometric Theory*, **16**, 502–523.

Linton, O. and J. Nielsen (1995), "A Kernel Method of Estimating Structured Nonparametric Regression Based on Marginal Integration," *Biometrika*, **82**, 93–100.

Linton, O., E. Mammen, and J. Nielsen (1999), "The Existence and Asymptotic Properties of a Backfitting Projection Algorithm under Weak Conditions," *Annals of Statistics*, **27**, 1443–1490.

MacKinnon, J. (1992), "Model Specification Tests and Artificial Regressions," *Journal of Economic Literature*, **30**, 102–146.

Mammen, E. (1991), "Estimating a Smooth Monotone Regression Function," *Annals of Statistics*, **19**, 724–740.

Mammen, E. (1992), *When Does Bootstrap Work?* New York: Springer-Verlag.

Mammen, E. and C. Thomas-Agnan (1999), "Smoothing Splines and Shape Restrictions," *Scandinavian Journal of Statistics*, **26**, 239–252.

Mammen, E. and S. Van de Geer (1997), "Penalized Quasi-Likelihood Estimation in Partial Linear Models," *Annals of Statistics*, **25**, 1014–1035.

Matzkin, R. (1994), "Restrictions of Economic Theory in Nonparametric Methods," in R. Engle and D. McFadden (eds.), *The Handbook of Econometrics,* Vol. IV, Amsterdam: North Holland, 2524–2559.

McLeish, D. L. (1974), "Dependent Central Limit Theorems and Invariance Principles," *Annals of Statistics*, **2**, 620–628.

Mukarjee, H. (1988), "Monotone Nonparametric Regression," *Annals of Statistics*, **16**, 741–750.

Mukarjee, H. and S. Stern (1994), "Feasible Nonparametric Estimation of Multiargument Monotone Functions," *Journal of the American Statistical Association*, **89**, 77–80.

Munk, A. and H. Dette (1998), "Nonparametric Comparison of Several Regression Functions: Exact and Asymptotic Theory," *Annals of Statistics*, **26**, 2339–2368.

Nadaraya, E. A. (1964), "On Estimating Regression," *Theory of Probability and Its Applications*, **10**, 186–190.

Newey, W. (1994a), "The Asymptotic Variance of Semiparametric Estimators," *Econometrica*, **62**, 1349–1382.

Newey, W. (1994b), "Kernel Estimation of Partial Sums," *Econometric Theory*, **10**, 233–253.

Newey, W. and K. West (1987), "A Simple Positive Semi-definite Heteroskedasticity and Autocorrelation-Consistent Covariance Matrix," *Econometrica*, **55**, 703–708.

Newey, W., J. Powell, and F. Vella (1999), "Nonparametric Estimation of Triangular Simultaneous Equations Models," *Econometrica*, **67**, 565–603.

Pagan, A. and A. Ullah (1999), *Nonparametric Econometrics*, Cambridge: Cambridge University Press.

Pendakur, K. (1999), "Semiparametric Estimates and Tests of Base-Independent Equivalence Scales," *Journal of Econometrics*, **88**, 1–40.

Phillips, P. C. B. (2001), "Bootstrapping Spurious Regression," Cowles Foundation, Yale University.

Pinkse, C. and P. Robinson (1995), "Pooling Nonparametric Estimates of Regression Functions with Similar Shape," in G. S. Maddala, P. C. B. Phillips, and T. N. Srinivasan (eds.), *Advances in Econometrics and Quantitative Economics*, Oxford: Blackwell, 172–197.

Pollard, D. (1984), *Convergence of Stochastic Processes*, New York: Springer-Verlag.

Powell, J. (1987), "Semiparametric Estimation of Bivariate Latent Variable Models," working paper 8704, Social Systems Research Institute of Wisconsin, University of Wisconsin, Madison.

Powell, J. (1994), "Estimation of Semiparametric Models," in R. Engle and D. McFadden (eds.), *The Handbook of Econometrics,* Vol. IV, Amsterdam: North Holland, 2444–2523.

Powell, J., J. Stock, and T. Stoker (1989), "Semiparametric Estimation of Index Coefficients," *Econometrica*, **57**, 1403–1430.

Racine, J. (1997), "Consistent Significance Testing for Nonparametric Regression," *Journal of Business and Economic Statistics*, **15**, 369–378.

Ramsay, J. (1988), "Monotone Regression Splines in Action," *Statistical Science*, **3**, 425–461.

Ramsay, J. (1998), "Estimating Smooth Monotone Functions," *Journal of the Royal Statistical Society, B*, **60**, 365–375.

Rice, J. (1984), "Bandwidth Choice for Nonparametric Regression," *Annals of Statistics*, **12**, 1215–1230.

Rice, J. (1986), "Convergence Rates for Partially Splined Models," *Statistics and Probability Letters*, **4**, 203–208.

Rilstone, P. and A. Ullah (1989), "Nonparametric Estimation of Response Coefficients," *Communications in Statistics, Theory and Methods*, **18**, 2615–2627.

Robertson, T., F. Wright, and R. L. Dykstra (1988), *Order Restricted Statistical Inference*, New York: Wiley.

Robinson, P. (1988), "Root-N-Consistent Semiparametric Regression," *Econometrica*, **56**, 931–954.

Schlee, W. (1982), "Nonparametric Tests of the Monotony and Convexity of Regression," in B. V. Gnedenko, M. L. Puri, and I. Vincze (eds.), *Nonparametric Statistical Inference*, Vol. 2, Amsterdam: North Holland, 823–836.

Schmalensee, R. and T. Stoker (1999), "Household Gasoline Demand in the United States," *Econometrica*, **67**, 645–662.

Schott, J. R. (1997), *Matrix Analysis for Statistics*, New York: Wiley.

Scott, D. (1992), *Multivariate Density Estimation*, New York: Wiley.

Seifert, B., T. Gasser, and A. Wolf (1993), "Nonparametric Estimation of Residual Variance Revisited," *Biometrika*, **80**, 373–383.

Serfling, R. (1980), *Approximation Theorems of Mathematical Statistics*, New York: Wiley.

Shao, J. and D. Tu (1995), *The Jackknife and Bootstrap*, New York: Springer.

Silverman, B. W. (1986), *Density Estimation for Statistics and Data Analysis*, New York: Chapman and Hall.

Simonoff, J. (1996), *Smoothing Methods in Statistics*, New York: Springer-Verlag.

Speckman, P. (1988), "Kernel Smoothing in Partial Linear Models," *Journal of the Royal Statistical Society, B*, **50**, 413–436.

Sperlich, S., D. Tjostheim, and L. Yang (1999), "Nonparametric Estimation and Testing of Interaction in Additive Models," *Econometric Theory*, **18**, 197–251.

Stengos, T. and Y. Sun (2001), "A Consistent Model Specification Test for a Regression Function Based on Nonparametric Wavelet Estimation," *Econometric Reviews*, **20**, 41–60.

Stoker, T. (1986), "Consistent Estimation of Scaled Coefficients," *Econometrica*, **54**, 1461–1481.

Stoker, T. (1991), *Lectures on Semiparametric Econometrics*, CORE Foundation, Louvain-La-Neuve.

Stone, C. (1980), "Optimal Rates of Convergence for Nonparametric Estimators," *Annals of Statistics*, **8**, 1348–1360.

Stone, C. (1982), "Optimal Global Rates of Convergence for Nonparametric Regression," *Annals of Statistics*, **10**, 1040–1053.

Stone, C. (1985), "Additive Regression and Other Nonparametric Models," *Annals of Statistics*, **13**, 689–705.

Stone, C. (1986), "The Dimensionality Reduction Principle for Generalized Additive Models," *Annals of Statistics*, **14**, 590–606.

Ullah, A. (1988), "Nonparametric Estimation and Hypothesis Testing in Econometric Models," *Empirical Economics*, **13**, 223–249.

Utreras, F. (1984), "Smoothing Noisy Data under Monotonicity Constraints: Existence, Characterization and Convergence Rates," *Numerische Mathematik*, **47**, 611–625.

Van de Geer, S. (1990), "Estimating a Regression Function," *Annals of Statistics*, **18**, 907–924.

Van Praag, B. M. S. and M. F. Warnaar (1997), "The Cost of Children and the Use of Demographic Variables in Consumer Demand," in M. R. Rozenzweig and O. Stark (eds.), *Handbook of Population and Family Economics*, Vol. 1A, Amsterdam: Elsevier Science, North Holland, 241–273.

Varian, H. (1985), "Nonparametric Analysis of Optimizing Behaviour with Measurement Error," *Journal of Econometrics*, **30**, 445–458.

Varian, H. (1990), "Goodness of Fit in Optimizing Models," *Journal of Econometrics*, **46**, 141–163.

Varian, H. (1992), *Microeconomic Analysis*, 3rd ed., New York: W. W. Norton.

Venables, W. and B. Ripley (1994), *Modern Applied Statistics with S-Plus*, New York: Springer-Verlag.

Villalobos, M. and G. Wahba (1987), "Inequality-Constrained Multivariate Smoothing Splines with Application to the Estimation of Posterior Probabilities," *Journal of the American Statistical Association*, **82**, 239–248.

Wahba, G. (1990), *Spline Models for Observational Data*, CBMS-NSF Regional Conference Series in Applied Mathematics, No. 59, Society for Industrial and Applied Mathematics.

Wahba, G. and S. Wold (1975), "A Completely Automatic French Curve: Fitting Spline Functions by Cross-Validation," *Communications in Statistics, Series A*, **4**, 1–17.

Wand, M. P. and M. C. Jones (1995), *Kernel Smoothing*, New York: Chapman and Hall.

Watson, G. S. (1964), "Smooth Regression Analysis," *Sankhya, Series A*, **26**, 359–372.

Whang, Y. and D. Andrews (1993), "Tests of Specification for Parametric and Semiparametric Models," *Journal of Econometrics*, **57**, 277–318.

White, H. (1980), "A Heteroskedasticity Consistent Covariance Matrix Estimator and a Direct Test for Heteroskedasticity," *Econometrica*, **48**, 817–838.

White, H. (1985), *Asymptotic Theory for Econometricians,* New York: Academic Press (new edition).

Wolak, F. (1989), "Testing Inequality Constraints in Linear Econometric Models," *Journal of Econometrics*, **41**, 205–235.

Wooldridge, J. (1992), "A Test for Functional Form Against Nonparametric Alternatives," *Econometric Theory*, **8**, 452–475.

Wright, I. and E. Wegman (1980), "Isotonic, Convex and Related Splines," *Annals of Statistics*, **8**, 1023–1035.

Wu, C. (1986), "Jackknife, Bootstrap and Other Resampling Methods in Regression Analysis," *Annals of Statistics*, **14**, 1261–1350 (with discussion).

Yatchew, A. (1988), "Some Tests of Nonparametric Regressions Models," *Dynamic Econometric Modelling*, Proceedings of the Third International Symposium in Economic Theory and Econometrics, W. Barnett, E. Berndt, and H. White (eds.), Cambridge: Cambridge University Press, 121–135.

Yatchew, A. (1992), "Nonparametric Regression Model Tests Based on Least Squares," *Econometric Theory*, **8**, 435–451.

Yatchew, A. (1997), "An Elementary Estimator of the Partial Linear Model," *Economics Letters,* **57**, 135–143. Additional examples contained in *Economics Letters* 1998, **59**, 403–405.

Yatchew, A. (1998), "Nonparametric Regression Techniques in Economics," *Journal of Economic Literature*, **XXXVI**, 669–721.

Yatchew, A. (1999), "An Elementary Nonparametric Differencing Test of Equality of Regression Functions," *Economics Letters*, **62**, 271–278.

Yatchew, A. (2000), "Scale Economies in Electricity Distribution," *Journal of Applied Econometrics*, **15**, 187–210.

Yatchew, A. and L. Bos (1997), "Nonparametric Regression and Testing in Economic Models," *Journal of Quantitative Economics*, **13**, 81–131, available at http://www.chass.utoronto.ca/~yatchew.

Yatchew, A. and W. Härdle (2001), "Dynamic State Price Density Estimation Using Constrained Least Squares and the Bootstrap," manuscript, University of Toronto and Humboldt University zu Berlin.

Yatchew, A. and A. No (2001), "Household Gasoline Demand in Canada," *Econometrica*, **69**, 1697–1709.

Yatchew, A. and Y. Sun (2001), "Differencing versus Smoothing in Nonparametric Regression: Monte Carlo Results," manuscript, University of Toronto.

Yatchew, A., Y. Sun, and C. Deri (2003), "Efficient Estimation of Semi-parametric Equivalence Scales with Evidence from South Africa," *Journal of Business and Economic Statistics*, **21**, 247–257. See also www.chass.utoronto.ca/~yatchew.

Young, S. G. and A. W. Bowman (1995), "Nonparametric Analysis of Covariance," *Biometrics*, **51**, 920–931.

Zheng, J. (1996), "A Consistent Test of Functional Form via Nonparametric Estimation Techniques," *Journal of Econometrics*, **75**, 263–289.

Index

References followed by fig. refer to figures. References followed by n refer to notes. References followed by t refer to tables.